MENTAL HEALTH AND MENTAL RETARDATION

MENTAL HEALTH AND MENTAL RETARDATION

Bridging the Gap

Edited by
Frank J. Menolascino, M.D.
Professor of Psychiatry and Pediatrics
University of Nebraska Medical Center
Omaha, Nebraska

and

Brian M. McCann, Ph.D.
Director
Research and Demonstration Institute
Association for Retarded Citizens of the United States
Arlington, Texas

UNIVERSITY PARK PRESS   Baltimore

UNIVERSITY PARK PRESS
International Publishers in Science, Medicine, and Education
300 North Charles Street
Baltimore, Maryland 21201

Copyright © 1983 by University Park Press

Typeset by University Park Press, Typesetting Division

Manufactured in the United States of America by
The Maple Press Company

Library of Congress Cataloging in Publication Data
Main entry under title:
Mental health and mental retardation.
Includes index.
1. Mentally handicapped—Mental health. 2. Mentally
handicapped—Mental health services. 3. Community
mental health services. I. Menolascino, Frank J., 1930-
II. McCann, Brian M. [DNLM: 1. Mental health—
Congresses. 2. Mental retardation—Congresses. WM 300
M5475 1981]
RC451.4.M47M46   1983   362.2'0880826   82-21746
ISBN   0-8391-1784-1

Contents

PART III
TRAINING CHALLENGES

PART IV
CONCLUSION

Contributors

The contributors to this volume are all actively involved in the fields of mental retardation and mental health. Each made a formal presentation at the first national conference on this topic, which was jointly sponsored by the National Association for Retarded Citizens and the National Mental Health Association in the fall of 1979. The original formal conference presentations were all updated in the summer of 1982.

Sidney W. Bijou, Ph.D.
Professor Emeritus
University of Illinois
Adjunct Professor of Psychology
  and Special Education
University of Arizona
Tucson, Arizona 85721

Brian M. McCann, Ph.D.
Director
Research and Demonstration
  Institute
Association for Retarded Citizens
  of the United States
2501 Avenue J
Arlington, Texas 76011

John J. McGee, Ph.D.
Assistant Professor of Medical
  Psychology
University of Nebraska Medical
  Center
42nd and Dewey Avenue
Omaha, Nebraska 68105

Frank J. Menolascino, M.D.
Professor of Psychiatry and
  Pediatrics
University of Nebraska Medical
  Center
42nd and Dewey Avenue
Omaha, Nebraska 68105

Michael J. Monfils, A.C.S.W.
Instructor in Psychiatric Social
  Work
Nebraska Psychiatric Institute
602 South 45th Street
Omaha, Nebraska 68106

Paul H. Pearson, M.D.
Professor of Pediatrics
University of Nebraska Medical
  Center
42nd and Dewey Avenue
Omaha, Nebraska 68105

Philip Roos, Ph.D.
National Director
Association for Retarded Citizens
of the United States
2501 Avenue J
Arlington, Texas 76011

Richard L. Rubin, M.D.
Clinical Assistant Professor
Division of Child and Adolescent
Psychiatry
University of Miami School of
Medicine
9655 South Dixie Highway
Miami, Florida 33156

Donald A. Swanson, M.D.
Associate Professor of Psychiatry
University of Nebraska Medical
Center
Clinical Director
Adult Outpatient Service
Nebraska Psychiatric Institute
602 South 45th Street
Omaha, Nebraska 68106

Michael G. Tramontana, Ph.D.
Bradley Hospital;
Section of Psychiatry and Human
Behavior
Brown University
Providence, Rhode Island 02912

**H. Rutherford Turnbull, III,
LL.B., LL.M.**
Professor of Special Education
and Law
Haworth Hall
The University of Kansas
Lawrence, Kansas 66045

Luke S. Watson, Jr., Ph.D.
Therapeutic Homes, Inc.
1379 Lantern Drive, SW
Fort Myers, Florida 33907

James E. Wilson, Pharm.D.
Assistant Professor
Colleges of Pharmacy and Medicine
University of Nebraska Medical
Center
42nd and Dewey Avenue
Omaha, Nebraska 68105

Foreword

Professionals and volunteers have long ignored persons who are mentally retarded and who also demonstrate difficulty in managing their ongoing emotional stability. The coexistence of the symptoms of both mental retardation and mental health has remained as a continuing challenge; however, the past two decades have witnessed a dramatic reinvolvement of mental health professionals in the life adjustment challenges of mentally retarded citizens. During this period of time, the national movement to find alternatives to institutionalization has brought increased numbers of multihandicapped retarded citizens into the mainstreams of our society, especially those with associated symptoms of mental illness.

This volume, through the collective professional experiences and knowledge bases of the cadre of professionals who have contributed to it, has extended further excellent insights into this complex issue. The contributors to this volume are uniquely qualified to examine the problems that have long frustrated parents, therapists, and administrators due to the lack of treatment and special facilities to provide services for this challenging dual-diagnosis population. The editors exemplify the overall quality of these contributors. As a practicing psychiatrist and a former president of the Association for Retarded Citizens of the United States, Dr. Frank J. Menolascino has directly experienced the paucity of professional coordination efforts between mentally handicapped persons and their families, mental health professionals, and the mental retardation personnel who directly provide services to mentally retarded persons. Dr. Brian M. McCann, a psychologist and Director of the Research and Demonstration Institute, Association for Retarded Citizens of the United States, recognizes the persistent deficiencies in planning efforts to provide these services at the national, state, and community levels. The professional collaborations and writing and editing experience of these editors, in concert with the contributors to this volume, provide extensive insights not previously shared.

In the wake of the national deinstitutionalization movement, the personality and behavioral dimensions of mental retardation have taken on new urgency and interest for mental health professionals. Increasingly, they are being asked to provide understanding and effective treatment-management interventions to a very large group of mentally retarded citizens who have the *combined* symptoms of mental retardation and mental illness. These dual-diagnosis individuals present a major challenge to mental health workers. In the past, mentally retarded individuals with allied mental illness have not typically been clinical challenges in the training settings of the majority of today's mental health practitioners. Indeed, there are precious few mental health personnel who have had extensive exposure to the didactic or clinical dimensions of mental retardation, not to mention when this symptom appears in conjunction with signs or symptoms of mental illness. This book is intended to fill this past professional training void while simultaneously sharing the diagnostic and treatment challenges which so globally permeate this topical area.

Ironically, at the turn of the century, ongoing clinical experiences and active teaching-research activities in mental retardation *had* been an integral dimension of the mental health professional's interest and involvement. During the first two decades of the 20th century, however, this dynamic involvement ceased because of the following major changes in professional and societal views: 1) the individualized psychiatric case study approach became displaced by the rapid psychometric intelligence testing approach; and 2) the mentally retarded citizen became erroneously viewed and labeled as the result of fixed genetic causes, which seemingly produced the vast number of rather unsavory "deviants" in our society. Acting in concert during the early 1920s, the professional and societal changes wiped out the individualized humanistic professional postures that had produced a very fine record of mental health involvement in maximizing the developmental potentials and personality adjustment of the mentally retarded.

As mental health training interest and ongoing professional efforts in mental retardation went into eclipse, so did the accompanying professionals enthusiasm for finding ways to serve the mentally retarded person. This documented retreat of mental health professions ushered in four decades (1920–1960) of backward custodial care for the "hopeless" in large institutional settings. This state of affairs persisted until the early 1960s, and the psychiatric aspects of mental retardation tended to be regarded as a narrow and fruitless area for professional involvement.

With the advent of the President's Panel on Mental Retardation and President John Kennedy's benchmark federal legislation in 1963, however, the field of mental retardation came alive once again. This renaissance of interest and involvement—actively joined in by professionals and parent volunteers alike—brought back the earlier professional mental health postures of help and hope. As a result of the new national commitment, improvement in the diagnostic, treatment, and management dimensions of mental retardation flowed from research to training, service provisions, and social policy changes, and was spurred onward by reconceptualization of societal responsibilities and modern professional viewpoints (e.g., normalization and the developmental model). The quality of life issues for the mentally retarded again became a focal point for professional approaches. Examples are the increasing elucidation of modern treatment approaches, civil rights considerations that brought into sharp question the validity of segregating retarded citizens in remote large institutions, renewed involvement in actively supporting parents of the mentally retarded, and national focus on initiating community-based services for these families and their retarded sons and daughters.

The national policy of deinstitutionalization, formulated by the President's Committee on Mental Retardation, focused in the 1970s on community-based services in the redefinition of residential services for mentally retarded individuals. It successfully reduced the population of institutionalized mentally retarded citizens, and directly flowed from the above-noted major changes in the 1960s. The population of the public institutions for the mentally retarded was successfully reduced from its zenith of 190,000 (in 1970) to 125,000 (in 1982). Yet this major "site of treatment" change has ushered in the current state of affairs wherein previously institutionalized mentally retarded citizens have had great difficulty in *shifting* from past experiences (and allied expectancies) of institutional passivity and dependency to acquiring the interpersonal skills necessary to "make it" in community-based service settings. Indeed, it is the very lack of these needed interpersonal skills (e.g., modes for successfully handling interpersonal conflict, impulse control, and adaptive interpersonal approaches to co-workers in sheltered work settings) that has underscored the pressing necessity for greatly increased professional awareness, knowledge, active involvement, and research in the personality and mental illness parameters of mentally retarded citizens.

The aforementioned has attempted to place in perspective the reason why many professionals involved in mental health and mental retardation activities have tended, until the recent past, to consider these two areas as irreconcilable as oil and water. Both of these topical areas present unique challenges, and thus require different approaches. Accordingly, some professional and advocacy groups have fought strongly to keep them separate in the funding of the many programs and services in the various state departments of mental health and mental retardation.

Although frustrations and problems of everyday living can be the cause of personality adjustment problems in mentally retarded individuals, the majority are not mentally ill. However, mentally retarded individuals experience mental illness at a higher rate than the general public and can have all forms of mental illness, just as nonretarded persons. This unique set of circumstances presents another whole set of problems for parents of mentally retarded persons. Such a family member can lend additional pressures to the parents' own basic anxieties, and professional assistance is often needed to cope with the day-to-day stresses of rearing a mentally retarded person.

Although the basic mental health needs of mentally retarded persons and their parents have long been obvious, these needs have frequently been neglected by both community and institutional mental health and mental retardation services. One reason for their neglect has been that mental retardation often is confused with mental illness, a situation that has caused many misunderstandings and led to inappropriate professional recommendations or services. For these reasons it is important to ensure that appropriate mental health services are accessible for both retarded persons and for their families.

In the recent past, the President's Committee on Mental Health, with the support of studies conducted by the President's Committee on Mental Retardation, published the *Liaison Task Force Report on Mental Retardation* (1978), which assessed the variety and types of mental health services that were being provided for the mentally retarded throughout our country. Close study of this Report reveals that it is fully pertinent to the concerns addressed in this volume. For example, although several key federal programs benefitting mentally retarded citizens have been placed into law in the past decade, the Task Force Report recognized that many of these programs are in need of revision or redirection. This is particularly urgent in the areas of income support, housing, health care, education, rehabilitation, and supportive family and social services. The President's Committee was especially concerned about these particular national program areas because they enable parents—or mentally retarded individuals themselves—to obtain appropriate care. They are vitally necessary for improving the mental health adjustment and overall quality of the mentally retarded individual's life.

Although mental retardation, as a condition, is not a form of mental illness, it is not a guarantee against mental illness. Thus, mentally retarded persons may, and often do, develop mental illness, as do nonretarded persons. Yet, when this "dual diagnosis" does occur, these individuals typically fall between the cracks of the criteria for admission to mental health or mental retardation systems of service. This volume is designed to address this significant problem since it systematically covers the major issues relevant to the presence (i.e., diagnosis, treatment, and management) of mental illness in mentally retarded individuals. First, there is an overview of the available information regarding the nature and prevalence of the mental health need of retarded persons—and the major challenges facing today's mental health-mental retardation professionals who provide these services. Next, there is a review of the mental health needs of parents of the mentally retarded, and examples of successful as well as inappropriate service approaches to them. There follows a review of successful individual treatment-management approaches—including behavioral, psychotherapeutic, and psychopharmacologic techniques—of instances of mental illness in the mentally retarded. The role of schools, vocational rehabilitation, and community-based consultation services are then explored as they relate to the mental health needs of mentally retarded persons.

In summary, the renaissance of professional mental health reinvolvement and the recent dynamism of approaches in the field of mental retardation have begun to illuminate the nature and types of mental illness in the mentally retarded and—more importantly— how citizens with both symptoms may be effectively rehabilitated.

Drs. Menolascino and McCann are to be congratulated for this well prepared volume that focuses upon the major dimensions of mental illness in mentally retarded persons. Through their collective sharing of specific information, fellow professionals will better understand and serve this complex dual-diagnosis population. I am confident that the content of this volume will significantly contribute to the current and future informational base of clinically applicable techniques that directly focus on what *can* be done effectively for mentally retarded citizens whose lives have become complicated by the inroads of mental illness.

Fred Krause
Executive Director
Presidents' Committee on
Mental Retardation

Preface

Mental health and mental retardation—to many of us these two areas often have seemed through the years as irreconcilable as oil and water. Both of these topical areas present unique challenges and thus require different approaches. Accordingly, the National Association for Retarded Citizens has fought strongly to keep them separate in funding in the many programs and services in the various state departments of mental health and mental retardation. Although this separateness remains valid, it is important to recognize that mentally retarded citizens and their families may have varying degrees of mental health needs. The frustrations and problems of everyday living can be the cause of emotional problems in mentally retarded individuals. The majority are not mentally ill; however, mentally retarded individuals experience mental illness at a higher rate than the general public. They can have all forms of mental illness, as can nonretarded persons.

This presents another whole set of problems for parents with a mentally retarded child. Such a family member can lend additional pressures to the parents' own basic anxieties. Parents may need assistence in coping with the day-to-day stress of raising a retarded child. Also involved is their own emotional reaction to this set of demanding circumstances. For these reasons, it is important to ensure that mental health services are accessible to retarded people and their families.

CURRENT AREAS OF CONCERN

The basic mental health needs of retarded people and their parents have long been obvious. Again and again they have been noted by parents of the retarded; however, these needs have been frequently neglected by both the community mental health and mental retardation services.

One reason for their neglect has been that mental retardation often is confused with mental illness. This has caused many misunderstandings and has led to inappropriate professional services. As a result, community mental health delivery systems for mentally retarded persons and their parents today are often described as unresponsive, woefully inadequate, and often nonexistent.

The National Association for Retarded Citizens has been seriously concerned about this matter. In the past, the association's leaders met with the President's Commission on Mental Health in its early planning stages for its now completed national study. The necessity for the commission to be careful not to include mental retardation as a form of mental illness was directly addressed. After the commission was established, it asked the President's Committee on Mental Retardation and the Association for Retarded Citizens to submit recommendations. The recommendations and findings that were submitted directly addressed the mental health needs of mentally retarded persons and their families. The majority of these recommendations and findings were incorporated into the formal report, which was later published by the President's Commission as the *Liaison Task Panel on Mental Retardation* (1978). This report recognized that many community mental health delivery systems are in need of revision or redirection. This is particularly urgent in areas of income support, housing, health care, education, rehabilitation, and supportive family and social services. The panel felt especially concerned about these service areas because they are so crucial to the families of mentally retarded persons. They enable parents or other individuals to provide appropriate care, and are vitally necessary for improving the quality of the retarded individual's life.

The panel reported that some people in the mental health field still respond to the myth that mentally retarded persons cannot profit from psychiatric intervention. These professionals often are unfamiliar with the basic facts of mental retardation and unable to distinguish between these facts and the myth of psychiatric nontreatability of the mentally retarded. Their unwillingness to treat mentally retarded persons very often can be attributed to their lack of knowledge and training in this area. Also, a low priority has traditionally been given to the referral of retarded persons to local mental health clinics; frequently they are directly referred to state institutions. There are some states, however, that do have limited mental health services available for mentally retarded persons in local community health centers. An example of the type of working relationship that can be achieved between mental health and mental retardation professionals is at the Nebraska Psychiatric Institute (NPI), Omaha. This program works directly with the regional system of community-based services for retarded citizens, the Eastern Nebraska Community Office of Retardation (ENCOR), and the local Pilot Parent organization (i.e., a program of the Greater Omaha Association for Retarded Citizens which is designed for parents to help other parents of developmentally disabled persons). Since the early 1970s, the NPI has served as a community mental health center backup for the ENCOR system's clients. It has provided a full range of modern mental health services, including emergency, outpatient, inpatient, day hospital, and community consultation services. Another excellent example is a program at the Macomb-Oakland Regional Center (MORC) in Mount Clemens, Michigan. It has been utilizing the services of mental health clinics in the community for its retarded citizens. The clinics participate in the interdisciplinary team process, and provide MORC clients with psychologic and psychiatric testing and evaluation, medication review, individual and group counseling, and behavioral programs. In addition, the clinics also provide inservice training for staff and parents. One of these clinics is the Center for Behavioral Psychiatry and Psychology, known as the Behavior Center, in Birmingham, Michigan. It began serving MORC in June 1978, and currently is seeing approximately 60 of its clients. The Behavior Center's staff visits schools, group homes, and workshops, in addition to seeing clients in their own homes.

PRELUDE TO A NATIONAL CONFERENCE—AND THIS BOOK

The National Association for Retarded Citizens made plans to help meet the above noted challenges by hosting a national conference on the mental health needs of mentally retarded persons and their families in the late fall of 1979. The conference brought together a wide array of mental health and mental retardation specialists in order to examine the specific stresses and problems that mentally retarded persons and their families experience. A major focus of this national conference was to develop workable strategies for meeting these mental health needs.

The findings of the previously noted panel submitted to the President's Commission on Mental Health served as one source of input for developing new approaches, and the presentations at the national conference—which are reviewed in this book—also embellished on what can be done to aid mentally retarded citizens who have allied mental health problems. However, this book also provides a splendid opportunity to lead the way by actively cooperating with other concerned groups in developing strategies to successfully combine mental health and mental retardation technology.

Accordingly, this book is a review of the key presentations at the first major national conference on the mental health needs of mentally retarded persons and their families. For too long retarded people with mental health problems have fallen into the gap that has separated mental health from mental retardation services. Typically these persons' needs have been totally unmet, as both services have been incapable of addressing them. This conference was long overdue, and its theme, Bridging the Gap, is extremely appropriate. Individuals who have been closely identified with the field of mental retardation have striven for years to clarify the distinction between mental retardation and mental illness. Often they have been frustrated by the general public's confusion of the two conditions and the tendency of some professionals to inappropriately apply mental health approaches to mental retardation. Not too long ago, for example, some psychiatrists defined mental retardation as a form of mental illness, and they used this faulty concept to justify the application of the medical model to mental retardation services. Fortunately, this and similar erroneous interpretations are now rapidly becoming past history. The developmental model has been generally adopted as the most appropriate basis for mental retardation services, and no longer does any profession claim dominance over the field of mental retardation, which is now recognized—as it should be—as requiring a transdisciplinary approach to treatment.

Although it is known that mental retardation is not a form of mental illness, they often coexist in the same person. Thus, retarded people may develop emotional problems and mental illnesses, as can nonretarded people; yet when this occurs, they typically fall between the cracks. The previously noted national conference and this book were both designed to address this significant problem. They were both organized to systematically cover the major issues relevant to the presence of mental illness in mentally retarded individuals. First, there is an overview of currently available information regarding the mental health needs of retarded people and the major issues and challenges facing the professionals who provide these services in our country today. Next, there is a review of the mental health needs of parents of retarded people and examples of successful as well as inappropriate approaches. There follows a review of successful approaches to intervention and remediation, including behavioral, psychotherapeutic, and psychopharmacologic tactics. Then the role of schools, vocational rehabilitation, and community-based mental health services are explored as they relate to the mental health needs of retarded people living in the community. Legal issues are explored in depth, with particular emphasis on such concepts as the least restrictive environment, competence, commitment, and criminal justice procedures. Finally, approaches to preparing personnel to meet the mental health needs of retarded people are explored, with special attention given to the role of University-Affiliated Programs and the Community Mental Health Centers.

Perhaps the spirit of the national conference (which was sponsored by the Association for Retarded Citizens in association with the National Mental Health Association) and this book (which documents the new direction for both of these helping associations) was most clearly expressed by the President of the National Mental Health Association (Mrs. Beverly Benson Long), who stated:

> It was a pleasure to contribute to the National Conference and to the Preface of this excellent book. The mental health needs of the retarded had been brought to my attention as a Past President of the Georgia Division of the National Mental Health Association and during my service on the President's Commission on Mental Health. We are pleased to be a cooperating agency in this endeavor and want to lend any support that we can to your efforts. It is my hope that firmer common bonds are forged between the national advocacy efforts for the mentally retarded and the National Mental Health Association's advocacy for the mentally ill, and that these bonds will continue to become stronger and stronger. Though the antecedent conditions and life problems in each of these groups of disabled citizens are different, many of the barriers to fulfillment of potential are the same. Public understanding is necessary in order to obtain appropriate resources to establish a continuum of services that will support *all* of the major needs relating to mental health and mental retardation. Not only should these two service systems support each other, but eventually they should be integrated with parents, peers, and the community, and with education, employment, and all other social services to provide a thoroughly coordinated human services delivery system. I think that is what we are all working toward. We are a long way off, but together we can bring it to fruition.

We look forward to a continuum of services that will support all of the major needs relating to mental health and mental retardation. This book, with its primary focus on the mental health needs of the mentally retarded, may further clarifiy the nature of this dual diagnosis that hampers the lives of many citizens. Hopefully, it will help

hasten the day wherein we can offer a helpful therapeutic environment that embodies maximal self-development and personal affirma-
tion for both our mentally retarded and mentally ill citizens and their
families.

Beverly Benson Long
President
National Mental Health
Association

Joseph A. Buonomo
President
Association for
Retarded Citizens
of the United States

MENTAL HEALTH AND MENTAL RETARDATION

PART I

NATURE OF THE DUAL DIAGNOSIS OF MENTAL RETARDATION AND MENTAL ILLNESS

Chapter 1

Overview

Bridging the Gap between Mental Retardation and Mental Illness

Frank J. Menolascino

The diagnostic and treatment challenges in providing services for mentally retarded citizens who have allied mental health needs is a topic that has taken on increased importance in view of significant recent changes in society's care and treatment of its retarded citizens. Specifically, the impact of deinstitutionalization has not only changed the physical site of service delivery, but has also dramatically altered the need for mental health services for the mentally retarded.

The recent movement of the retarded from institutional back wards into the community has literally changed the definitions of normal and abnormal behavior. Behaviors that were traditionally viewed as expected in institutionalized retarded citizens are now viewed as abnormal within the mainstreams of society. For example, the clinical phenomena of rocking, rumination, and head banging are frequent behavioral occurrences in institutionalized retarded; within the institutional setting, they are traditionally viewed as expected behaviors and their abnormality is tolerated. Such behaviors are rarely seen in retarded citizens raised at home.

Allied behavioral treatment issues secondary to the deinstitutionalization movement have been the questionable merits of high psychoactive medication usages (i.e., their singular usage as chemi-

3

cal restraints versus their potential role as programming aids) and the paucity of available mental health services for normalization (i.e., by aiding the retarded person's personal-social adaptations to community mainstream environments).

These issues underscore the need for bridging the gap between the roles of mental retardation and mental health programs in meeting the individual needs of all retarded citizens. Increasingly, joint habilitation efforts between mental retardation and mental health colleagues can be seen. These efforts include crisis intervention services, the provision of backup inpatient mental health facilities for regional mental retardation programs, provision of mental health outreach consultative services (e.g., patient-centered and program-centered consultations) to community-based mental retardation programs, specialized mental health programs solely for mentally ill-mentally retarded persons, and the use of parents of the retarded as paraprofessionals for other parents and their mentally ill-mentally retarded son or daughter.

DEFINITIONS

There are a number of major concepts, issues, and trends relevant to the relationship(s) between emotional disturbance and mental retardation. The definition of mental retardation as found in the diagnostic system of the American Association on Mental Deficiency (Grossman, 1976) posits the presence of subaverage intellectual functioning and associated deficits in social-adaptive behavior. The majority of the disorders listed as capable of producing the symptom of mental retardation, however, are more descriptive of syndromes, rather than specifically understood diagnostic entities (especially in AAMD categories VII and VIII; see Table 1.1). It should be noted the definition or description of causes of the symptom of mental retardation says little about expected behaviors beyond rough guidelines as to social-adaptive accomplishments at differing levels of retardation.

Similar perplexity may exist in the delineation of the causes and manifestations of mental illness in a given individual. A widely accepted diagnostic classification of mental illness is the *Diagnostic and Statistical Manual on Mental Disorders*, 3rd Ed., (DSM-III) of the American Psychiatric Association (1980). It is synopsized in Table 1.2.

In Table 1.2, one notes a number of mental illnesses that can embody the symptom of mental retardation; (e.g., the organic mental

Table 1.1   Classification of the causes of mental retardation: American Association on Mental Deficiency (Grossman, 1976)

O.	Infections and intoxications (e.g., prenatal and postnatal infections)
I.	Trauma or physical agent (e.g., prenatal injury, childhood trauma)
II.	Metabolism or nutrition (e.g., inborn errors of metabolism)
III.	Gross brain disease (postnatal) (e.g., neurocutaneous dysplasia)
IV.	Unknown prenatal influence (e.g., malformations of the brain)
V.	Chromosomal abnormality (e.g., Down's syndrome)
VI.	Gestational disorders (e.g., prematurity)
VII.	Following psychiatric disorder (e.g., childhood schizophrenia)
VIII.	Environmental influences (e.g., psychosocial disadvantage)
IX.	Other conditions (e.g., defects of special senses)

disorders); or can include mental retardation as a *transitory* finding in the clinical picture (e.g., in the regression often noted in schizophrenia); or the mental illness can display pervasive developmental delays, which may be separated only with great difficulty from similar manifestations of mental retardation (e.g., infantile autism).

When the uncertainty of primary causes in mental retardation is combined with the problems of clinical description in mental illness, an area of possible clinical confusion arises: symptomatic behaviors that although produced by different causes, can have the *same* final symptom pathway—abnormal behavior. For example, the origins of a retarded child's hyperactivity may range from motor expression of anxiety to manifestations of cerebral dysfunction, or it may be due to both. Similarly, a shortened attention span may be the end product of determinants ranging from inadequate parenting relationships in infancy (suggesting that the parents were unable to operate as a selective stimulation barrier for the child) to impaired (i.e., neurologic) midbrain screening of incoming stimuli. The adult moderately retarded person can surely have a seizure disorder and also display schizophrenia, along with his or her symptoms of mental retardation. Combined diagnoses become more clearly indicated in these frequent instances of mixed disorders. Failure to describe and/or delineate these multiple disorders in the same individual

Table 1.2.   Types of mental illness (DSM-III, 1980)[a]

A. General
   Organic mental disorders (e.g., Alzheimer's disease)
   Substance use disorders (e.g., Amphetamines)
   Schizophrenic disorders
   Affective disorders (e.g., manic-depressive psychosis)
   Paranoid disorders (e.g., acute paranoid disorders)
   Anxiety disorders (a phobia)
   Adjustment disorders (e.g., work inhibition)
   Psychosexual disorders (e.g., exhibition)
   Personality disorders (e.g., antisocial personality)
B. Disorders in childhood and adolescence
   Attention deficit disorder (e.g., hyperkinetic syndrome)
   Conduct disorders (e.g., undersocialized-aggressive)
   Anxiety disorders (e.g., separation anxiety disorders)
   Eating disorders (e.g., anorexia nervosa)
   Stereotyped movement disorders (e.g., Tourette's disorder)
   Pervasive developmental disorders (e.g., infantile autism)
   Specific development disorders (e.g., developmental language
   disorders)

[a]For extended discussion of each of these diagnostic entities in relatively non-technical language the reader is referred to *Psychiatry: Medical Outline Series,* 4th Ed. (Eaton, Peterson, and Davis, 1980).

sharply limits both professional understanding and effective treatment. The symptomatic nature of mental retardation, however, coupled with possible multifactorial causes of an associated behavioral manifestation not only increases the possible number of causes, but also presents challenging possibilities for professionals to initiate a wide array of specific treatment interventions in these complex dual diagnostic challenges.

Because abnormal behaviors in retarded individuals are discussed at some length later in this chapter, it seems timely to review a current definition (Chess and Hassibi, 1978) of normal behavior we may use as a baseline; "He gets along reasonably well with his parents (or mate), siblings, and friends, has few overt manifestations of behavioral disturbance, is using his apparent intellectual potential close to its estimate, and is contented for a reasonable proportion of time" (p. 32).

DSM-III (American Psychiatric Association, 1980) embraces the symptomatic and developmental parameters that are such important considerations here. These considerations suggest that a description of mental illness in the mentally retarded should include behavioral patterns that produce serious conflicts within retarded individuals, their families, and in the greater circle of their community transactions. The presence of a disturbing personality trait, such as pervasive anxiety, may significantly reduce their effectiveness and efficiency as to intellectual and social-adaptive capabilities.

A valuable concept in assessing mental illness in mentally retarded persons (especially children) is that of *developmental contingencies*. This concept stresses both the timing and interaction of extrinsic and intrinsic factors, which may be major determining factors in symptom production at different neuronatomical, physiologic, and/or developmental states of physical or personality development. The concept of developmental contingencies requires that a careful review of the personal and clinical histories be done for any given child, with an overriding concern for capturing the dynamic flow of developmental events that produces the present set of symptoms of mental illness in the child. Figure 1.1 reviews some of the factors that can be assessed in such a developmental-interactional approach to seeking the possible significant determinants of symptomatic behavioral manifestations in the retarded.

Figure 1.1 illustrates the complexity of evaluating the impact of different developmental contingencies in any given child (or adult). It also illustrates, by its relative complexity, the wide variety of dimensions that clinicians may assess and attempt to alter therapeutically. Indeed, many of the factors listed in Figure 1.1 have become key points in the translation from the theoretical domain to the clinical setting for mental health workers. These considerations underscore the dynamic interplay between constitutional factors, validated cerebral trauma, and the quality and quantity of parenting.

HISTORICAL OVERVIEW

Prior to the 1900s it is difficult to speak of the scientific study of mental retardation because, like mental illness, its early history was dominated by primitive thinking that tended to attribute the problems to various supernatural causes. Except for the work of Hippocrates and a few of his contemporaries, mental retardation or any identifiable description of it does not appear in the medical writings of antiquity. The caregivers of the first 18 centuries of the Christian era had little interest in mental retardation (or mental illness) and its manifestations. Readers who are particularly interested in the early historical aspects will find relevant material in Kanner (1964) and Menolascino (1970).

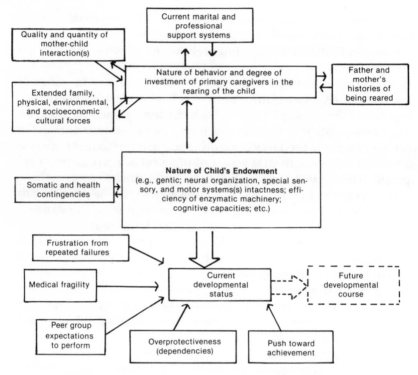

Figure 1.1.   Developmental contingencies of personality functioning.

At the dawn of the 19th century, a French psychiatrist, Jean-Marc-Gaspard Itard, published a report on his 5-year project of "educating the mind" of Victor, known as The Wild Boy of Aveyron. Itard's report sparked the beginnings of widespread scientific and professional concern with "idiocy" (mental retardation). His project arose from earlier successful efforts to educate the deaf and his conviction that Victor's mind could be educated by a system of sensory input and allied habit training. Itard's work clearly illustrated what a creative, humanistic, and highly structured approach to a developmentally delayed individual could accomplish. He recognized the significance of motivation, transference, and what is now called ego development and the strengthening of ego controls through the use of identification. Accordingly, Itard's *De l'Education d'un Homee Sauvage* (1801) (Itard, 1932) can be viewed as the first detailed report on dynamic psychotherapy.[1]

---

[1]An excellent review of Itard's benchmark work is provided by Lane (1976).

Edouard Seguin's book, *The Moral Treatment, Hygiene, and Education of Idiots and Other Backward Children* (1846), is another landmark in the literature of mental retardation. Seguin, a specialist in education of the deaf, was inspired by Itard's reported work with Victor. Under the leadership of Samuel G. Howe, a Boston psychiatrist specializing in the education of deaf mutes, Seguin's system was introduced to America in the mid-1800s when Dr. Howe became the director of the first state-supported school for the retarded in Boston. At the same time, for political reasons, Seguin fled France, and with Howe's encouragement, came to the United States. From then on (circa 1850) he was active in assisting 19th century America in establishing schools for "idiots and other feebleminded persons" and residential centers for their humane care.

During this second half of the 19th century, mental health professionals further involved themselves with some of the key issues of retardation. The American Association on Mental Deficiency was founded in 1876; all of its charter members were psychiatrists. They and many other psychiatrists who followed in their footsteps were dedicated to the proposition that through the application of psychotherapeutic principles and dynamically oriented education, "idiotic" and "imbecile" children could be substantially improved.

In the last decade of the 19th century, however, another fateful trend developed. The Parisian School of Psychiatry and Neurology turned its attention to possible causative factors that could produce the symptom of mental retardation. While describing mental retardation in psychologic and behavioristic terminology, this group firmly adhered to the thesis that the ultimate nature of these conditions lay in some form of brain impairment. This one-dimensional view was expressed in a variety of "defect" theories, which implied a distinct limitation on the retarded person's learning and/or adaptive ability. Because of "damaged internal mechanisms," the symptom of retardation was seen as beyond the scope of extrinsic (i.e., educational or treatment) manipulation. There is no doubt that this particular defect concept played a dominant part of shifting the role of mental health workers from one of positive therapeutic intervention to that of the custodial gatekeeper.

The defect concept was also utilized to "explain" some occasional manifestations associated with mild mental retardation that were being recognized more frequently. One particular area drew a great deal of attention: maladaptive social behavior. Most retarded individuals with such problems were identified in adolescence and came to the "idiot asylums" as social misfits, neglected children, or both. Evident limitation in the "learning of letters" and the frequent association with social failure prompted the English psychiatrists to term these individuals *moral imbeciles*. For all practical purposes, Goddard (1912, 1914) later equated "moral imbecility" with his definition of the "moron," and attributed the condition to heredity.

In summary, borne along on the crest of a dawning social conscience, the 19th century initially witnessed the recognition of mental retardation as a condition in which the intellectual faculties have never developed sufficiently. It witnessed "educating the minds of idiots"; and for almost 90 years, mental health workers had a well established and well documented role of leadership in promoting the best interests of the mentally retarded. It should be noted that many "new developments" in the care, training, and education of the mentally retarded have been anticipated (and practiced) with sophisticated skill by 19th century mental health professionals. As the 20th century approached, two trends were noted: the rise of the brain impairment concept in professional thinking, and a move away from the concept of sheltering the retarded from society. This latter approach was drastically altered to one of protecting society from the retarded. Concomitantly, the attitude of benevolence toward the retarded faded away.

At the beginning of the 20th century, important trends coalesced into a *tragic interlude,* which left a lasting imprint on the professional mental health worker's involvement in the field of mental retardation. In a time span of only 20 years (1900-1920), the interest of mental health professionals shifted away from mental retardation. Three crucial developments, operating in a symbiotic relationship, administered the coup de grace to the earlier enthusiasm and challenge of mental retardation for the mental health profession in the United States: 1) the introduction of the Binet Test to America in 1908; 2) the publication of Goddard's monograph on *The Kallikak Family* in 1912; and 3) defect theories introduced in the last decade of the 19th century. These three developments served to alienate the mental health professional's interest from mental retardation.

Almost overnight, the Binet Test and its subsequent modifications gained acceptance as a crucial diagnostic technique for mental retardation. Indeed, it soon came to be utilized as the one and only guide for educational programs and even for the prognosis of social effectiveness. The mental status interview and assessment approach were replaced by the mental test approach, and professional mental health services became expendable. The discovery of vast numbers of "morons in our midst" through the use of mental tests soon became a matter of widespread concern, especially because so many of the mildly retarded seemed to be social misfits. The fact that it was mostly the social misfits that came under scrutiny was over-looked, and the conclusion was drawn that all retarded individuals were social problems, or potentially so.

Goddard was not alone in sounding this eugenic alarm. Others contributed to the growing consensus that, in time, reached four distinct conclusions: 1) there were more retarded persons than people realized; 2) the mentally retarded accounted for virtually all of the current social ills; 3) heredity was the major cause of mental retarda-tion; 4) because the "decadent" retarded seemed to reproduce faster than nonretarded citizens, society would soon be destroyed unless drastic measures were taken.

While these concepts about mental retardation were taking hold, American mental health professionals were rapidly assimilating the dynamic concepts of psychoanalysis into mental health evaluation and treatment. Psychotherapeutic efforts with the psychoneuroses served to entice mental health professionals away from the more "prosaic" activities in mental retardation, and Itard's psychopeda-gogic efforts with Victor were forgotten.

It is interesting to note that the early roots of child psychiatry had a strong beginning in this same period in the Judge Baker Clinic in Boston. Here some of the same "morons" were being evaluated as juvenile delinquents; yet, the evaluation setting (community-based) of this clinic and the professionals involved (the prototype of the multidisciplinary treatment team) were not greatly different from current models of diagnosis and treatment. The resultant psychody-namic formulations and treatment recommendations were both wel-come and helpful. Indeed, it seems that the previously noted mental health ferment in the mental retardation institutions was trans-posed directly to the community-based work in juvenile delinquency, although the retarded were not viewed as good treatment candidates in this new focus on community- and family-based treatment efforts.

The tragic interlude stimulated major financial commitments on a national scale to the construction of ever larger institutions in which to incarcerate "dangerous" retarded citizens. In rapid succes-sion, restrictive marriage and sterilization laws and lifelong segrega-tion ("warehousing") of retarded individuals in inexpensive institu-tions produced what Vail (1966) aptly describes as the professional mental health worker's posture of "dehumanization." The role of mental health professionals in mental retardation rapidly became that of a jailer, and the prevailing professional-societal expectations left little room for the humane and therapeutic models that had typified the earlier role of mental health professionals in mental retardation. This change alone was enough to repel many professionals who earlier had been motivated by a humane ambition to rehabilitate retarded persons.

As noted by Wolfensberger (1969), the period from 1925 to the very recent past was characterized by the prevailing institutional practices and a continuation of the practices that evolved from these outdated professional rationales. The pictoral overview entitled *Christmas in Purgatory* by Blatt and Kaplan (1974), reports of the President's Committee on Mental Retardation (1978, 1979), and Poling and Brvening (1982) document this aimless continuity. During this same period, major organizational changes occurred in the structure of professional mental health organizations, which also reflected these changes. The bulk of rapidly evolving child psychiatry services became noninstitutionally oriented, a trend that has continued and strengthened during the last 25 years. The rapid drift of mental health professionals away from mental retardation in the 1920s and 1930s culminated in a significant organizational restructuring in the American Psychiatry Association: its section on Mental Deficiency was formally replaced by a new section on Child Psychiatry in 1959. This change gave organizational support to psychiatry's disenchantment with mental retardation and a formal separation resulted. The work of many dedicated mental health professionals in the area of mental retardation continued, but they became lost voices in a wilderness in which national professional mental health organizations simply tolerated mental retardation as its Cinderella (Menolascino, 1970; Potter, 1964; Tarjan, 1966) and gave little else to it.

It seems then that mental retardation attracted the interest and participation of outstanding mental health professionals throughout the 19th century and for the first decade or so of the 20th century. By the 1920s, the interest of the mental health disciplines in the mentally retarded had begun to deteriorate. From then until 1960, the topic of mental retardation and the clinical challenges of the mentally retarded occupied but a peripheral position in the training and practice of mental health professionals.

CURRENT PERIOD OF MENTAL HEALTH REINVOLVEMENT

First, diagnostic clarifications were made of the wide variety of causative agents (or processes) that can produce the symptom of mental retardation. This work led to a sharpened focus on the similarities and differences between mental retardation and mental illness (see Table 1.3).

Second, increasing consensus was reached on an operational definition of mental illness; e.g., "An abnormality of behavior, emotions or relationships—which abnormalities are sufficiently marked and/or prolonged as to handicap the individual himself and/or distress his family or the community—and which continue up to the time of assessment" (Chess, 1969).

Third, research studies of the biomedical, educational, and psychosocial determinants of mental retardation attracted ever in-

Table 1.3. Similarities and differences between mental retardation and mental illness

Mental retardation	Mental illness
1. Retardation refers to subaverage intellectual functioning	1. Mental illness has nothing to do with IQ. A person who is mentally ill may be a genius or may be subaverage
2. Retardation refers to impairment in social adaptation	2. A mentally ill person may be very competent socially but may have a character disorder or other aberration
3. Incidence: 3% of general population	3. Incidence: 16–20% of general population
4. Retardation is present at birth or usually occurs during the period of development	4. Mental illness may have its onset at any age
5. In mental retardation, the intellectual impairment is permanent but can be aided through full development of the person's potential	5. Mental illness is often temporary and in many instances is reversible. It is not a developmental disability
6. A retarded person can usually be expected to behave rationally at his or her operational level	6. A mentally ill person may vacillate between normal and irrational behavior
7. Erratic and/or violent behavior are rarely noted in retarded persons secondary to the cause of their retardation	7. In some types of mental illness the presence of erratic or even violent behavior is a hallmark (e.g., paranoid schizophrenia)
8. Symptoms of failure to adjust to societal demands are secondary to limited intelligence and social-adaptive responses	8. Symptoms are secondary to a break with reality and/or emotional interference with responses

creasing numbers of investigators to the scientific study of the personality characteristics in the retarded.

Fourth, citizen advocacy groups (e.g., the Association for Retarded Citizens of the U.S.) joined forces with professionals to demand that more scientific attention be addressed to research on the adjustment potentials of the retarded.

These contributions to the interrelationships between mental retardation and mental illness have reflected this renaissance of professional interest. Indeed, the bulk of the literature on this topic has appeared since 1960 (Balthazar, Stevens, and Gardner, 1969; Beier, 1964; Bernstein, 1970; Bialer, 1957; Garfield, 1963; Menolascino, 1970; 1977; Szymanski and Tanguay, 1980). Particular professional focus has been placed on: 1) frequency and types of emotional disorders in the retarded; and 2) treatment-management approaches that have been employed to ameliorate these coexisting entities. Before addressing these specific topical areas, a brief overview may help identify the major viewpoints and contributions that have ushered in the current period of mental health reinvolvement in the area of mental retardation and the challenges faced in the 1980s.

It is very popular in mental retardation circles to focus on the acceptance of the principle of normalization (Nirje, 1969) and the developmental model (Menolascino, 1977) as the keystones to progressive ideologies and treatment. Yet these concepts evolved directly from major contributions of mental health professionals to knowledge of early personality development and child care principles. Indeed, the changes in the care of the mentally retarded, to a very great extent, had their roots in the advances made in mental health over the last 30 years. These changes fall into four main areas: 1) improved understanding of early personality development; 2) delineation of the nature of mental illness in the retarded; 3) models of care and their impact on the mental health of the mentally retarded; and 4) the understanding of the frequency and types of mental illness most commonly observed in the mentally retarded.

Developmental Issues

The work of Spitz (1946), Bowlby (1951), and others regarding the effects of early object loss and institutionalization has had a profound effect on all child-rearing practices. For orphaned children who are not identified as emotionally or mentally handicapped, this work has virtually eliminated the large institutional orphanage in favor of foster care. This change could have been justified for humanitarian reasons alone, but it has far greater implications for society in preventing the syndrome of the detached institutionalized adult who is too crippled to function in normal family relationships. For retarded individuals, the same principles apply. As recently as 10 years ago some of the most familiar sights in institutions for the retarded were individuals who tended to manifest two basic expressions of the syndrome of detachment. One was the retarded child with chronic affect hunger who would indiscriminately approach any visitor in a pathetic attempt to gain attention; the other was the individual who had given up trying to reach people and had withdrawn to spend countless hours in some type of ritualized, often bizarre, self-stimulating behavior. These types of behavior were frequently cited as reasons for continuing institutional care: "See how she approaches any stranger; she would never be safe in the community"; and, "Look at all the psychotic rituals; he could never be managed in the community." The work of Spitz and Bowlby indicated that frequently it was not the underlying mental retardation, but rather the impersonal care of the institution that led to a number of these behavioral characteristics of detachment.

As these newer principles of care were applied, it became more apparent that much of the behavior thought to be most typical of the retarded person is actually an expression of emotional detachment, and is therefore preventable if retarded individuals are placed in small settings where they will have a limited and consistent group of caregivers. Attention to these critical developmental periods (Connolly and Bruner, 1974) and events has underscored the importance of giving children this type of care if they are to acquire (and sustain) higher levels of competence.

Nature of Mental Illness in the Retarded

One of the reasons frequently given for institutionalization of the retarded was the concern about unmanageable behavior of retarded persons as they approached midadolescence or adulthood. Although there is a higher incidence of epilepsy, motor, special sensory, and allied handicapping conditions in the retarded (Menolascino and Egger, 1978), the tremendous improvements in medical treatment of these various problems during the last 20 years has made possible revolutionary changes in the management of retarded persons. Similarly, improved mental health treatment modalities have permitted a dramatic decrease in highly structured institutional treatment approaches. Isolation rooms, restraints, and excessive pharmacologic regimes are increasingly becoming the exception rather than the rule.

These improvements in treatment of mental illness in the mentally retarded have flowed from an increased understanding of the nature (i.e., developmental determinants) and manifestations (i.e., symptoms) of mental illness in the retarded. Further exploration of the at-risk nature of the retarded has made it abundantly clear that any condition which renders one *less* capable of handling reality-based demands makes one *more* susceptible to mental illness. Table 1.4 enumerates these at-risk factors that make retarded individuals vulnerable to mental illness.

Influences of Level of Retardation   The factors noted in Table 1.4 are further augmented by the *level* of mental retardation that is present. For example, in the *severely retarded* the presence of major central nervous system impairment tends to impair greatly their ability to access or participate in social transactions. Without gentle and stable interpersonal support systems, the severely retarded tend to respond adversely to interpersonal stress with stereotyped and out-of-contact behaviors that mimic autism. Similarly, severe language delay, which is usually present, hinders the development of complex personality development, thus enhancing vulnerability to emotional under- or overreactivity. A study by Chess, Horn, and Fernandez (1971) clearly noted that if severely retarded infants (who were also blind and deaf secondary to rubella) were provided with early and ongoing interpersonal and developmental stimuli, they tended to show delayed and primitive behavior that was consistent with their level of retardation. They also noted, however, that in those instances where these early sets of experiences were *not* provided, the infants displayed "blindisms," rocking, obstinancy, and "organic autism." Thus, if the handicaps were energetically treated, the impact would be developmentally delayed but behaviorally intact; if these intervening treatment experiences were absent, then the impacts would be very disturbed and out-of-contact.

In the *moderately retarded,* a set of personality characteristics are noted that can either be programmed for maximal developmental growth or become the focal point for mental illness. Specifically, during an extensive study of young moderately retarded children, Webster (1970) noted a consistent set of personality characteristics that he termed the primary psychopathology of moderately retarded youngsters:

1. Benign autism
2. Repetitiousness (nonobsessive)

3. Relative inflexibility (rapid external changes—heightened propensity for personality disorganization)
4. Passivity (a protective posture secondary to perceived failure)
5. Simplicity of the emotional life (secondary to delayed personality development and allied symptoms such as motor and special sensory handicaps)
6. Marked language delay

It should be noted that the benign autism, nonobsessive repetitiousness, relative inflexibility, passivity, and simplicity of the external life are *all* fertile ground for both the initiation of a mental illness (if a highly supportive family or necessary program services are not provided) and misdiagnosis. Regarding the latter, one must be careful not to view the personality characteristics of the moderately retarded as signs or symptoms of mental illness. The few available autobiographies of moderately retarded individuals may be helpful in this regard (e.g., Hunt, 1967); here these basic personality features are noted *without* the presence of symptoms or signs of allied mental illness.

Mildly retarded individuals have a unique set of stresses. Their often nearly normal appearance tends to preclude their easy identification by others as being handicapped individuals. This can lead to unrealistic expectations on the part of the individual and/or his or her loved ones and a series of major interpersonal failures. At the same time, these individuals are capable of developing some insight into their limitations.

Emotional disturbances in the *mildly retarded* often result when the individual is labeled as deviant and is enmeshed in the dynamic interplay of disturbed family transactions. The frequent delay in establishing that these youngsters have a distinct handicap (usually not confirmed until 6 to 9 years of age) is a common source of anxiety for the mildly retarded individual. Low self-esteem is very frequent in the mildly retarded; the stigma of attending special classes and adverse encounters with the social-interpersonal environment tends to make them feel ineffective and different.

This may be compounded by the individual's inability to integrate the normal developmental sequences at the appropriate time in his or her life. For example, during the late childhood period of personality integration, the mildly retarded person has considerable difficulty in understanding the symbolic abstractions of schoolwork and the ongoing complexities of social-adaptive expectations from both family and peer group. It is at this stage that they often gain some understanding of their limitations. Unfortunately, by early

Table 1.4   At-risk factors for mental illness in the retarded

1. Relative inability to understand the demands of their culture second-ary to the presence of intellectual and social-adaptive limitations.
2. Major handicaps secondary to central nervous system impairments, often lead to secondary behavior manifestations (e.g., self-stimula-tion as an external replacement for impaired inner resources)
3. Constricted emotional and personality growth secondary to delayed self-concept (i.e., differentiating the self from the nonself). Allied components are: a) sensory and motor handicaps; and b) delayed in-tegrative functions: poor reality perceptions, retaining of primitive thinking (e.g., magical thinking, confusion of reality/fantasy; prob-lems in handling aggression, difficulty in pinpointing sources of frustration)
4. Delayed language development, with particular reference to delayed ability to express appropriate needs, and decreased exploration of the world. Their lack of ability to understand the interpersonal world around them leads to a very concrete cause-and-effect understanding of that world
5. Impaired memory and transfer of learning leads to lowered inner con-trol and decreased ability to delay responses and plan alternative methods of action. Thinking tends to be concrete and rigid; this leads to poor responses to external and internal stress.
6. Low self-esteem is fostered by early attendance at special schools; leads to a sense of "differentness" and, eventually, a self-image of deviancy. Perceives he or she has failed the parents; leads to an in-creased need for praise and approval. Repeated nonapproval from peers leads to an increasing sense of incompetence and ineffec-tiveness. Peer rejection and lowered family and group expectations are reflected in lowered individual motivation
7. Atypical personality defenses include increased obsessional behav-ior; helps to control new situations and control and/or cope with the environment. Fears, however, are retained longer and defenses are more fixed leading to rigidity of life-style and increased utilization of nonadaptive defenses (e.g., denial, compulsive rigidity, withdrawal, regression, projection, etc.)
8. Vulnerability in adulthood. Continuation of the previously noted fac-tors in childhood and adolescence directly leads to longer depen-dence, social and vocational limitations, and interference with heter-osexual experiences. Failure to master key adaptational tasks at developmentally appropriate milestones in childhood and adoles-cence, when compiled with the lowered global intelligence, culmi-nates in poor judgment.

adolescence they have all too often established an identity that incor-porates both retardation and deviance. The mildly retarded are not as likely to be buffered or redirected by loved ones into new interper-sonal coping styles that can help correct earlier misconceptions about the self. Without a source of ongoing family or community support and direction, the mildly retarded are at high risk to develop mental illness or marginal identities in our society.

The persistent concerns about heightened sexual activity and/or aggressive proclivities in the mildly retarded have been clarified. Rather than the old view of greater or lesser than normal sexual-aggressive drives (Barr, 1904), it is clear that the strength of these drives is not as important as the ability to manage them. Successful personal managing depends on the nature of the individual's personality growth and defenses, social opportunities to express these drives, and specific training in modulating or redirecting them. All of these considerations are recognized areas of conflict that are very amenable to psychotherapy approaches. Needless to say, the mildly retarded *are* prime candidates for such treatment.

Emotional Adjustment Problems Related to Different Models of Care   An alternative way to view the emotional adjustment problems of the retarded (in addition to the levels of retardation) is to consider the problems as they seem to relate to different models of parenting and the care provided to the individual during his or her formative years. Providing optimal care for the retarded at home, in the community, or in an institutional setting is extremely difficult because there is no average retarded person. In a general way, some grouping can be done on the level of retardation; however, a striking aspect is the great variation of abilities often seen within each of these persons. This variability, plus the difficulty that primary caregivers have in fully understanding the individual retarded person, seems to be the basis for a number of the emotional problems seen in the retarded. The most common types of caregiver errors in the retarded involve the caregivers having either overly limited or excessive expectations for the individual retarded person. Errors in either direction seem to contribute significantly to a great many of the emotional problems seen in the retarded.

Problems in Care Models Reflecting Limited Expectations   Too few expectations, combined with too little effort on the part of the caregivers for retarded persons, create problems. These individuals tend to show a pattern of underachievement and a detachment syndrome. One characteristic problem is profound and often indiscriminately expressed affect hunger. The moderate and mildly retarded often have had no extended experiences with significant or meaningful object relations; they are accustomed to living amidst large numbers of minimally involved people. As a result, the retarded's indiscriminant approach to strangers can be a serious problem; this lack of social sense is often cited as part of the syndrome of retardation and a reason for continued institutionalization (Donaldson and Menolascino, 1977). A variant of this detachment syndrome is more often seen in the severely retarded. Instead of exhibiting indiscriminant approach behaviors, this group often withdraws into themselves, developing a pattern of primitive and self-stimulating behaviors that are similar to those seen in infantile autism.

Another care model variant is seen when the caregivers actually do too much instead of too little; this caregiving model of overprotection in the retarded fosters dependence and smothers initiative and learning. Prior to the availability of community-based programs, parents who were faced with the singularly unhappy choice of sending their children to an institution sometimes felt that the only acceptable solution was to care for the afflicted family member at home. All too often this was done in an isolated part of the home away from the nest of the family and external social contacts. Here the devoted mother tended to the child's every need, thus increasing his or her dependency and almost eliminating any capability for developing effective social-adaptive functions. This may cause even more serious emotional adjustment problems when the child's physical maturation or the parent's advancing years make home care no longer possible.

Whereas the detached mildly or moderately retarded person is at risk to develop the counterpart of a character disorder in a person of normal intelligence, the overprotected retarded person is more likely to show symptoms of inflexibility, autistic thinking, and separation anxiety. The retarded may also tend to show stereotypic behavior as a pattern of self-stimulation. As might be expected, the detached individual leaving the institution is at risk to show active but indiscriminant behavior in community placement efforts; the retarded person with a history of overprotective isolation is more likely to respond with anxiety and anger to the social and self-help demands of the community or even to future institutional placement.

Excessive Expectations   At the other end of the spectrum, there are caregivers with unrealistically high expectations. One of the most common problems in very young moderately retarded children who do not have physical stigmata is the parents' failure to recognize their children's intellectual limitations before the normal time of language acquisition. It is not unusual for an autistic-like psychosis to occur in a sensitive, intelligent appearing (but nevertheless retarded) child when his or her conscientious parents do all the "right" things during the second year of life to facilitate language skills. Verbal demands to name objects often cause the moderately retarded child with a language disability to react with increasing anxiety and a variety of avoidance behaviors that reflect this lack of pleasure in verbal interactions. On the contrary, if retardation in these children is detected early (by age 2 or 3 years) and if ways are found to relate to them that do not depend unduly on verbal productions, they are frequently able to abandon their autistic-like behavior. Similar examples of the effects of excessive expectations are seen occasionally in innovative institutional or community programs in which more severely retarded children may be subjected to overly intense efforts to maximize their capabilities. In some cases this has resulted in more frequent seizures or a pattern of autistic withdrawal quite similar to that noted above. One of the most distressing problems with older children in this group is outbursts of violent behavior when excessive expectations have been maintained for too long; such children are frequently placed on high dosages of medication in an effort to control aggression that is actually reactive in nature and not a symptom of psychosis.

In summary, information concerning models of care that are appropriate for the management of the mentally retarded can provide valuable guidelines for maximizing their developmental potential. Expectations based on observed behaviors (rather than expected behaviors), level of retardation, and the typically beneficial role of early educational and socialization programs help define the model and principal programs that the retarded need. Conversely, inappropriate expectations and lack of early developmentally oriented programs will only heighten the vulnerability of retarded individuals to mental illness.

Frequency and Types of Mental Illness in the Retarded A few introductory comments on clinical diagnostic assessment seem in order before discussing the frequencies and types of mental illness in the mentally retarded.

The 1970s brought mental health and mental retardation professionals to a realization that mental illness can frequently hinder the intellectual and social adaptive growth of mentally retarded individuals. Nevertheless, there has been only small change in the management of the mentally ill-mentally retarded child or adult; his or her clinical diagnostic assessment is too often accomplished only with much difficulty and with too little understanding of the manifestations of mental illness in the retarded person. Accordingly, it may be timely to focus on general and specific issues of clinical diagnostic assessment to help professionals better recognize mental illness in retarded persons.

It should be stressed at the outset that the mental status examination of a mentally retarded individual—whether to confirm the primary diagnosis of mental retardation, to assess whether it is an instance of "pseudoretardation," or to confirm the coexistence of mental illness and mental retardation—*cannot* be accomplished in isolation from general diagnostic procedures. In short, the mental health professional should (ideally) carry out his or her own physical and neurologic examinations, and should be able to interpret pediatric and internal medicine and neurologic consultations, as well as such studies as psychologic evaluations and electroencephalograms. Following this process, the mental health professional is in a much better position to see the whole person, and thereby piece together the diagnostic puzzle that mental illness can present in the mentally retarded person.[2] To cast the mental health professional in the role of a "complete professional" may be viewed as "asking too much," but failure to assess clearly all parameters of a child's or adult's behavior can result in many of the major diagnostic errors made with the retarded. It seems that exclusive focus on the mental status examination has perpetuated the classic split between the *psyche* and the *soma* in evaluating and treating the retarded.

Studies concerning the frequency and types of mental illness in the mentally retarded have some major methodologic problems. The early studies (pre-1960) were carried out primarily in institutional and/or hospital settings. Frequency rates reported ranged from 16% (Penrose, 1966) to 28% (Beier, 1964) and 40% (Pollock, 1958). These studies as well as more recent investigations of institutionalized retarded (Balthazar and Stevens, 1975; May and May, 1979; Menolascino, 1972, 1975) are questionable guides to the true frequency of mental illness in the mentally retarded because institutionalization traditionally has been used as a societal mechanism for managing retarded citizens with social-behavioral difficulties. The more recent studies may also reflect the increasing referral of "community program rejects" to institutions (Menolascino, 1972). In other words, are these individuals disturbed because of personality deficits secondary to their underlying mental retardation, or are they disturbed because of the way they are treated by society? For example, a study of the incidence of mental illness in a sample of institutionalized individuals with Down's syndrome revealed that 35% of the total sam-

---

[2]If a University-Affiliated Program or similar diagnostic similar team in a Community Mental Health Center is available, then an in-depth professional background in the individual diagnostician is not an essential element.

ple were mentally ill at the time of the study. There were clear indications, however, that 56% of the total sample had displayed clear indices of major mental illness at the time of their admission to the institution (Menolascino, 1967). The question arises, why were they sent to an institution for the retarded rather than to a mental health facility? Because institutions for the retarded traditionally have employed a meager cadre of mental health professionals, the admission of these mentally ill-mentally retarded individuals to such an institution was (and is) quite inappropriate.

A series of reports on mentally retarded individuals who lived with their primary families and/or in their primary community at the time of the study has appeared (Berman, 1977; Chess, 1962, 1970; Chess and Hassibi, 1978; Dewan, 1948; Eaton and Menolascino, 1966, 1967, 1982; Menolascino, 1965, 1967; 1969; O'Connor, 1951; Webster, 1971). These studies report that the mentally retarded fall prey to the same types of mental illness that befall people with normal intellectual abilities. Recent professional literature repeats the theme that in the retarded the full range of psychoses, neuroses, personality disorders, behavior disorders, and adjustment reactions exist as are noted in the general population. Other workers report a higher incidence and a different spectrum of mental illness among the retarded than in the general population (Beier, 1964; Garfield, 1963; Phillips and Williams, 1975). Some suggest that there are qualitative differences as well, so that some psychiatric conditions seen in the retarded may represent unique syndromes (Bender, 1970; Menolascino and Eggers, 1978; Webster, 1971). Yet there have been few studies that have looked specifically at the frequency and types of mental illness in this population.

May and May (1979) thoroughly reviewed the types and frequency of mental illness noted in the mentally retarded. The data in Table 1.5 summarizes the types of mental illness noted in their literature survey.

Even if mentally retarded persons are emotionally well adjusted, they will experience some difficulty functioning independently or semiindependently in their community. If their lives are complicated by a mental illness, their adjustment difficulties are obviously compounded. Recent studies rather consistently reported a 20 to 35% frequency rate of emotional disturbances and suggested strongly that clinical focus must be placed on the diagnosis and subsequent treatment of the combined findings of mental illness and mental retardation.

Table 1.5.   Most frequently reported mental illnesses in the mentally retarded

Psychoses
  Schizophrenia
    Paranoid ⎱ Propfschizophrenia
    Catatonic ⎰ (Lanzkron, 1957)
  Manic-depressive psychosis
  Psychotic depression

Neuroses
  Conversion reaction
  Anxiety reaction
  Depressive reaction

Personality disorders
  Schizoid personality
  Passive aggressive
  Antisocial personality

Transitional-situational
  Adjustment reaction to stress
  Alcoholism
  Suicide gestures

Syndrome associated
  Stereotyped behaviors (e.g., Lesch-Nyhan syndrome; self-destructive acts)
  Confusional/aggressive episodes (e.g., seizure disorders)

Interestingly, the presence of these combined findings may also reflect a professional bias: the symptom of mental retardation may be viewed as a signal *not to treat* the retarded person's accompanying mental illness. This bias was clearly identified by Woodward, Jaffe, and Brown (1970) when they noted:

There are two prevalent attitudes on the part of many practicing child psychiatrists in the New York area with which we differ strongly: 1) There is the attitude that a psychiatric diagnosis must be made in terms of either "organicity" or "non-organicity." Those holding this view seem unable to conceive of a mixed picture. Our experience would suggest that a mixed picture is common. To us it is irrational to say that a child with brain damage can have only one form of pathology, and this explains everything. Why can't a child have mixed brain damage and a psychoneurosis? 2) There is the attitude that a child who has any evidence of brain damage at all, even an isolated abnormal electroencephalogram without other evidence of central nervous system involvement, should not be offered psychotherapy. This attitude exists in spite of the known fact that many disturbed children respond poorly to psychotherapeutic programs, and have no evidence of organic lesions. We believe that the decision whether a child should have psychotherapy depends on the estimate of his ability to profit by it, regardless of the presence of organic pathology (p. 290).

This pair of attitudinal biases may have added unduly both to the past and current reports of high frequency of mental illness in the retarded, with little evidence of effective efforts to treat the mental illness in these individuals. Indeed, these professional blind spots may have incorrectly pushed some retarded citizens into institutional patienthood as "chronically disturbed retarded persons."

A Recent Study Eaton and Menolascino (1982) recently completed a clinical study that had as its primary purpose the determination of the types and frequency of mental illness noted in a community-based population of mentally retarded citizens. It is significant that this study was carried out in a community setting because the majority of previous studies on this topic have assessed retarded citizens in institutions wherein a higher prevalence of mental illness and more severe levels of retardation are usually noted. Furthermore, the study assessed both retarded children and adults, whereas previous community-based studies often focused on only one chronologic age segment of the retarded. The setting for this study was a community-based program for the mentally retarded (the Eastern Nebraska Community Office of Retardation; see Menolascino, 1977), which has been operational for a decade and serves a five-county region of Nebraska which includes the city of Omaha. The population base is 482,000, and it is 80% urban. To be eligible for this program, an individual had to be functioning in the mentally retarded range as determined by an interdisciplinary team evaluation. Since 1968, there has been a trend in Nebraska to decrease the number of retarded citizens in its institutions; those who were discharged to the catchment area automatically became patients in this program. The program was well known in the area and received referrals from local schools, health practitioners, and directly from families of retarded individuals. Accordingly, the resulting population of mentally retarded in the program was a representative cross-section of retarded citizens in this catchment area.

From January 1976 to June 1979, a total of 168 retarded individuals, or 21% of the total enrollment (i.e., 798) in the ENCOR system during this time span were referred for psychiatric assessment. Each was individually evaluated. Of the initial 168 referrals, it was determined by the psychiatric consultant that 115 were both mentally ill and mentally retarded. These 115 individuals became the study group; they represented 14.6% of the entire mentally retarded population in the ENCOR program.

The chronologic age range of the study group was from 6 to 76 years. Six percent of the group were 10 years of age or under, and teenagers comprised 43%. Adults made up 51% of the study group, with 20 year olds accounting for 32% and those over 50 years, 2%. The group was 66% male because of a disproportionately large number of boys between the ages of 6 and 15 years; there were 25 boys but only 11 girls in this age range in the study group. For all other age groups, distribution of males and females was fairly equal.

The diagnostic entities that were seen most frequently are listed in Table 1.6. As to formal psychiatric diagnosis, organic brain syndrome (OBS) grouped with behavioral or psychotic reactions was the most frequent diagnostic group. In the present study, diagnostic criteria for the OBS diagnosis was evidence of an OBS by mental status, physical-neurologic examinations, and/or history of etiologically significant factors. The diagnosis of OBS with behavioral reaction was used for the subgroup that frequently displayed inappropriate acting-out behaviors (e.g., emotional lability, impulsivity, poor social judgment, frequent angry tantrums), but did not have psychotic symptoms. The subgroup with evidence of OBS and clear psychotic symptoms presented a different clinical picture than schizophrenia because: 1) the organic signs and symptoms of the disorder were prominent; 2) the out-of-contact behaviors were not the type commonly seen in schizophrenia (e.g., no thought disorder or hallucinatory experiences); and 3) their personality structures did not show the progressive involvement of multiple segments of personality functioning which is characteristic of schizophrenia. Using these criteria, 21% of the study group were found to have OBS with behavioral reaction and 13% were diagnosed as OBS with psychotic reaction.

Personality disorders comprised 38% of this sample; almost half of this group were classified as passive-dependent. Schizoid personality and emotionally unstable personality disorders were found in 6%, and the one patient with a paranoid personality disorder comprised 3% of this category.

The 24 patients diagnosed as schizophrenic included 17 with chronic undifferentiated schizophrenia (four of these had been diagnosed as childhood schizophrenics earlier in their lives); three pa-

Table 1.6. Types of psychiatric disorders in a community-based sample of retarded persons

Diagnosis	Age (years)									
	6-10	11-15	16-20	21-25	26-30	31-35	36-40	41-45	46-50	50+
Schizophrenia (N = 24)										
Childhood		3								
Chronic paranoid										1
Chronic undifferentiated			5	7	2		1	1		
Acute undifferentiated				1	3					1
Personality disorders (N = 31)										
Emotionally unstable				2			2			
Paranoid personality							1			
Antisocial personality				1	1	1				
Schizoid personality		1		2	1			2		
Passive-dependent		2		2	1			1		
Passive-aggressive			2	4	1	3			1	
Anxiety disorder (N = 1)				1						
Adjustment disorder (N = 24)	5	7	4	3	1	2	1	1		
Organic brain syndrome[a] (N = 34)										
With transient psychotic reaction	2	4	5	2		2	1			
With transient behavioral reaction		12	4	3						
Totals (N = 115)	7	29	20	28	9	8	6	5	1	2

[a]Although one could argue that *all* mentally retarded citizens have an OBS (especially the low-moderate and severely retarded), this OBS designation is utilized herein in an effort to be consistent with the DSM-III nomenclature.

tients displayed chronic paranoid schizophrenia.[3] Once acute undifferentiated schizophrenia reaction was also noted. The patient diagnosed as having a neurosis was a 26-year-old woman with a chronic anxiety reaction. The clinical dimensions of each of the major diagnostic categories will now be discussed.

It was not unusual to note combined diagnoses such as childhood schizophrenia and moderate mental retardation, or an unsocialized aggressive reaction of adolescence and mild mental retardation. Certain diagnostic categories such as the neuroses were underrepresented in this sample, while other categories were seen with relative frequency (e.g., schizophrenia and adjustment reactions).

Childhood Schizophrenia and Mental Retardation

Psychotic reactions of childhood have presented a major challenge to the clinician because the psychotic child frequently functions at a mentally retarded level. Early observers believed that all psychotic children "deteriorated." In 1943, "early infantile autism" was described (Kanner, 1943); yet to label a child autistic presents some formidable diagnostic and treatment problems. A number of follow-up studies (Bender, 1959, 1970; Menolascino, 1965; 1960; Rimland, 1964; Rutter and Schopler, 1978; Schain and Yannet, 1960) coupled with the literal rediscovery of the wide variety of primitive behavioral repertoires in the retarded, have tended to mute the earlier clinical enthusiasm concerning the interrelationship between functional psychoses and early infantile autism.

In this study, the presence of bizarre behavior, persistent withdrawal, echolalic speech, and the affective unavailability of some persons in early adolescence who had clearly experienced regressive symptomatology from an earlier higher level of functioning was striking. Three adolescents illustrated the superimposition of childhood schizophrenia (i.e., by past history the schizophrenic illness in all three had begun between ages 4 and 6 years) upon etiologically clear instances of mental retardation (e.g., one had Down's syndrome, one was post-rubella, and the third had a major cranial malformation as the cause of his mental retardation).

---

[3]All of these patients had clearly documented clinical histories or examination findings of *both* mental retardation (primary disorder) and schizophrenia, thus representing instances of propfschizophrenia (Lanzkron, 1957) rather than the symptom of mental retardation being a secondary sign of global personality regression (e.g., secondary to schizophrenia).

Because treatment-prognosis guidelines may differ for youngsters with autistic reactions, and the combined mental retardation-childhood schizophrenia syndrome noted herein, this differential diagnosis is therapeutically significant beyond academic interests. For example, the vast majority of autistic youngsters seem to profit greatly from mental retardation services and secondary mental health consultations (Rutter and Schopler, 1978). Conversely, the retarded youngster who develops schizophrenia has a primary need for mental health services, with mental retardation services being utilized in a secondary role (until his or her functional psychosis subsides).

Adult Schizophrenia and Mental Retardation

Significantly, instances of paranoid schizophrenia were noted in both verbal and nonverbal patients. Included in the sample of the latter were three adults who drew out on paper their "attackers," replete with nonverbal gestures. One young man labeled his separate fingers as the "source" of his common delusions, which he portrayed symbolically in crude drawing. In the entire group of combined diagnoses of mental retardation and schizophrenia, it was noted that the altered affective responses, bizarre rituals, and utilization of interpersonal distancing clearly marked the observed behaviors as schizophrenic.

Personality Disorders

Personality disorders are characterized by chronically maladaptive patterns of behavior (e.g., antisocial personality, passive-aggressive personality, etc.), which are qualitatively different from psychotic or neurotic disorders (APA, 1980). It is interesting to note that although the schizoid personality has been reported only rarely in the retarded, it was noted in five patients in this study. These personality disorders occurred in individuals wherein the behavior was based primarily on extrinsic factors, all had no causal relationships to the symptom of mental retardation. The presence of personality disorders in 28% of this sample suggests that they are a frequent accompanying handicap for mentally retarded citizens.

Anxiety Disorders

Early reviews (Beier, 1964; Garfield, 1963) of the occurrence of psychoneurotic disorders in the retarded suggested that their frequency was quite low and the types of psychoneuroses reported were limited (e.g., anxiety and depressive reactions). Recent reviews (Balthazar and Stevens, 1975; May and May, 1980) however, dispute the concept of incompatibility between neuroses and retardation. They are quite explicit regarding the diagnostic criteria, and attribute the neurotic phenomena to factors associated with atypical developmental patterns associated with disturbed family functioning. For example, anxiety disorders in retarded children clearly link symptoms of anxiety (e.g., fear of failure and insecurity) to exogenous factors such as chronic frustration, unrealistic family expectations, and persistent interpersonal deprivations. Interestingly, these reports suggest that psychoneurotic disorders are more common in individuals in the high-moderate and mild levels of mental retardation; this has prompted speculation that the complexity of psychoneurotic transactions is beyond the adaptive limits of the more severely retarded. The findings reported by these authors are not consistent with the experience of this study wherein only one mentally retarded individual with an anxiety neurosis was noted.

Adjustment Disorders (of Childhood, Adolescence, or Adults)

Although this category of psychiatric disorders is perhaps overutilized in the assessment of the nonretarded, it is only infrequently employed during clinical assessment of emotional disturbances in the retarded population.

In this study, the highest frequency of psychiatric diagnoses were adjustment disorders: 24 (or 29%) of the total sample. Because mentally retarded individuals have a predisposition to overreact to stimuli and a limited understanding of social-interpersonal expectations they are more likely to exhibit personality disorganization after minimal interpersonal stress. These adjustment disorders may be caused by continuing inappropriate social-adaptive expectations or unexpected and frequent changes in externally imposed life patterns. Clinically, these disorders respond rapidly to environmental adjustment (when coupled with realignment of parental, residential, and educational personnel's expectations or goals), brief utilization of psychopharmacologic adjuncts, and/or supportive psychotherapy.

In summary, this study noted that retarded persons, because of their high incidence of central nervous system impairment and their diminished interpersonal coping abilities, present a greater than average risk for developing associated mental illness. As noted in the discussion of the relationship between mental illness and mental retardation, the reported frequency of mental illness in the mentally retarded also suffers from the myopia of the reporters. As May and May (1979) noted, well recognized forms of major personality dysfunctions (i.e., the symptom clusters noted in alcoholism or suicide) are only rarely reported in the current literature on the dual diagnosis of mental retardation and mental illness.

Finally, the frequency figures reported in the literature concerning the relationship between emotional disturbances and mental retardation must be placed in proper perspective by reviewing the expected frequency rates of emotional disturbances in the nonretarded. The Report of the Joint Commission on Mental Health in Children (1969) suggested that emotional disturbances complicated the lives of 14% to 18% of the child population, whereas epidemiologic studies on mental illness in adults (e.g., Leighton, 1959; Strole, 1962) suggest that the incidence of mental illness in the general population approaches 25%. From this perspective, the reported ranges of frequency of emotional disturbances in the mentally retarded suggest only a moderately increased susceptibility for them as a group.

The Mentally Retarded Offender

The mentally retarded individual who displays delinquent or criminal behavior has, like the sociopathic personality, raised questions about the role of these behaviors as a sign of emotional disturbance in the retarded; however, there is little reported information available to support the hypothesis. During the first three decades of this century, it was believed that virtually every mentally retarded individual was a potential juvenile delinquent, and that most criminals had overt manifestations of mental retardation (Goddard, 1914). Since the time of Goddard's "scientific investigations," approximately 450 separate studies on the intelligence of juvenile delinquents have been published; in fact it is probable that no other single characteristic of the juvenile delinquent has been so thoroughly studied. Still, these investigations have not provided conclusive evidence regarding the relationship between general intelligence and delinquent or criminal behavior. There has been considerable divergence of conclusions in the various studies; such divergence includes: 1) the retarded are a type of "born criminal" (i.e., "moral idiots"); 2) retardation is a hereditary characteristic, and, following Mendel's Law, it accounts for the preponderance of male retarded offenders; 3) the retarded characteristically commit antisocial crimes of assault and sexual assault; 4) retarded individuals commit crimes in the absence of inhibiting social factors because they lack the capacity to grasp the social values of their culture, including its social and legal definitions of right and wrong; 5) the retarded cannot be deterred by the threat of punishment; 6) the retarded are suggestible, and so respond to the criminal leadership of brighter persons; and 7) retarded individuals more frequently are reared in families and neighborhoods where their day-to-day identification with delinquent models is common (Menolascino, 1975).

The rationale for these opinions range from the biologic to the biosocial. The biologic concept of the retarded person as a "moral idiot" or a Mendelian "criminal type" historically preceded the biosocial view of the mentally retarded offender as a product of social interaction. During the early decades of this century, there was predisposition to view the triad of mental retardation, delinquency, and dependency as inevitably associated with the biosocial phenomena. Even Sumner, in his brilliant source book, *Folkways* (1979), cited these three characteristics as representative of the "submerged" (i.e., maladjusted) tenth of the general population who are at the bottom of the social class ladder.

As Beier (1964) noted in a review on this topic, the early estimates of the frequency of mental retardation in the offender ranged from 0.5% to 55%, with the majority of the earlier studies reporting estimates at a higher percentage range. These widely divergent poin ts of view have persisted to the present time (Allen, 1966, 1968). The literature on this topic is interesting to review because the conclusions range from one extreme to the other:

Delinquency and criminality are frequent phenomena in the mentally retarded population and the treatment potentials are low.
Delinquency and criminality are infrequent phenomena in the retarded, are dependent on environmental-familial factors, and proper treatment will effectively quell these acting-out behaviors.

Studies have indicated that the types of crimes most often committed by the retarded are qualitatively different from those most frequently committed by nonretarded offenders, with the former showing a significantly higher incidence of crimes against the person (Allen, 1970). These studies point to the relatively higher incidence of mental retardation among the socially, economically, and culturally deprived segment of our population (which also produces a greater proportion of prison inmates than does the general population), and suggest that mental retardation and crime are more significantly related to these environmental factors than they are to each other. This literature also generally concludes that there is a relatively higher percentage of arrests and convictions of mentally retarded persons charged with crime than of the total criminal population. Both points are well taken, and additional research is necessary before any judgments can be made about cause and effect relationships.

Allen, Fester, and Rubin (1978) have brought a new perspective to this old problem of the retarded offender. Their methodology and resultant findings are most commendable, especially in contrast to the armchair viewpoints that seemed to dominate discussions of this topic in the past. Allen recommends an "Exceptional Offenders Court" for the early identification of those mentally retarded offenders in need of treatment, rather than criminal prosecution in order to expedite diversion to other community resources, and offers the following summary of a modern view of the mentally retarded offender:

> Historically, society has pursued three alternative courses with the mentally retarded offender: we have ignored his limitations and special needs; or we have sought to tailor traditional criminal law processes to fit them; or we have grouped him with psychopaths, sociopaths, and sex deviates in a kind of conventicle of the outcast and hopeless. What is suggested here is a "fourth way" (e.g., the "Exceptional Offenders Court") a way not of rejection and despair, but of acceptance and hope (Allen, 1970, p. 607).

Another critical problem in the provision of services stems from the rejection of responsibility for retarded offenders on the part of many health and correctional professionals. For different reasons, each group rejects the mentally retarded as unsuitable for their respective treatment programs. As noted by Brown and Courtless (1967):

> Mental hospitals claim such an offender is not mentally ill; the traditional institutions for the retarded complain that they do not have appropriate facilities for the offender . . . correctional institutions would like to remove such persons from their population on the grounds that programs available in the correctional setting are totally inadequate and in many cases inappropriate for application to retarded persons (p. 373).

Three viewpoints regarding retarded offenders that seem most consistent with the findings of reported studies are worthy of note:

1. The mentally retarded are as capable of delinquent criminal acts as are their intellectually normal brethren; however, factors other than intellectual ones seem to be more important in the

etiology of such behavior, and these factors are those commonly cited as important to the development of delinquent and criminal behavior in the general population.

2. The lowered social adaptive abilities of the retarded (e.g., concrete thinking, lack of social insight, etc.), coupled with a relative lack of supervision, may make him or her more prone to such acts.

3. Societal views toward specific behavioral maladjustments especially sexual acting-out in girls who come from broken homes or lower socioeconomic levels (Saenger, 1960) may result in legal charges against or institutionalization of a retarded person. The same behavior in a retarded individual of differing social class or family background, however, may not result in legal action. For example, delinquent behavior in a retarded girl from an intact home and upper socioeconomic class typically eventuates in a referral to child guidance clinic, whereas her counterpart from a broken home and lower socioeconomic class is admitted to a juvenile detention facility (Kugel, Trembath, and Sagor, 1968).

There is an evolving treatment-management focus that stresses clarification of community-based treatment and management of the retarded offender. One of the new models of community-based approaches to this challenge is the "Structured Correctional Service" of ENCOR (Menolascino, 1977). This service is specially staffed with personnel experienced both in corrections and mental retardation.

In summary, the relationship of intelligence and delinquency is still the subject of some dispute, but the areas of controversy today differ from those prevailing prior to and shortly after the first investigations into the subject. The developments that have led to the gradual acceptance of a more humanistic attitude toward the retarded offender are inextricably bound to an improved understanding of mental retardation and juvenile delinquency, as well as advances in the methodology of social science research.

A SUGGESTED FRAMEWORK FOR VIEWING
MENTAL ILLNESS IN THE MENTALLY RETARDED

An alternative approach to current professional thinking concerning types of mental illness in the mentally retarded will now be discussed. Although the herein proposed conceptual framework is nontraditional as to current diagnostic systems in mental health, it has been helpful as an approach to everyday clinical challenges in both the diagnosis and—especially—the treatment and management of individuals with *both* mental illness and mental retardation. This approach is based on the author's extended clinical experiences with three general types of mentally retarded individuals with associated mental illness: those with *primitive* behavior, those with *atypical* behavior, and those with *abnormal* behavior. These three types, with the typical diagnostic-treatment challenges that each present, will now be reviewed.

Primitive Behavior

Primitive behavior usually is manifested by severely or profoundly retarded individuals who also display gross delays in their behavioral repertoires. Primitive behaviors include very rudimentary utilization of special sensory modalities, particularly touch, position, sense, oral explorative activity, and minimal externally directed verbalizations. In the diagnostic interview, primitive behaviors such as mouthing and licking of toys, excessive tactile stimulation, autistic hand movements, and skin picking and body rocking are noted. From a diagnostic viewpoint, the very primitiveness of the children's overall behavior, in conjunction with much stereotyping, initially may suggest a psychotic disorder of childhood. These children, however, do make eye contact and will interact with the examiner quite readily, despite their very minimal behavioral repertoire.

Similarly, one might form the initial impression that both the level of observed primitive behavior and its persistence are secondary to intrinsic and/or extrinsic deprivation factors; however, at the same time, these children display multiple indices of developmental biologic arrest that are of primary or congenital origin. It should be noted that these children do not possess a functional ego at the appropriate chronologic age, and there is an amorphic (or minimal) personality structure. The following case history illustrates this primitive behavior type.

Case History One: Primitive Behavior A 6½-year-old boy was seen at the request of the ward team (i.e., a developmental specialist, social worker, physician, and psychologist); the purpose of the psychiatric consultation was to provide diagnostic clarification and treatment recommendations. The youngster had been admitted for observation at the request of both his parents and the staff of the previous treatment setting, with the following transfer impression: "Functions at the severely retarded level, but physically he looks so normal. He is not a very warm child. We wonder if he isn't an autistic child."

The personal history revealed that he was the last of three children, born after an uneventful pregnancy to a 26-year-old mother who had no prior history of obstetrical complications; family history was negative for hereditary disease. His birth weight and clinical status in the early neonatal period were all within normal limits. By the age of 6 months, the child was described as passive; early developmental milestones were markedly delayed, and he displayed generalized muscle hypotonicity. By the end of the first year, his developmental attainments were those of a 4-month-old child and he had undergone a variety of medical evaluations. No definite diagnostic impressions were obtained, and the parents were counseled to provide general stimulation for their youngster. Because this family placed a high premium on child care, they were not satisfied with such nonspecific diagnostic and management recommendations. Accordingly, between the ages of 12 months and 48 months, the boy underwent six more evaluations in different parts of the country. By the age of 5 years, formal psychometric assessment indicated that the child was functioning at the 12 to 16 months developmental level; his family was perplexed and still shopping for diagnostic-treatment recommendations that would "really help him to grow like he should" (mother's statement). Medical reevaluation at age 6 was followed by parent rejection of the diagnosis of severe mental retardation. The boy had been admitted to the present institution for the retarded for further diagnosis, observation and possible treatment. As previously noted, the admitting impression was "possible autism."

Psychiatric examination of this youngster revealed no physical signs or symptoms of delayed development except for primitive finer hand movements, dull and vacant eyes, and the absence of any structured language. He occupied himself continuously with quick hand movements approximately 12 inches from his eyes, and he periodically picked at a spot on his left wrist. Initially, he was only passively compliant with the examiner. With a little inducement, however, he interacted with the examiner through eye contact, and gingerly participated in attempts at playing Pat a Cake and rolling a ball back and forth. The previously noted hand movements promptly disappeared as his attention was occupied.

Treatment recommendation focused upon stopping the diagnostic merry-go-round, while stressing the need for closer interpersonal relationships (e.g., foster grandparent contacts on a regular basis), continuity of similar passive-dependent relationships, and involvement in a highly structured, developmentally oriented program to stimulate and develop self-help skills. During a follow-up observation period, the child care workers had begun to work actively with this youngster on self-help skills and small group interactions, and they showed rather remarkable success. Simultaneously, ongoing family interviews helped to relieve parental anxiety and gave them more realistic expectations for their child.

This type of primitive behavior is frequently seen in severely and profoundly retarded children who are from rather perplexed families and who have received "the works" in diagnostic procedures. This type of emotionally disturbed-mentally retarded child essentially is an "untutored child" whose primitive behavior has been allowed to persist while parents and professionals have focused their concern on differential diagnostic issues. The family slowly loses its tolerance and empathy for the child as their initial high expectations and ongoing investments of energy result only in slow dissolution of their hopes.

There is a lingering myth that retarded children, especially the more severely retarded, must "look retarded." It would seem that normal physical appearance in the presence of markedly delayed developmental milestones (e.g., in motor and language) and primitive behavior are viewed as incongruous (and/or incompatible) by both lay and some professional observers. Yet a number of severely and profoundly retarded children have won "beautiful baby" contests. Frequently, the initial physical impression of these children and the complexity of their family interpersonal transactions, against the backdrop of severe mental retardation, results in an erroneous diagnosis of a psychotic disorder of childhood. This error is compounded by the treatment-management approaches that accompany such a diagnosis, and the effects upon the attitudes of the child, parents, and professionals. In contrast, realignment of parental and professional expectations, clarification of diagnoses, and focus upon specific treatment are the keys to providing effective help to retarded individuals who display primitive behaviors.

Atypical Behavior

Another frequently referred behavioral challenge is that of the adolescent retarded person who is committed to an institution because of ongoing adjustment difficulties within his or her home community, but not necessarily within the primary family structure. Atypical behaviors displayed by such retarded persons include poor control (as evidenced by emotional outbursts), impulsivity, sullenness, obstinacy, mild legal transgressions, and generally poor adaptation to prevocational or vocational training programs.

After such an individual arrives at the institution, psychiatric consultation most commonly is requested because: 1) the youngster refuses to cooperate with the training or group social-living expectations of the institutional setting; or 2) continual abrasive comments and/or contact from the family belittle the institution's ability to help their family member. A result of such family conduct is the retarded person's questioning: "Why was I put here?" and "Why are you keeping me?" The family denies the reality of the youngster's social-adaptive problems, while at the same time they harass the institutional staff for focusing upon and attempting positive modification of these problem behaviors.

These instances of atypical behavior are *only atypical for the institutional settings in which such youngsters find themselves* (i.e., they are really quite typical within the primary family subculture). Etiologic diagnosis usually is in the area of "cultural-familial mental retardation" or "idiopathic mental retardation." The following case history is illustrative of this clinical challenge.

Case History Two: Atypical Behavior—Response to Complex Intrafamilial Communication Patterns The patient was a 14-year-old, mildly retarded boy whose parents had a common-law marriage. Delayed development became more obvious when he entered school; then increasing behavioral difficulties were noted. Later, a series of minor altercations with the police occurred, culminating in a car theft which necessitated his removal from the community. His parents tended to blame the school for his poor performance and subsequent maladjustment; his institutionalization was very much against their wishes, and they felt that they were being persecuted (e.g., "The law is against us. He is a good boy if other people will just leave him alone."). Adjustment to institutional placement was characterized by frequent temper outbursts when demands were made upon him. He manifested continual sullenness and refused to involve himself in any of the institution's programs, except to demand that his parents be allowed to visit him weekly. Psychiatric consultation was requested to identify methods the staff might use to motivate the boy toward a more positive role in his ongoing training program.

Psychiatric examination revealed a tall young man of awkward physical appearance who was rather dressed up for the interview. He opened the interview by asking, "Who put you up to talking to me? Why? I'm not retarded and don't belong here despite what *they* say, or what *you* try to get me to say!" Following this initial salvo, he tended to limit his remarks to monosyllabic answers, nods, and grunts. He did state, "I was sent for training but they can't teach me nothing here. I know as much as they do!" He would anticipate and/or avoid questions about his personal history by sullenly staring at the examiner, looking toward the door, or appearing greatly bored by the entire transaction. Sullen defiance, personality immaturity, and interpersonal manipulations were very much in evidence. At the end of this rather exasperating interview, he stated, "You talk to my folks; they know me and they don't like the crap I've been getting from these jerks around here."

Discussion of the case with staff revealed that they minimized the importance of the family's anger toward the institution and the negative effect of this attitude upon the son's adjustment. Collectively, members of the treatment team provided information gleaned from letters, telephone calls, and family visits, all of which repeated the common theme that the family was not responsible for his placement, and continued to convey the message to him, "You can come home whenever they will let you." It would have been extremely difficult for any individual staff member to be aware of the total clinical picture and associated treatment challenges; however, with clarification and direction, staff members were able to devise some imaginative intervention techniques. In a planned conference with both the parents and the boy present, the parents were told that they could take their son home if they so desired. The family responded by listing numerous factors that they would have to consider; they then became quite uncomfortable and announced that they would telephone their decision to the boy. When the staff insisted that the boy be told of their decision in person and in the presence of staff members, the mother asked the boy to leave the room; she then stated that she couldn't tell him that she didn't want him to live at home because "He will be mad at me." When the boy was told of the family's decision by the mother, he responded (as predicted) with an angry outburst directed toward his family. In the follow-up plan, the family's visits were restricted in number; a specific member of the treatment team was present during these visits. The staff was instructed to meet his angry outbursts with the disclaimer that they were there only to help him and were not holding him against the wishes of the family.

Mild mental retardation is far more frequent than all other levels of retardation combined; yet the overwhelming majority of them are not institutionalized. Many of the youngsters who are institution-alized are admitted to protect them from severe emotional and mate-rial deprivation (Benda, Squire, Ogonik, et al., 1964; Eisenberg, 1958, 1972). Unfortunately, they usually are the last to be identified as mentally retarded and already may have spent their formative years in deprived settings. Not only have they been identified with dyssocial and antisocial pathologic living conditions, but their atti-tudes, defenses, and personality patterns usually are well en-trenched by the time of institutionalization.

It would seem that former institutionalized mentally retarded individuals with atypical behavior increasingly are "flunking out" of community-based services programs and continue their persistently atypical behavior within a social system other than primary family. Management is difficult unless very close coordination exists be-tween the administrative segments of institutional treatment teams (Beitemann, 1970); yet it is in these very cases that the total environ-ment of an institution setting can modify motivational potential, ef-fect changes in the patient's value systems, and achieve more posi-tive social-adaptive approaches to interpersonal transactions and the world of work (Slivkin and Bernstein, 1970).

Abnormal Behavior

Most of the clearly abnormal behavior challenges encountered in in-stitutionalized or community-based samples of retarded individuals primarily encompassed instances of psychotic behavior. It is truly remarkable that in the 1980s, one still sees psychotic children who have literally been dumped into institutions for the mentally re-tarded because of the lack of specific treatment programs in their home communities, or because of treatment nihilism toward the psy-choses of childhood. Treatment nihilism is a major problem: one typically notes a clinical history of great enthusiasm when treat-ment is initiated, then the slowness of the child's response "wears out" the treatment team and the child is referred as untreatable, the frequently accompanying personality regression is extrapolated to imply mental retardation, and the prognosis is viewed as hopeless. A broad view of these individuals' developmental potentials and psy-chotic characteristics must be wedded to specific treatment goals if this type of treatment failure is to be avoided.

In the clinical interview, children with psychotic disorders pre-sent the following behavioral dimensions: 1) bizarreness of manner, gesture, and posture; 2) uncommunicative speech; 3) little or no discrimination between animate and inanimate objects (one of the primary signs of psychosis in childhood, an entity sharply delineated from the primitive behavior previously noted); 4) identification with mostly inanimate objects; 5) display of deviant affective expressions; 6) little if any relationship with peers; 7) passive compliance to external demands or stimuli; and 8) marked negativism (e.g., if pushed into an interpersonal setting, the child initially exhibits negativism, followed in rapid succession by withdrawal and out-of-contact behavior, i.e., psychosis.

A case history is presented to illustrate the features of a psychotic reaction in late childhood.

Case History Three: Psychotic Behavior The patient was a 12-year-old boy who had been admitted to an institution for the retarded at age 7 because of frequent temper tantrums, noisy screeching, carrying a large screwdriver at all times, and cruelty to animals. A personal history review noted that at age 3 he was considered somewhat precocious by his parents, but was noted to display periodic elective mutism; a hearing loss was suspected. Shortly thereafter he became mute and regressed in his intellectual and motor achievement. At the time of admission he was considered "different and slow" and was unable to function in available special education options. The staff was concerned about his withdrawal as well as his bizarre behavior, reporting that he watched the linoleum tile patterns quite carefully, turning to the right on every 22nd tile interval.

On direct examination he grimaced frequently, making no affective contact despite the lengthy interview period; he made bizarre hand movements, and alternately chewed on a small ball or his left wrist, while mumbling incoherently to himself. When pushed to interact, he physically withdrew to a corner of the room and excitedly addressed the walls, in a high pitched voice: "Elephant dogs, elephant dogs. . . ." The diagnosis was mental retardation secondary to a major psychiatric disorder, childhood psychosis.

A treatment plan was devised for this patient which included the use of psychotropic drugs and provision of a milieu that focused on activities and closer interpersonal contacts. The chronicity of the boy's psychosis and his interpersonal unavailability was approached via a behavior modification paradigm with focus on reestablishing both self-help skills and interpersonal contacts. Specific management foci included developing a repertoire of skills that would permit him to function in a less restrictive environment (e.g., community-based sheltered workshop and/or a residential hostel facility).

The treatment results noted in this case example provide much greater personal fulfillment than the passive participation in an endless merry-go-round of residence in an institution for the mentally retarded, followed by referral to a mental hospital, and then discharge (after having obtained "maximal hospital benefits") back to the institution for the mentally retarded. Many institutions for the retarded have built up large backlogs of such psychotic patients whose definitive treatment needs have gone unmet. These patients are referred elsewhere during their acute episodes, and are typically returned in a subacute remission state. Because institutional staff personnel frequently view these psychotic patients as "odd or dangerous," often the individual patient's psychotic process is refueled by apprehensive staff members until he or she is pushed once again into an acute state.

A major current trend in institutions for the mentally retarded is to provide regional resource programs and facilities to backup the emerging community-based programs. Because mentally ill-mentally retarded individuals are often rejects from community-based programs, they present a major challenge to members of the institutional staff. This challenge demands that the focus of professional staff members be sharply attuned to the behavioral dimensions of mental retardation, and the needs of families worn out by the primitive-atypical-abnormal behaviors of their mentally retarded sons and daughters.

The previously reviewed descriptive diagnostic considerations and the general and specific treatment-management plans strongly suggest that a variety of treatment approaches must be utilized to help these individuals. For example, a mentally retarded individual with a psychotic disorder may need a specific type of milieu setting, psychoactive drugs to reduce motor overactivity and mood fluctuation, ongoing citizen advocate contacts, behavior shaping to stimulate positive reinforcement of specific adaptive behaviors, and active involvement of the family support system. Due to the complexity of these treatment ingredients, the team approach is a prime pathway for providing a wide spectrum of individualized services for the mentally ill-mentally retarded individuals.

In summary, three patterns of behavior noted in these individuals with both mental retardation and mental illness have been presented. The increasing admission rate of such individuals to institutions for the mentally retarded demands a reevaluation of these individuals. How they can be evaluated, and the spectrum of global and specific treatment-management modalities that are available for them have been reviewed. Finally, some administrative implications and suggested guidelines for implementing necessary diagnostic and treatment approaches are presented within the context of redirected goals for institutions for the mentally retarded—as regional resource centers—for the currently burgeoning community-based programs for the mentally retarded.

TREATMENT AND MANAGEMENT MODALITIES

Early literature on the treatment and management of mental illness in the mentally retarded presented approaches and attitudes paralleling: 1) early humanistic educational activities; 2) the negative historical-societal postures toward those viewed as "deviants," and the accompanying tragic interlude during which the defect position and the eugenic alarm ushered in an era of custodialism to "protect society from the retards"; 3) the resurgence of professional and public interest and involvement in the plight of the retarded at the midpoint of this century.

Concurrent with these trends, professional reports on the treatment and management of mentally ill-mentally retarded individuals reflected the "dementia" prototype, the early educational approaches on "amentia," the suppressive approaches (e.g., isolation, restraint, sedatives, etc.) during the early part of this century, followed by specific treatment approaches to the psychotic, the juvenile delinquent, the brain damaged, and, finally in the early 1960s, some specificity of treatment and management approaches toward mentally ill-mentally retarded individuals. From 1915 to 1960, clinical descriptive studies focused on low behavioral treatment expectations, and the monotonous recommendation for institutionalization were the clinician's standbys. This trend is even more remarkable considering that this same time period witnessed the establishment of the child guidance clinics in the United States. These clinics used such treatment-management approaches as individual psychotherapy and family therapy to serve mentally ill children and adolescents—with or without the allied symptom of mental retardation.

Since 1950, there has been an increasing stream of reports on the treatment and management of mental illness in the retarded. Treatment approaches have ranged from individual psychoanalytically oriented psychotherapy to therapeutic nursery schools with associated family therapy, psychoactive drugs, group therapy, play therapy, behavioral modification, and combined approaches (see especially the contributions of Rubin, Monfils, Wilson, and Watson in this volume; also Menolascino, 1970). Each of these trends over the last two decades has grown in its range of utilization, although the psychoanalytic approach has remained rather sharply focused on the severe and complex disorders of early childhood. The therapeutic nursery school approach has expanded to serve a variety of levels and types of both retardation and emotional disturbance in the older age groups. All of these approaches are based on a treatment plan that begins with an in-depth study of the child and his or her family in order to determine the nature and extent of their adjustment difficulties, and then to refine intervention techniques to resolve them. Reviews of psychotherapeutic techniques that are both useful and successful with the mentally retarded emphasized the prevalent fallacy that psychotherapy is not applicable to the mentally retarded (Bialer, 1957, 1970; Katz, 1972; Lott, 1970). Similar results concerning the value of group psychotherapeutic efforts in institutional and community-based programs (see Monfils in this volume; also Mowatt, 1970; Slivkin and Bernstein, 1970; Zisfein and Rosen, 1974) have also been reported frequently.

In contrast, Rogers and Dyamond (1954) stated that psychotherapy was not indicated for the mentally ill-mentally retarded individual because it requires insight, a high level of verbal communication, a capacity for self-reliance, and other factors inherent in normal intelligence. Clearly, this point of view is outdated as evidenced by the changing attitudes about the retarded and the body of clinical experience to date indicates that this point of view is invalid. In brief, it should be underscored that therapeutic relationships that stress warmth and acceptance are keyed to differing developmental levels of personality functioning and are equally if not more important in assessing response to psychotherapy than excessive focus on the criterion of intellectual and/or cognitive functions.

The rise of regional mental retardation resource centers and clinics in the community, such as the university-affiliated programs, has greatly facilitated the availability of manpower to carry out more of these individual and group treatment-management interventions. These resources provide a cadre of interested professionals and available community resources—necessary ingredients for the individual family approach. This movement has brought increased professional involvement in the emotionally complicated instances of retardation in community-based samples. Even in its proper milieu, however, the community-based programs such as the university-affiliated programs have many limitations. First, it is in many ways a direct descendent of the child guidance center model and has carried along with it many of the professional rigidities (e.g., types of personnel utilized) that have adversely plagued that model. Second, the rather cumbersome administrative guidelines and very high financial costs of such programs tend to limit their ability to serve the large number of mentally ill retarded individuals who are in need of such services. Wolfensberger (1965), in a provocative article entitled "Diagnostic Diagnosed," suggested that the "diagnostic preoccupation" of such clinics is: 1) not needed; 2) too costly; and 3) being continued at the cost of precluding the actual delivery of services which can be accomplished more effectively and cost beneficially elsewhere in the community.

Behavior Modification as a Treatment Modality

Behavior modification is a treatment-management approach that has been applied to a wide range of diagnoses. This approach has been used for over three decades in individual and group approaches to the retarded. Because Chapter 6 in this volume provides an overview of this treatment-management approach to the mentally retarded, only a brief review of its potential impact is presented.

The use of behavioral modification to treat the mentally ill-mentally retarded individual will serve both to unite *past viewpoints* and *illuminate new horizons of treatment response and prognosis*. In contrast to past therapies, the behavioral modification approach: 1) strongly focuses on the precise descriptions of primitive, atypical, or abnormal behaviors; 2) describes predictable phenomena; 3) does not consider formal diagnostic dimensions to be sacrosanct, and hence does not permit them to limit full descriptive analyses of observed behavior.

The observed descriptive parameters are utilized as the basis for a hierarchy of treatment interventions. Treatment-management contacts, based on the following objectified hierarchy of treatment needs can then give direction to the treater(s), the troubled individual, and his or her family:

Alternative Treatment Programs for
Antisocial or Self-injurious Behaviors[4]

1. Rewarding an alternative activity
2. Selectively withdrawing social rewards

---

[4]These and similar techniques are treatment options. They must focus on the need to transfer or generalize the improvements obtained to other treatment/residential settings. The goal is to carry over the treatment ingredients and results to all dimensions of the mentally ill-mentally retarded person's life situations.

3. Isolating or restricting the individual
4. Push to perform incompatible responses

This treatment approach can be objectively assessed by cost-service benefit guidelines, and holds much promise for resolving the justified concern with the cost of human management services. The flexibility of the behavioral modification approach permits the focus on a symptom (e.g., head banging) or a syndrome-symptom complex (e.g., psychoneurotic phobic reaction). Studies of this aspect of behavioral modification have posed serious challenges to cherished notions about the overdetermined nature of either singular symptoms or syndromes of behavior. Interestingly, most retarded persons and their parents have, in the author's experience, shown a singular lack of interest in such professional debates, and have been more impressed by the results of behavior modification for symptom alleviation.

In conjunction with the current renaissance of professional interest in treatment-management approaches to mental illness in the mentally retarded, many excellent ongoing contributions strongly suggest that future reviews of this topic area will reflect a continuing emphasis on behavior modification intervention techniques.

Parental Counseling

Parental counseling is a frequent ingredient of many treatment approaches to the emotionally disturbed mentally retarded, and Roos presents an extended discussion on this subject in Chapter 3 of this volume. It is sufficient here, then, to comment briefly on this approach.

First, it should be noted that counseling the parents of the retarded has many unusual features. Although there are over 150 publications dealing with or very relevant to the topic (mostly appearing since 1950), only a small number of experimental studies have been conducted.

Early professional views on parental responses to their retarded children were heavily influenced by psychoanalytic thought. Major emphasis was placed on the role of guilt, which was seen as a near universal phenomenon in parents of all types of handicapped children. These parents were commonly viewed as conflicted and almost certain to use defense mechanisms such as denial and projection; it was expected that such defenses would be of neurotic proportions. The psychoanalytic interpretation reached its apex with two elaborations. One of these by Beddie and Osmond (1955) equated parental response to a retarded child as equivalent to a "child loss" (death of a normal child) and required "grief work" in order to be overcome. Institutionalization was seen as a "death without the proper rites." The other elaboration by Solnit and Stark (1961) coined the term *chronic mourning* for the "object loss" to which the advent of the retarded child was equated.

Usually, management did not go much beyond this because, on the one hand, parents were now assumed to be able to make the best adjustment possible under the circumstances; on the other hand, there was a pessimistic, even nihilistic view about the retarded child. Thus, there seemed to be little to do in a concrete way except perhaps to recommend institutional placement and to help make the necessary arrangements.

More recently, stress has been placed on the realistic demands and burdens that parents of retarded children often bear. Parents were seen as being under a great deal of situational and external stress, and symptoms of such stress were perceived as essentially normal or at least expected under the circumstances. The neurotic interpretation of parental reactions was specifically attacked and rejected by Olshansky (1962, 1966). He pointed to certain social factors of our culture that induce the parent to feel devalued for having a damaged child and to other coexisting factors that inhibit the parent's ability to externalize this sorrow so as to dissipate it. Such conflict was seen as likely to result in long-term internalization of a depressive mood, which Olshansky termed "chronic sorrow" or "an understandable non-neurotic response to a tragic fact" (Olshansky, 1966, p. 21). The management suggested by Olshansky emphasized ventilation of parental feelings, readiness on the part of the professional to act as a scapegoat or a focus of anger to the parent, and provision of concrete services such as nursery schools, special classes, sheltered workshops, and guidance with practical problems of child rearing.

Counseling parents of mentally ill-mentally retarded children frequently requires general supportive measures and guidelines regarding future management. For example, Menolascino (1978) noted that the most common parental reactions were situational depressive features about their responsibility and their mixed feelings (which were most commonly based on anger about the narcissistic injury done to them and anxiety concerning their child's future). The problem of guilt is a further unique dimension to be considered in counseling approaches to the parents of these children. In the primary emotional disorders of childhood, the parents can usually project a good portion of their "blame" or guilt onto the child and scapegoat situations are frequently produced. In the retarded child, there is usually no direct way to externalize the guilt; this continuing problem may present formidable resistance to any counseling attempts (MacKinnon and Frederick, 1970). Thus, parents of children with both mental retardation and emotional disturbance have multiple levels and types of inner turmoil that can cause some of their child's behavioral problems.

Psychopharmacologic Adjuncts to Treatment

The psychopharmacologic agents currently utilized in the treatment of the mentally ill all affect neurotransmitter activity in some way. Some of these agents tend to block or diminish neurotransmitter activity, whereas the stimulants and antidepressants tend to enhance the activity of certain neurotransmitters. As a result of the experience with these various drugs over the past three decades and the recent studies of the metabolism of neurotransmitters in various comparative mental illnesses, there has developed an improved understanding of the probable neurotransmitter abnormality in certain psychiatric conditions (Cohen, 1976). For example, it seems that children without physiologic signs of anxiety who exhibit impulsive motor hyperactivity tend to be catecholamine deficient; they are likely to respond positively to stimulant or antidepressant medication. Similarly, physiologically anxious, hyperalert children tend to have high norepinephrine levels; they generally respond well to the more sedative phenothiazines, whereas children with stereotyped ritualistic behavior seem to have high dopamine levels and tend to respond best to the more potent antipsychotic medication. Thus, if the clinician is able to correlate the probable neurotransmitter abnormality in a given psychiatric condition with the pharmacologic action of various psychoactive medications, the probability of selecting an appropriate medication will be increased.

Many clinicians might argue (correctly) that medication is not the ultimate answer to the emotional and personality problems of the retarded (Freeman, 1966, 1970, 1971); these medications may adversely affect the individual via their toxicity or their exclusive use instead of developmental programs (Lipman, 1970) and the disadvantages of medication may outweigh their advantages (Colodny and Kurlander, 1970). Even with these factors clearly in mind, the proper use of medication can often provide an excellent treatment intervention via the rapid diminuation of offending symptoms when unacceptable behavior has caused the family or school to demand immediate movement toward more restrictive placement alternatives. This entry (i.e., behavioral queiescence) must be the first step to a total program of treatment involvement, and not the last step or the narrow chemical-restraint approach of the recent past.

A more extensive review of this complicated and challenging treatment modality is provided by Wilson in Chapter 7 of this volume and Brevning and Poling (1982).

A Systematic Approach to Management

Key elements of a systematic approach toward treatment include:

Careful Diagnosis The diagnosis of individuals who are both mentally retarded and mentally ill requires an open-minded approach. This is the first basic principle for the clinician who plans for these individuals and it is an important professional posture throughout treatment. Often problems are related to multiple causes and therefore will require a variety of interventions. Periodic reevaluation often reveals developmental surprises which underscore the need for a flexible diagnostic-treatment-prognostic attitude. Social, psychologic, and biologic factors contributing to the mentally ill-mentally retarded person's dysfunction must be clearly identified so that the most effective means of intervention can be determined.

Active Family Involvement and Education The second principle in treatment planning is to engage the family through active participation as early as possible. The family is the key to any effective treatment program. The clinician's attitudes and level of interest frequently determine the success of this endeavor; thus, future cooperation (or lack of it) on the part of the family may reflect his unspoken, as well as spoken attitudes at the time of initial contact. The therapist needs to convey to the family his willingness to share the facts he learns as part of the first step in treatment. Treatment plans become a cooperative process that the parents and clinician work out over the course of time. It is valuable to indicate in an early contact that treatment planning rarely results in a single recommendation; it is something that may shift in focus and alter its course as the retarded individual continues to develop. Early implementation of diagnostic and treatment flexibility helps develop the clinician's ability to view the total child and encourages a referral to other special sources of help as indicated. This may forestall the "doctor shopping" that often occurs if the parents seek a series of opinions concerning some special allied problem.

Much has been written about grief reaction of families with handicapped members, and it frequently occurs in parents of mentally retarded individuals. Clinicians evaluating these children must always be aware of this grief reaction especially at the time of interpretation to parents or in subsequent interviews. Assessment of family interaction and strengths is a necessary part of the total evaluation because these assets are essential to planning a comprehensive treatment program.

Principles of Primary and Secondary Prevention   A third consideration in a comprehensive system approach to treatment is early diagnosis and treatment. In the more severely retarded, this process is likely to occur in conjunction with a medical evaluation during infancy or in the preschool years. In relatively mild cases in disadvantaged families, screening programs prior to school entry or in the school become relatively more important. Much can be done to prevent the alienation of borderline and mildly retarded children if their limitations are identified early. This has the advantage of preventing their suffering the effects of unrealistic expectations and also allows the school to develop appropriate special programs for the child. In all areas, early diagnosis facilitates identification of problems, which in turn is essential if one is to formulate realistic therapeutic goals and overall expectations for the child. If this is done, frustration is reduced and fewer secondary psychiatric problems are encountered. In this sense, prevention becomes a cohesive part of the ongoing work for the child and his family. This total approach requires continued follow up, and periodic reevaluation must be done so that appropriate shifts in treatment and overall levels of expectation may be carried out.

Principles of Tertiary Prevention   The fourth principle focuses on the maximation of development potential. It involves a different type of goal setting from the usual treatment plan because the focus must often be on what the retarded individual *can do* rather than anticipation of a cure. The goal then becomes one of maximally and at the same time realistically helping to habilitate the patient. If done well, the retarded person will avoid the problem of inappropriate expectations.

Normalization   The principle of normalization (Nirje, 1969) has literally revolutionized the field of mental retardation. Normalization implies that services will be provided within the communities; it stresses that the overwhelming majority of retarded persons are able to enjoy and profit from the rich variety of human experiences that are found there. These considerations include the opportunity to enjoy life experiences in a family setting or a small group home, to have a work or school experience in a location separate from their dwelling, and to have developmentally appropriate activities within the context of a larger community. This trend became federal mandate via the deinstitutionalization policy of 1971, and as a result a tremendous number of community support services, including mental health services, are necessary. In some instances, it may be helpful for mental health professionals to take the lead in creating such services as group homes for the retarded, day-care programs, or appropriate educational and vocational training opportunities. A relatively small percentage of mentally ill-mentally retarded individuals will require short- or long-term inpatient mental health placement for behavioral management because they are dangerous to themselves or others. Some retarded individuals may require long-term care when they present with intractable psychotic conditions. Parenthetically, these psychotic retarded individuals should be treated in mental health facilities in or near their home communities, in contrast to the nontreatment that they have often received in the large public institutions for the retarded. The special needs of these more handicapped patients typically exceeds the capabilities and expertise of most community-based programs, and short-term crisis care inpatient facilities should be used as backup support services to the rapidly evolving community-based mental retardation programs.

Coordination of Services Coordination of the many services needed for individuals with dual diagnoses requires awareness of the various services available in a given community and a professional attitude that permits active collaboration. It necessitates sharing of the overall treatment plan with the retarded individual (when appropriate), the family, and with community resources (e.g., teachers, group home personnel, etc.). Close attention to the clarity and continuity of communication is essential.

In summary, it is necessary to remember that *combined* or balanced treatment approaches are frequently indicated when one attempts to provide modern treatment intervention for these dual-diagnosis individuals:

1. Counseling (guidance; individual and/or group psychotherapy)
2. Behavioral modifications
3. Psychoactive drugs
4. Parent counseling
5. Social ecology⟶residential
6. Vocational habilitation⟶ work

7. Social —► recreational
8. Follow along services

The balanced treatment approaches noted in the list above quickly reveal that a number of these approaches may need to be utilized simultaneously. Indeed, failure to use such balanced treatment approaches (due to the specialist's lack of interest and/or knowledge or because of fixed professional-ideologic blind spots to certain of these techniques) is the most commonly noted reason for treatment-management failures in this clinical area. The approach outlined below has been found to be helpful in sequentially (and successfully) treating mentally ill-mentally retarded individuals:

1. Clearly identify the problem(s)
2. Define it (them) objectively
3. Identify and list three possible *alternative* solutions
4. Pick *one* and implement; observe outcome
5. Take your time. Have the proposed treatment(s) been fully implemented, data collected and analyzed, attitudinal problems addressed (e.g., burned-out staff with countertransference problems), intercurrent (i.e., new) factors recently accessed?
6. If not satisfied with outcome:
   a. Generate new alternatives that have resulted from information gleaned from the initial intervention attempt and implement
   b. Select an alternative from the original list and implement
7. Take your time
8. Repeat step 6 if necessary

As with any human development variable, behavior slowly changes in a directional manner over time (i.e., the developmental model); thus, points 5 and 7 should be adhered to closely.

True, this is a rather large expectation of and from the professional; yet less elaborate or less balanced treatment interventions too often miss the goals of the needed combined treatment intervention, which must often be simultaneously initiated in these complex individuals.

CURRENT MENTAL HEALTH
APPROACHES TO SERVE THE MENTALLY RETARDED

The treatment of retarded persons by mental health personnel requires a systems approach (or a community psychiatry model) rather than traditional insight-oriented psychotherapy for the identified patient. Although many neurotic children or acutely troubled adolescents may require a considerable amount of individual therapy or family therapy oriented toward clarifying communication problems, these patients typically require a more direct approach. Some parents of the retarded will need traditional psychotherapeutic approaches as they work through grief or unrelated emotional problems that might interfere with their ability to care for their child. Nearly all parents will require specific information and recommendations regarding the many problems they will face. Here, the need for long-term support and guidance is stressed in order to help them most effectively manage a "problem" that has been thrust upon them. In this respect, the care of the retarded is quite similar to the care of many other dependent populations and can be compared to the community aspects of child psychiatry or geriatric psychiatry. These and similar dimensions of this topic are noted in Table 1.7.

Many of the mental illness disorders of the retarded will require that mental health personnel be relatively more active, more direct, and more concrete in the interview or treatment setting, and will also require that they become accustomed to the delayed language development so often seen in the retarded.

In addition, it is important that mental health personnel be aware of the many community services that may be needed to serve the retarded; they must also be aware of the specific needs of different types of retarded patients. Often, conventional programs are not adequate. For example, although the staffing ratio and the degree of supervision required in group home care of mildly retarded adolescents may not seem to differ significantly from that required in group homes for moderately or severely retarded patients, the latter typically require much higher staffing ratios, more strict building and health codes, and greater medical-nursing supervision.

With regard to younger retarded children who are treated in day-care programs, it is important to provide a diversity of activities that will allow for the varying developmental levels of the children. Not only is there likely to be a considerable variation of abilities from one retarded child to another, it is not unusual to see significant variability from skill to skill within one such child. Accordingly, these special day-care programs for the retarded will require a more intense staffing pattern and a higher degree of staff experience than conventional day-care programs.

Another crucial difference in mental health consultation is the more frequent need to focus on the amelioration of a retarded in-

Table 1.7. What mental health professionals can learn from those in mental retardation

1. Focus on the descriptive level of the handicap (i.e., mild level, severe level—not etiology) and on observed behaviors over time (i.e., the pattern of the disturbance).	v.	Excessive focus on etiology, diagnosis; insight is overly stressed, and prognosis. Observation often takes a back seat to a subjective view of dynamics.
2. Acceptance of chronicity and focus on maximizing the abilities of the retarded via support systems for living, work, and social-recreational alternatives.	v.	Relative nonacceptance of chronicity. Acute episodes become occasions for much therapeutic activity; non-acute (i.e., chronic behaviors) viewed as noninteresting and/or "nontreatable."

3. Cultivate attitude of cooperation/collaboration in the family's habilitation of their retarded son or daughter. In contrast, the mental health approach too often sets up an adversarial or blame-casting posture toward the parents.
4. *Full* acceptance that nonprofessionals can offer much in the treatment-management of *any* troubled citizen (that is literally one-half of the basis of the normalization principle). The mental health model is too oriented to hierarchical decision making, which leaves little room for nonprofessionals' inputs.
5. Modern mental retardation systems of services focus on sheltered or partially sheltered vocational and residential placements as the *crux* of a community-based program of rehabilitation and treatment, instead of assuming, as in the current non-care of chronic mentally ill patients, that patients will have the supports and shelter they need in the community.
6. Organized parent groups (e.g., the Association for Retarded Citizens of the U.S.) have focused on the active recruitment of parental and general public advocates, professionals, and interested citizens for help and the effective changing of public attitudes toward the mentally retarded. A far less active advocacy (especially parents of the mentally ill) and professional general public advocates group (e.g., National Mental Health Association) is currently operative. Finally, the professionalism of mental consultations and public education thrusts stresses unduly on the need for professionals rather than parents or lay citizens in these roles.

dividual's personality difficulties while simultaneously providing support and developmentally oriented special curriculum guidance to the day-care program personnel (Group for the Advancement of Psychiatry, 1979). For example, in the past, mental health personnel excessively focused on resolving the disturbed retarded child's roadblocks to learning (i.e., the concomitant mental illness) without giving equal attention to the child's ongoing special developmental needs. Parental counseling and individual therapy with the child can often be interwoven into a developmentally oriented curriculum which focuses on language stimulation and the acquisition of self-help skills. Without this type of consultation focus, the child's emotional status may improve while he or she is *negatively slipping* past critical developmental periods for skill acquisition. In these consultations, it is appropriate to consider mixed modality approaches such as an individual psychotherapeutic focus on the child, counseling for his family, a behavioral modification approach to initiate or extend ongoing learning tasks, and the utilization of specific medications when indicated.

Mental health personnel are aware of the federal legislation (PL 94-142) that mandates that local school systems provide appropriate educational opportunities for all handicapped children. As a result of this legislation, many special programs are already functioning in most communities. Unfortunately, the quality of these services and their specific educational programs may vary widely from community to community. Therefore, it must be the responsibility of mental health professionals to become familiar with the services provided by local programs. They may be rather surprised to note both the variety and complexity of the excellent community-based programs for the retarded that have come into being during the last 10 years. The very newness of many of these programs demands that mental health personnel keep fully abreast of developments in early childhood education. This aspect of care had not been sufficiently stressed previously in most mental health training programs. Similarly, mental health consultation to special education programs in the schools demands an awareness of current trends, whether one is making specific recommendations to meet the special needs of one child or making recommendations regarding entire school programs.

This frequently observed quality of family strength does affect the manner in which the mental health professional interfaces with retarded persons and their families. These parents, through their establishment of a national movement of concern 30 years ago, have become a well organized force for seeking changes in treatment approaches and service delivery for their sons and daughters. Indeed, most of the major national changes in the field of mental retardation have come from the parent advocacy movement, the Association for Retarded Citizens of the U.S.

Some of the social changes of the 1950s and early 1960s resulted in the Report of President Kennedy's Panel on Mental Retardation and his benchmark legislation on behalf of the mentally retarded in 1963. The National Association of Retarded Citizens helped to translate the President's Panel Report into action by giving support to the direly needed research efforts, to strong public policy actions at the federal and state levels, to the initiation and support of alternative community-based service programs, and to greater public education efforts. The association's governmental affairs actions stimulated the federal government to establish both a series of 12 mental retardation research centers to further basic research in mental retardation and university-affiliated programs for training the necessary large cadres of professionals in mental retardation. Many child psychiatry programs were major beneficiaries of these programs.

Working with the their local Association for Retarded Citizens, mental health professionals can help parents in their advocacy for new services while simultaneously fulfilling the professional's role as a positive change agent on behalf of these children and adults.

CLINICAL RESEARCH CHALLENGES

Throughout this chapter, many of the diagnostic and treatment-management challenges that confront those who are interested in the emotionally complicated instances of mental retardation have been underscored. The trends reviewed in this chapter strongly suggest that mental health professionals know where the mountain is, its height, and physical characteristics, and have begun basic and applied programs of professional involvement that are meaningful first attempts at reconnaissance.

In the area of the mentally ill-mentally retarded, such reconnaissance can extend to the following areas:

1. Descriptive studies that directly assess the behavioral myths of the past (e.g., the "Prince Charming" behavioral description of the individual with Down's syndrome (Menolascino, 1965) should be undertaken.
2. Nonspecific descriptive behavioral phrases (e.g., infantile autism) should be replaced with more specific behavioral delineations.
3. The appreciation of *coexisting* symptoms and/or disorders must become widespread so that complex disorders are not reduced to unitary diagnostic-treatment formulations.

4. Detailed studies of the subgroups of the mentally retarded and their physical and emotional etiologies need to be made. For example, the study entitled "Psychiatric Disorders of Children with Congenital Rubella" by Chess, Horn, and Fernandez (1971) was focused on the question, does the symptom of mental retardation render an individual more prone to certain types of mental illness or maladaptive defenses? It clearly showed that the extent of handicaps in their sample was highly associated with the presence of mental illness, especially in the psychotic reactions noted. Does this relationship hold true for other etiologic subgroups of the retarded?

5. Studies of the types of emotional disturbances noted in the different levels of mental retardation are long overdue. Do the retarded have personality defenses that are akin to the normal? Are there specific personality dimensions which result because of the symptom of mental retardation? The review of this topical area by Berkson and Landesman-Dwyer (1977) is a healthy step toward unraveling these issues.

6. Further evaluation of current treatment-management approaches are badly needed.

7. The interrelationships between the evolving scales for social-adaptive behavioral assessment and traditional assessment techniques should be studied.

8. The confounding variables that may alter what mental health professionals see, what they treat, and why and how they do either need to be examined and conceptualized. For example, the bulk of the reports in the literature on the dual diagnosis of mental illness-mental retardation concern institutionalized retardates and it may be a literature quite distinct from that which is currently evolving from community-based services. Can these reported studies and results truly be compared?

9. More information is needed on the relative impact of early developmental experiences on both mental retardation and emotional disturbance, either singularly or as combined phenomena.

10. There is a need for more direct observational data on the attitudes, feelings, and experiences (phenomenologic transactions) of mentally retarded individuals so as to delineate why the majority of retarded individuals do not become mentally ill (Zigler and Balla, 1973).

CONCLUSION

Retarded persons are subject to the same basic types of mental illness as the general population. Because of their tendency toward central nervous system impairment and diminished overall coping ability, they present somewhat greater than average risks for psychosis, long-term behavioral disturbances, and transient adjustment disorders.

During the last three decades, the traditional and overly simplified behavioral views of the retarded have been changed. The extraordinary historical events that led to psychiatry's relative withdrawal from the field of mental retardation resulted in a number of stereotyped views or blind spots that mental health professionals characteristically exhibited as they related to the retarded. For example, only recently have child psychiatrists and other mental health members begun to shake off the all too frequent past posture of viewing the retarded as brain-damaged children and youth, hopeless, or not worthy of treatment intervention. Once again it has become respectable and challenging for mental health personnel to become involved in mental retardation. The multiple facets of this renaissance are clearly reflected by the wide variety of involvements noted in the contribution to this volume. This reinvestment of mental health resources has been enhanced by the rise of the CMHCs—especially their recent inclusion of services for the retarded—and the persistent demands of organized parent groups of the retarded.

The rejuvenation of the mental health professional's interest in mental retardation has come at a most opportune time—when the bulk of modern mental health training and service provisions are located in the community—because this exactly coincides with the "rediscovery" of the community as the normalizing site for retarded citizens to live. The latter statement is not a guesstimate, but is based on changing public attitudes, recent federal government policies (e.g., deinstitutionalization), and markedly altered professional viewpoints and expectations.

Additional crucial features in the current remarriage of mental health and mental retardation are the rapidly increasing numbers of mental health personnel and developmentally oriented pediatricians, psychologists, teachers, and social workers (i.e., a significant manpower pool is becoming available), the presence of a well organized and highly effective advocate group (the Association of Retarded Citizens of the U.S.), and the recent benchmark legal decisions on behalf of the retarded which stress their full legal rights to education and treatment in the least restrictive settings possible.

In the past, many retarded persons were unnecessarily institutionalized because of allied mental illness. Today, in nearly all cases, the retarded can be maintained in the community with the help of mental health professionals who are willing to provide short-term and supportive care for them and their families. Because these treatment challenges are now readily handled by mental health workers in community-based settings, the care can and should occur outside an institution for the great majority of the retarded. All of these events have led to significantly increased independent and semi-independent functioning for many retarded persons, and have made possible the development of significant systems of service where the focus on developmental maximation has greatly improved the quality of life for the retarded.

The recent renaissance of involvement of mental health personnel with mentally ill-mentally retarded persons will greatly help retarded citizens to remain in their home communities and maintain close relationships; to live, work, and socialize in the mainstreams of our society; and to have sources of sophisticated mental health services readily available for them.

REFERENCES

Allen, R. 1968. Legal norms and practices affecting the mentally deficient. Am. J. Orthopsychiatry 38(4).

Allen, R. 1970. The law and the mentally retarded. In: F. J. Menolascino, (ed.), Psychiatric Approaches to Mental Retardation. Basic Books, New York.

Allen, R., Ferster, E., and Rubin, F. 1978. Readings in Law and Psychiatry. Johns Hopkins Press, Baltimore.

American Psychiatric Association, Committee on Nomenclature and Statistics. 1980. Diagnostic and Statistical Manual of Mental Disorders. 3rd Ed. American Psychiatric Association, Washington, DC.

Balthazar, E., and Stevens, H. 1975. The Emotionally Disturbed Mentally Retarded: A Historical Contemporary Perspective. Prentice-Hall, Inc., Englewood Cliffs, NJ.

Balthazar, E., Stevens, H., and Gardner, W. 1969. International Biology of Literature on the Emotionally and Behaviorally Disturbed Mentally Retarded: 1914–1969. State of Wisconsin Department of Health and Social Services, Madison.

Barr, W. 1904. Mental Defectives: Their History, Treatment and Training. Blakiston's Son & Co., Philadelphia.

Beddie, A., and Osmond, H. 1955. Mothers, mongols, and mores. Can. Med. Assoc. J. 73:167.

Beier, D. 1964. Behavioral disturbances in the mentally retarded. In: H. Stevens and R. Heber, (eds.), Mental Retardation: A Review of Research. Chicago University Press, Chicago.

Beitemann, E. 1970. The psychiatric consultant in a residential facility for mentally retarded. In: F. J. Menolascino, (ed.), Psychiatric Approaches to Mental Retardation. Basic Books, New York.

Bender, L. 1959. Autism in children with mental deficiency. Am. J. Ment. Defic. 63(8).

Bender, L. 1970. The life course of children with autism and mental retardation. In: F.J. Menolascino, (ed.), Psychiatric Approaches to Mental Retardation. Basic Books, New York.

Berkson, G., and Landesman-Dwyer, S. 1977. Behavioral research on a severe and profound mental retardation. Am. J. Ment. Defic. 81:428–454.

Berman, M. 1977. Mental retardation and depression. Ment. Retard. 5(6):19–21.

Bernstein, N. 1970. Diminished People: Problems and Care of the Mentally Retarded. Little, Brown & Company, Boston.

Bialer, I. 1970. Emotional disturbances and mental retardation: Etiologic and conceptual relationships. In: F. J. Menolascino, (ed.), Psychiatric Approaches to Mental Retardation, pp. 68–90. Basic Books, New York.

Bialer, I. 1957. Psychotherapy and adjustment techniques with the mentally retarded. In: A. Baumeister, (ed.), Mental Retardation: Appraisal, Education, Rehabilitation, pp. 138–180. Aldine Publishing Co., Chicago.

Blatt, B., and Kaplan, F. 1974. Christmas in Purgatory: A Photographic Essay in Mental Retardation. Human Policy Press, Syracuse.

Bowlby, J. 1951. Maternal Care and Mental Health. World Health Organization, Geneva.

Brown, B., and Cortless, T. 1967. The Mentally Retarded Offender. The President's Commission on Law Enforcement and Administration of Justice, Washington, DC.

Chess, S. 1962. Psychiatric treatment of the mentally retarded child with behavioral problems. Am. J. Orthopsychiatry 32:863–869.

Chess, S. 1969. An Introduction to Child Psychiatry. 2nd Ed. Grune & Stratton, New York.

Chess, S. 1970. Emotional problems in mentally retarded children. In: F. J. Menolascino (ed.), Psychiatric Approaches to Mental Retardation. Basic Books, New York.

Chess, S., and Hassibi, M. 1978. Behavioral deviations in mentally retarded children. In: S. Chess, and A. Thomas (eds.), Annual Progress in Child Psychiatry and Child Development. Brunner/Mazel, Inc., New York.

Chess, S., and Hassibi, M. 1978. Principles and Practices of Child Psychiatry. Plenum Publishing Corp., New York.

Chess, S., Horn, S., and Fernandez, P. 1971. Psychiatric Disorders of Children with Congenital Rubella. Brunner/Mazel, Inc., New York.

Cohen, D. J. 1976. The diagnostic process in child psychiatry. Psychiatr. Ann. 6:29–35.

Colodny, D., and Kurlander, L. 1970. Psychopharmacology as a treatment adjunct for the mentally retarded: Problems and issues. In: F. J. Menolascino (ed.), Psychiatric Approaches to Mental Retardation. Basic Books, New York.

Connolly, K., and Bruner, J. 1974. Competence: Its Nature and Nurture. Academic Press, London.

Donaldson, J., and Menolascino, F. 1977. Past, current, and future roles of child psychiatry in mental retardation. Am. J. Child Psychiatry 16:38–52.

Eaton, L., and Menolascino, F. 1966. Psychotic reactions of childhood: Experiences of a mental retardation pilot project. J. Nerv. Ment. Dis. 143:55–67.

Eaton, L., and Menolascino, F. 1967. Psychoses of childhood: A five-year follow-up of experiences in a mental retardation clinic. Am. J. Ment. Defic. 72(3):370–380.

Eaton, L., and Menolascino, F. 1982. Psychiatric disorders in the mentally retarded: Types, problems and challenges. Am. J. Psychiatry. 139:1297–1303.

Eaton, M. T., Peterson, M. E., and Davis, J. E. (eds.), 1980. Psychiatry: Medical Outline Series. 4th Ed. Medical Examination Publishing Co., Garden City, N.Y.

Eisenberg, L. 1958. Emotional determinants of mental deficiency. Arch. Neurol. Psychiatry 80:114–121.

Eisenberg, L., 1972. Caste, class and intelligence. In: R. Murry, and P. Rossner, (eds.), The Genetic, Metabolic, and Developmental Aspects of Mental Retardation. Charles C Thomas, Springfield, IL.

Freeman, R. 1966. Drug effects on learning in children: A selective review of the past thirty years. J. Spec. Educ. 1:17–44.

Freeman, R. 1970. Psychopharmacology and the retarded child. In: F. J. Menolascino, (ed.), Psychiatric Approaches to Mental Retardation, pp. 294–368. Basic Books, New York.

Freeman, R. 1971. Review of medicine in special education: Medical-behavioral pseudorelations. J. Spec. Educ. 5(9):93–100.

Garfield, S. 1963. Abnormal behavior and mental deficiency. In: N. Ellis, (ed.), Handbook of Mental Deficiency: Psychological Theory and Research. McGraw-Hill Book Company, New York.

Goddard, H. 1912. The Kallikak Family. Macmillan, New York.

Goddard, H. 1914. Feeblemindedness: Its Causes and Consequences. Macmillan, New York.

Grossman, H. 1976. Manual of Terminology and Classification in Mental Retardation. American Association on Mental Deficiency, Washington, DC.

Group for the Advancement of Psychiatry. 1979. Psychiatric Consultation in Mental Retardation. Mental Health Center, Washington, DC.

Hunt, N. 1967. The World of Nigel Hunt. Taplinger, New York.

Itard, J. 1932. The Wild Boy of Aveyron. (Original title: De l' Education d'un Homme Sauvage, 1801). Century, New York.

Joint Commission on Mental Health in Children. 1969. Crisis in Child Mental Health: Challenge for the 1970's. Harper & Row, New York.

Kanner, L. 1943. Autistic disturbances of affective contact. Nerv. Child. 2:217–250.

Katz, E. 1972. Mental Health Services for the Mentally Retarded. Charles C Thomas, Springfield, IL.

Kugel, R., Trembath, J., and Sagor, S. 1968. Some characteristics legally committed to a state institution for the mentally retarded. Ment. Retard. 2:8.

Kurlander, L., and Colodny, D. 1965. Panacea, palliation or poison: The psychodynamics of a controversy. Am. J. Psychiatry, 121:1168–1170.

Lane, H. 1976. The Wild Boy of Aveyron. Harvard University Press, Cambridge, MA.

Lanzkron, J. 1957. The concept of propfschizophrenia and its prognosis. Am. J. Ment. Defic. 61(3):544–547.

Leighton, A. 1959. My Name Is Legion. Basic Books, New York.

Lipman, R. 1970. The use of psychopharmacological agents in residential facilities for the retarded. In: F. J. Menolascino, (ed.), Psychiatric Approaches to Mental Retardation. Basic Books, New York.

Lott, G. 1970. Psychotherapy of the mentally retarded. In: F. J. Menolascino, (ed.), Psychiatric Approaches to Mental Retardation. Basic Books, New York.

MacKinnon, M., and Frederick, B. 1970. A shift of emphasis for psychiatric social work in mental retardation. In: F. J. Menolascino (ed.), Psychiatric Approaches to Mental Retardation. Basic Books, New York.

May, J., and May, J. 1979. Overview of emotional disturbances in mentally retarded individuals. Presented at the Annual Convention of the National Association for Retarded Citizens, Atlanta.

Menolascino, F. 1965. Autistic reactions in early childhood: Differential diagnostic considerations. J. Child Psychol. Psychiatry 6:203–218.

Menolascino, F. 1965. Psychiatric aspects of mental retardation in children under eight. Am. J. Orthopsychiatry 35:852–861.

Menolascino, F. 1967. Mental retardation and comprehensive training in psychiatry. Am. J. Psychiatry 124:249–466.

Menolascino, F. 1967. Psychiatric findings in a sample of institutionalized mongoloids. J. Ment. Subnormal. 13:67–74.

Menolascino, F. 1969. Emotional disturbances in mentally retarded children. Am. J. Psychiatry 126(2):54–62.

Menolascino, F. 1970. Psychiatry's past, current and future role. In: F. J. Menolascino (ed.), Psychiatric Approaches to Mental Retardation. Basic Books, New York.

Menolascino, F. 1972. Emotional disturbances in institutionalized retardates: Primitive, atypical and abnormal behaviors. Ment. Retard. 10(6):3–8.

Menolascino, F. 1975. Community psychiatry and mental retardation. In: L. Bellack, and H. Barten, (eds.), Progress in Community Mental Health. Brunner/Mazel, Inc., New York.

Menolascino, F. 1977. Challenges in Mental Retardation: Progressive Ideologies and Services. Human Sciences Press, New York.

Menolascino, F. 1978. Parents of the mentally retarded: An operational approach to diagnosis and management. J. Am. Acad. Child Psychiatry, 7(4):589–602.

Menolascino, F., and Egger, M. 1978. Medical Dimensions of Mental Retardation. University of Nebraska Press, Lincoln.

Mowatt, M. 1970. Group therapy approach to emotional conflicts of the mentally retarded and their parents. In: F. J. Menolascino, (ed.), Psychiatric Approaches to Mental Retardation, pp. 422–434. Basic Books, New York.

Nirje, B. 1969. The normalization principle and its human management implications. In: R. Kugel, and W. Wolfensberger, (eds.), Changing Patterns in Residential Services for the Mentally Retarded. U.S. Government Printing Office, Washington, DC.

Olshansky, S. 1962. Chronic sorrow: A response to having a mentally defective child. Soc. Casework 43:190–193.

Olshansky, S. 1966. Parent responses to a mentally defective child. Ment. Retard. 4(4):21–23.

Penrose, L. 1966. The contribution of mental deficiency research to psychiatry. British J. Psychiatry 112:747–755.

Phillips, I., and Williams, N. 1975. Psychopathology: A study of one-hundred children. Am. J. Psychiatry 32:1265–1273.

Poling, A. D., and Brevning, S. E. 1982. Overview of mental retardation. In: S. E. Brevning and A. D. Poling (eds.), Drugs and Mental Retardation. Charles C Thomas, Springfield, IL.

Pollock, H. 1958. Brain damage, mental retardation and childhood schizophrenia. Am. J. Psychiatry 115:422–427.

Potter, H. 1964. The needs of mentally retarded children for child psychiatry services. J. Am. Acad. Child Psychiatry 3:353.

President's Committee on Mental Retardation. 1979. Historical Overview. U.S. Government Printing Office, Washington, DC.

President's Committee on Mental Retardation. 1978. MR 78: The Edge of Change. U.S. Government Printing Office, Washington, DC.

Rimland, B. 1964. Infantile Autism. Appleton-Century-Crofts, New York.

Rogers, C., and Dyamond, R. 1954. Psychotherapy and Personality Change. University of Chicago Press, Chicago.

Rutter, M., and Schopler, E. 1978. Autism: A Reappraisal of Concepts and Treatments. Plenum Publishing Corp., New York.

Saenger, G. 1960. Factors in influencing the institutionalization of mentally retarded individuals in New York City. New York State Interdependental Health Resources Board, Albany.

Schain, R., and Yannet, H. 1960. Infantile autism. J. Pediatr. 57:560–567.

Seguin, E. 1846. The Moral Treatment, Hygiene, and Education of Idiots and Other Backward Children. Columbia University Press, New York.

Slivkin, S., and Bernstein, N. 1970. Group approaches to treating retarded adolescents. In: F. J. Menolascino, (ed.), Psychiatric Approaches to Mental Retardation. Basic Books, New York.

Solnit, A., and Stark, M. 1961. Mourning and the birth of a defective child. Psychoanal. Study Child 16:523–537.

Spitz, R. 1946. Hospitalism: An inquiry into the genesis of psychiatric conditions in early childhood. Psychoanal. Study Child 2:313–343.

Strole, J. 1962. Mental Health in the Metropolis. McGraw-Hill Book Company, New York.

Sumner, W. 1906. Folkways: A Study of the Sociological Importance of Usages, Manners, Customs, Mores and Morals. Ginn, Boston.

Szymanski, L., and Tanguay, F. (eds.), 1980. Emotional Disorders of Mentally Retarded Persons. University Park Press, Baltimore.

Vail, D. 1966. Dehumanization and the Institutional Career. Charles C Thomas, Springfield, IL.

Webster, T. 1971. Unique aspects of emotional development in mentally retarded children. In: F. J. Menolascino, (ed.), Psychiatric Aspects of the Diagnosis and Treatment of Mental Retardation. Special Child Publications, Seattle.

Wolfensberger, W. 1965. Diagnosis diagnosed. J. Ment. Subnormal. 11: 62–70.

Wolfensberger, W. 1969. The origin and nature of our institutional models. In: R. Kugel, and W. Wolfensberger (eds.), Changing Patterns in Residential Services for the Mentally Retarded. U.S. Government Printing Office, Washington, DC.

Woodward, K., Jaffe, N., and Brown, D. 1970. Early psychiatric intervention for young mentally retarded children. In: F. J. Menolascino, (ed.), Psychiatric Approaches to Mental Retardation. Basic Books, New York.

Zigler, E., and Balla, D. 1973. Personality factors in the performance of the retarded: Implications for clinical assessment. J. Am. Acad. Child Psychiatry 16:19–37.

Zisfein, L., and Rosen, M. 1974. Effects of a personality adjustment training group counseling program. Ment. Retard. 12(3):50–53.

Chapter 2

Application of Neuropsychologic Methods in the Evaluation of Coexisting Mental Retardation and Mental Illness

Michael G. Tramontana

A diagnosis—no matter how well it is substantiated by existing evidence—lacks utility unless it leads to clear and specific statements regarding a patient's treatment and prognosis. For example, the symptom of mental retardation when diagnosed by itself is too general a designation to guide specific decisions with respect to treatment and prognosis for mentally retarded individuals. Before specific treatment can be prescribed and prognosis specified, it is first necessary to have a clear and comprehensive appraisal of the various factors that contribute to the existing intellectual deficits and difficulties in adjustment of the retarded individual, including physical, psychologic, and social determinants. Brain impairment can be an important contributing factor in many cases, and therefore a careful appraisal of this must be included within the context of a general evaluation of the patient. A broad-based perspective such as this is all the more essential in the evaluation of individuals with the combined symptoms of mental retardation and mental illness, for the diagnostic possibilities are all the more complex.

This chapter focuses on neuropsychologic evaluation as one means of achieving greater diagnostic clarification as a prelude to specific treatment planning for individuals with coexisting mental retardation and mental illness. It begins with an overview of clinical neuropsychology—its applications and its present methods. The relevance of neuropsychologic evaluation to diagnosis and treatment planning for various cases of mental retardation with mental illness is discussed, and problems and prospects in the application of neuropsychologic methods to the mentally retarded are outlined. Emphasis is given to the comprehensive appraisal of brain function in specifying important determinants of behavioral and functional variation for the individual with mental retardation and psychiatric disturbance, and in suggesting the kinds of characteristics that an effective program of individualized intervention might include. Little attention has been given to the systematic application of comprehensive neuropsychologic methods to the mentally retarded. Thus, the chapter should be viewed as a proposal for future directions rather than a review of past efforts in this area. Although the focus is on coexisting mental retardation and mental illness, many of the issues pertaining to differential diagnosis and treatment intervention on the basis of a neuropsychologic evaluation apply to both mental retardation and mental illness taken separately, albeit in less complex form than when the two coexist.

STATUS OF CLINICAL NEUROPSYCHOLOGY: AN OVERVIEW

Current thinking in the field of neuropsychology recognizes that higher mental functions are neither discretely compartmentalized with respect to cortical location, nor that functions are organized thoughout the cerebral cortex in a way that is independent of location (e.g., Luria, 1966, 1973). It is never the case that a single, isolated cortical zone is exclusively responsible for the execution of a mental function. Rather, different and often distant cortical regions are recruited in a concerted fashion, each contributing its own role in the execution of the function. For example, there is not a reading "center" in the brain; instead, the complex function of reading requires a number of specific areas of the brain to be brought into a particular pattern of harmonious operation. The pattern and the areas themselves will differ, depending on the mental function involved and how it is performed.

Thus, when a particular mental function is impaired, it is not the case that only one area of the brain is implicated. A function can break down in any of a number of ways; *how* it has broken down (i.e., its qualitative features) suggests the brain areas that are likely involved. Moreover, because a complex mental function is not entirely dependent upon a single, circumscribed area of the brain means that it cannot be completely obliterated through a single, localized brain lesion. The potential for remediation exists so long as remaining capacities can be utilized to substitute for the lost component(s) of the function. Therefore it is important in evaluating the individual with brain injury to determine precisely those abilities that have been impaired and those that have been spared, and to devise a plan of rehabilitation based both on this appraisal and on a knowledge of brain-behavior relationships. This is the task of clinical neuropsychology.

Until recently, there was a lack of adequate assessment instruments for general use in clinical neuropsychology. Earlier methods for evaluating brain function consisted mainly of single-test approaches exemplified by the Bender Motor Gestalt Test (Bender, 1938) and other such instruments. In this approach, localization of function was largely disregarded, and it was presumed that the use of a general, all-purpose test would enable clinicians to detect most forms of brain dysfunction with reasonable accuracy. This is not so, and the drawbacks in relying upon single measures of "organicity" have been well documented (e.g., Golden, 1978; Reitan, 1974). Suffice it to say that not only is there the dual problem of false positives and false negatives in diagnosing brain dysfunction on the basis of a single test, but there is also the problem that no single test could ever provide the kind of detailed and comprehensive appraisal of brain function necessary for treatment planning. A *battery* of neuropsychologic tests is needed for this. Perhaps the two most widely used neuropsychologic batteries now available are the Halstead-Reitan Neuropsychological Battery and the more recently developed Luria-Nebraska Neuropsychological Battery. Both entail a comprehensive assessment of adaptive functions and abilities and are highly sensitive in detecting even subtle degrees of brain dysfunction. Moreover, each is a standardized set of procedures for which interpretation is based not only on the level of performance demonstrated on the various tests in the battery, but also depends on the pattern of performance, differences in performance between the two sides of the body, and specific pathognomonic signs (see Reitan and Davison, 1974; Golden, Hammeke, and Purisch, 1980, respectively, for a complete description of each battery.)

A particularly important area receiving increased attention lately has been the application of standardized neuropsychologic batteries in the diagnostic evaluation of persons with psychiatric disorders. Earlier efforts to distinguish between brain damage and a serious mental disturbance, such as schizophrenia, on the basis of neuropsychologic results proved to be largely unsuccessful. Indeed, discrimination rates were often no better than chance, especially among chronics (Heaton, Baade, and Johnson, 1978). Although it has since been shown that accurate discrimination can be achieved with either the Halstead-Reitan Battery (Golden, 1977) or the Luria-Nebraska Battery (Moses and Golden, 1980; Purisch, Golden, and Hammeke, 1978) the focus of inquiry has shifted somewhat. Rather than simply seeking ways of distinguishing mental disturbance from brain dysfunction, the fact that this has so often been very difficult to do suggests that in many instances it may be only a forced distinction, and that attention should instead be directed to determining the nature and extent of brain dysfunction that may actually exist in persons who are mentally disturbed. Obviously, the more chronic or treatment resistive the population of psychiatric patients one is dealing with, the more plausible this possibility becomes.

In the first of a series of studies devoted to a comprehensive neuropsychologic evaluation of children and adolescents with psychiatric disorders, Tramontana and his colleagues found a 60% rate of abnormality on the Halstead-Reitan Neuropsychological Battery for hospitalized psychiatric patients ranging from 9 to 15 years of age (Tramontana, Sherrets, and Golden, 1980). Impairment was found to be more prevalent among the more chronic subjects, was associated with a lag of two grades or more in school performance, and was more likely to be reflected in higher rather than lower functions of the cerebral cortex. Although no direct relationship between brain impairment and psychiatric disturbance was inferred, brain impairment in childhood or adolescence was seen as placing the affected youngster at particularly high risk for developing a psychiatric disturbance and for the disturbance to endure and to influence various areas of adjustment, including school performance.

Unfortunately, there are very few published reports on the application ofcomprehensive, standardized neuropsychologic procedures in the diagnostic evaluation of mental retardation (e.g., Matthews, 1974). Although it is probably true that some modification of procedure would be necessary for test administration with the moderately to severely retarded, there is no indication that existing procedures could not be appropriately administered to persons in the mild to moderate range of mental retardation. In most cases, if a mentally retarded individual can be administered a Wechsler or a Stanford-Binet successfully, there is no practical reason why the Halstead-Reitan or Luria-Nebraska could not also be used. Rather, there appear to be several more basic reasons for the underutilization of neuropsychologic methods with the mentally retarded. First, perhaps it is simply assumed that mental retardation is necessarily associated with some form of brain impairment (although its cause and even its very presence may often be elusive), so that evaluating this systematically would only amount to confirming what is really already "known." Second, there seems to be the tacit assumption that any existing brain impairment is of a diffuse and nonlocalizable nature among the mentally retarded, and, consequently, that a neuropsychologic appraisal would not provide information that would lend itself to differential treatment planning. The third reason seems to be a derivative of "black box" psychology, and has to do with questioning the value of relating observable deficits in behavior or abilities to inferred disorders of the brain.

RELEVANCE TO DIAGNOSIS AND TREATMENT PLANNING

Of all the various manifestations of mental retardation, assessing brain impairment is often most difficult in the case of mental retardation involving concurrent psychiatric disturbance. This is partly because of the lack of systematic study in this area, but perhaps more importantly is due to the increased diagnostic complexity that is involved when mental retardation and mental illness coexist. Accurate assessment is highly important, however, inasmuch as the patient's behavioral, emotional, and intellectual improvement can depend greatly on properly diagnosing and treating the neurologic aspects of the condition. Although it is not yet possible to estimate the prevalence of brain impairment among persons with coexisting mental retardation and mental illness, its nature and extent are likely to vary widely among those for whom it is actually a contributing factor. What is important in the individual case is to determine precisely *how* brain impairment may be contributing to existing intellectual deficits and psychiatric symptoms, to determine the kinds of situations in which the individual will be more or less limited, and to specify the conditions that are likely to help maximize the patient's capabilities and potential for adjustment.

In some cases, a neuropsychologic evaluation may reveal otherwise undetected abnormalities in brain function that significantly impede the individual's adaptability and responsiveness to therapeutic efforts. For example, consider the following hypothetical case:

> R.T. is a 13-year-old boy classified in the mild range of mental retardation and enrolled in a program for the educably retarded. Although he is described as typically subdued, almost depressed in his affect, and showing little in the way of emotional expression, there recently have been a number of aggressive outbursts in which he reportedly strikes out rather violently with little apparent provocation. Program staff are quite frightened and perplexed by these episodes, but tend to view them as an indication of excessive educational demands being placed on the boy, and have revised his curriculum accordingly. He is now being given more "room to breathe," with less one-to-one staff contact and more time in arts and crafts than in academic subjects. Neither these changes, however, nor a psychiatric referral that resulted in his being placed on tranquilizing medication seem to have brought about any improvement. If anything, R.T. appears to have grown worse.
>
> A neuropsychologic evaluation finds R.T. to be disproportionately impaired in the acoustic discrimination of pitch and rhythm, with spatial abilities as well as motor and tactile functions involving the left side of the body also being significantly impaired, although to a lesser extent. Taken together, the findings are suggestive of overall mild cortical impairment—predominantly of the right cerebral hemisphere— with focal involvement of the right temporal lobe. The latter finding, coupled with the reported pattern of R.T.'s problem behavior, raises the possibility that temporal lobe epilepsy may be involved in his aggressive outbursts. An electroencephalographic examination is undertaken and confirms the presence of a seizure disorder localized to the right temporal lobe. A careful review of his history, moreover, reveals that although a seizure disorder had actually been diagnosed and treated in early childhood, anticonvulsant medication was discontinued by the age of 7 without recurrence of seizures. Their recent resurgence, however, apparently coincided with the onset of puberty.

There are several aspects of the preceding case example that are particularly noteworthy. First, the neuropsychologic evaluation opened the way to the eventual diagnosis of temporal lobe epilepsy, a condition that for whatever reasons had not been taken into account in appraising the boy's aggressive outbursts. Moreover, with the pattern of results indicating right hemispheric impairment, one gains some understanding of the depressive features described in the case (e.g., see Tucker, 1981). One would also question the wisdom of revising the educational curriculum to emphasize arts and craft activities for a boy in whom spatial perception is among his greatest difficulties. Lastly, the case serves to underscore the importance of adopting a developmental perspective in evaluating brain function abnormalities in that changes can often occur with age.

In contrast to cases of retardation of the so-called cultural-familial variety in which undetected abnormalities in brain function may nonetheless significantly impede adjustment, there can be other cases in which brain damage is a known etiologic factor in the retardation, but its effects are overestimated. Consider the following example:

D.D. is a 30-year-old microcephalic woman with major motor seizures who is classified in the moderate range of mental retardation. An increase in bizarre and stereotypic behavior in her late teens, coupled with increased social withdrawal and apparent self-preoccupation, led to the additional diagnosis of chronic, undifferentiated schizophrenia—a diagnosis that she still carries. Her seizures have been well controlled with medication, but her response to antipsychotic medication has been judged as unsatisfactory in that she does not appear to have grown any more accessible or responsive to institutional staff and programmatic efforts. She shows little reaction to requests or comments put to her, even though she is able to speak and can often be heard engaging in "empty chatter." As one staff member put it, "You can't simply tell D.D. to do something; it's like you have to pick her up, lead her by the hand, and show her exactly what you want." The implicit concensus among staff seems to be that the upper limit of D.D.'s functioning has already been reached, and that there simply is too little "gray matter" present to permit any appreciable impact from intervention efforts.

A neuropsychologic evaluation shows, however, that although there is indeed a generalized impairment of adaptive abilities, D.D. is by far most impaired with respect to auditory perception and acoustic-motor responding, but does substantially better in processing and responding to either visual or tactile input. She is not deaf, but nonetheless the results suggest that it would be a mistake to devise any program of intervention in which feedback, guidance, and instruction would be given primarily through an auditory-verbal medium. Moreover, the pattern of performance, together with a knowledge of brain-behavior relationships, suggests that her memory and learning with auditory input could perhaps be maximized through the deliberate recruitment of either occipital or parietal cortex into the task, by the simultaneous provision of, respectively, either visual or tactile stimulation. In a sense, therefore, it is literally true that one would have to "lead her by the hand and show her exactly what is wanted" in facilitating her responding to verbal requests, for she necessarily would be dependent on such supplemental cues.

Thus, not only could a neuropsychologic evaluation provide clues as to what areas of function could best be worked with, but could also lead to testable hypotheses as to the means by which progress may most profitably be achieved. Apart from any predisposition to psychosis that may have existed from the outset in the preceding case, one might wonder whether the social withdrawal and severely regressed behavior that were eventually seen might have been minimized in earlier years had the social environment been better able to reach her through interactions capitalizing on the sensory pathways through which she was most readily accessible. As in this example, it is a mistake to assume that just because damage is widespread and evidently distributed throughout the cortex, all functions and adaptive abilities are necessarily impaired to the same extent. *Variation almost always exists*, even when the damage is highly diffuse and nonlocalizable (Golden, 1978). This is because brain pathology does not necessarily operate in an equable fashion, leaving neat, symmetrical zones of equivalent tissue destruction. Its distribution may be diffuse, but there are differences in the extent to which different cortical zones are affected. Impairment will also vary because the functions themselves differ with respect to cortical organization: those relying on few cortical areas for their execution are relatively more affected by *where* the areas of maximal involvement are, whereas those functions relying on many cortical areas would instead be influenced more by the total *amount* of tissue damage present (Luria, 1966, 1973). Thus, even if there were documented evidence of diffuse cortical atrophy (as indicated, for example, through computed tomography), and even if the areas of maximal involvement were known, this would not indicate precisely the functions that are most impaired nor the ones that are relatively spared. Here, a neuropsychologic evaluation—being a *direct* appraisal of brain function—is necessary to provide a precise delineation of the effects of known brain damage.

There are other cases in which localized rather than diffuse damage produces a highly generalized impairment. Distinguishing the specific nature of the impairment, however, can often be rather difficult. Consider, for example, a child with a focal lesion of the frontal lobe, including destruction to frontolimbic pathways:

> F.L. is a 10-year-old boy whose development is described by his parents as having been largely unremarkable up to about the age of 3. Thereafter, he was observed to become increasingly distractible, as well as delayed in his intellectual development. He also presented management difficulties, which became sufficiently pronounced to require his placement in an engineered classroom at the outset of his entry into school. Treatment with both Ritalin and a contingency management system has been only partially successful in that the boy continues to lag far behind his peers in school and fails to internalize rules which are set in the home. Problems of obesity and enuresis are present, in addition to symptoms of distractibility, behavioral disinhibition, perseveration, and impaired intellectual functions, especially memory. He

has now been admitted for a psychiatric evaluation preceding probable placement into a residential treatment facility. The admitting diagnoses are hyperactivity and mild mental retardation.

A neuropsychologic evaluation at that time shows that whereas F.L.'s basic sensory and motor functions are largely within normal limits, his higher mental functions—including memory and learning—are impeded by a susceptibility to the disrupting effects of extraneous stimulation. He is apt to be stimulus bound and to have major difficulty in maintaining a mental "set," and thus is likely to have difficulty in regulating his own thoughts and actions through internalized rules. Moreover, whereas language comprehension is intact, there is a mild difficulty in speech articulation. Although F.L. is right-handed, he fails to show an expected right-hand superiority on a variety of motor tasks.

Taken together, the findings suggest a focal impairment involving frontal portions of the brain, perhaps primarily on the left side and probably extending into associated subcortical structures as well. A computed tomography scan is performed and confirms the presence of a static lesion involving primarily prefrontal cortex, with partial destruction of frontolimbic pathways.

The neuroanatomical region involved in the preceding case is well known in its importance in the regulation of goal-directed behavior, cognition, and affect (e.g., Luria, 1966, 1973; Milner, 1964). When impaired, it can result in a pattern of disinhibitory symptoms closely resembling the syndrome of childhood hyperactivity (Newlin and Tramontana, 1980). If such a condition occurs early in development, it would not only disrupt present intellectual functioning, but would also impede the attainment of important skills and abilities in later developmental stages. In terms of measured intelligence, the individual might well be designated as mentally retarded and show a seemingly nonspecific impairment covering many areas of intellectual functioning. Assuming that the condition is static and does not reflect a progressive neuropathologic process, however, some reversibility of symptoms could conceivably be achieved by efforts aimed at reducing the individual's net level of stimulation (either medically or through environmental modifications), and by taking care to devise a rehabilitation program in which complex tasks and demands are broken down into much simpler components and in which reinforcement contingencies are not presented over an extended time frame. Obviously, prognosis would depend greatly on early detection and appropriate intervention.

Thus, a neuropsychologic evaluation may reveal more ability and adjustment potential than is perhaps apparent, especially when there is a more or less specific factor producing a highly generalized deficit. A related example involves the case of unilateral left hemispheric cerebral impairment:

L.H. is a 7-year-old autistic girl classified in the moderate range of mental retardation. She has shown an apparent failure to acquire or use language appropriately, along with pronounced deficiencies in social attachment and development that have been evident since infancy. The possibility that she might be deaf was even considered at one time because of her self-preoccupation and poor responsiveness to others, but this was later ruled out through observations of her fascination with musical and environmental sounds and her variable compliance with simple verbal requests. There was a history of possible birth trauma involving reported complications in her delivery, but there was never confirmation of any actual period of perinatal anoxia. There were abnormal findings on an earlier electroencephalographic examination, but a subsequent examination during her most recent psychiatric hospitalization was judged as unremarkable.

A neuropsychologic evaluation focusing on a detailed assessment of fairly basic sensory and motor functions was performed. This revealed substantial differences in performance between the two sides of the body, with significantly more recognition errors and a much higher discrimination threshold for the right side in various tactile tasks, along with inferior performance in simple motor tasks with her preferred right hand. These lateralizing features and the relative superiority of her performance in nonverbal tasks pointed toward a unilateral impairment of the left cerebral hemisphere.

The preeminent role of the left cerebral hemisphere for speech and language functions in most individuals is well documented (e.g., Gazzaniga, 1970). The neuropsychologic significance of this is especially relevant in the evaluation of autism and childhood schizophrenia because of the frequent association of these conditions with major abnormalities in language performance and development (Quay and Werry, 1979). An impairment of the left cerebral hemisphere may be involved, but its detection can often be obscured by the seemingly nonspecific nature of the child's deficits. Detection would have been quite difficult in the preceding case—apart from any supporting evidence that might have been obtained through computed tomography—had it not been for the presence of motor and tactile symptoms involving the contralateral side of the body. That is, whereas a severe emotional or mental disturbance unrelated to brain damage may produce a general interference with performance—including language—it is implausible that only certain functions or functions on predominately one side of the body would be affected. Valid neuropsychologic diagnosis in cases of this kind requires the presence of such localizing signs in order for dysfunctional language performance to be taken as indicative of left hemispheric damage (Tramontana and Wilkening, 1980).

Several other issues are raised by the preceding case example. The first has to do with the relation of L.H.'s possible anoxia at birth to her unilateral brain impairment. Although perinatal anoxia does not invariably lead to chronic brain dysfunction (Schain, 1977), indications are that the hemispheres differ with respect to their vulnerability to oxygen deficiency. Cerebrovascular asymmetries are such that the left hemisphere is likely to be affected sooner and more severely (Bruens, Gastaut, and Giove, 1960; Carmon, Harishanu, Lowinger, and Lavy, 1972; LeMay and Culebras, 1972). Perhaps this was the case with L.H. It is also possible that her having a substantial impediment in the use and comprehension of human communication so early in life constituted a significant obstacle to her socialization and attachment, and contributed to her withdrawal and autistic preoccupation. Her fascination with music and various environmental sounds need not be viewed as expressions of pathology that must be extinguished, but instead could be viewed as healthy expressions of function of her unimpaired hemisphere which are her primary means of contact with external reality. Because the right hemisphere does not "speak," it is not easy to assess its functions in a left hemisphere impaired individual. General intelligence can often be underestimated, as relatively intact functions of the right cerebral hemisphere are perhaps missed. It is important, however, that hemispheric differences be carefully appraised. Spatial abilities, constructional skills, as well as musical abilities and various forms of intuitive or impressionistic thinking (i.e., right hemisphere functions) could all be basically intact, but perhaps not utilized to maximal advantage. Such abilities can and should be drawn upon in developing and implementing treatment plans and in fostering the patient's contact with a reality in which mastery is possible.

It was indicated before that dysfunctional performance on a neuropsychologic evaluation can result not only from brain damage, but also can occur with serious psychiatric disturbances for which there may be no existing evidence of structural damage to the brain. Rather than debating whether the psychiatric disturbance is the cause or effect of neuropsychologic dysfunction or arguing that newly available technologies will perhaps reveal heretofore undetected brain anomalies in certain psychiatric disorders, suffice it to say that psychiatric conditions are often associated with neuropsychologic abnormality (Heaton et al., 1978; Tramontana et al., 1980). A distinction between brain damage and brain dysfunction is

implied; that is, whereas brain damage is one cause of brain dysfunction, brain dysfunction can occur from factors other than the destruction of brain tissue. It can be rather variable in psychoses (perhaps secondarily to neuropsychologic abnormalities), waxing and
waning in conjunction with the exacerbation and remission of manifest symptoms. It is this variability, coupled with the presence of
nonspecific attentional deficits, that often serves to distinguish neuropsychologic dysfunction associated with psychiatric disturbance.
Here, the neuropsychologic evaluation becomes more specifically an
appraisal of potential reversibility by distinguishing between brain
damage and brain dysfunction in the psychiatric patient with mental
retardation.

Consider the following case example:

> J.S. is a 21-year-old man who was recently hospitalized for an acute
> psychotic episode. His symptoms include persecutory delusions, audi-
> tory hallucinations, and loose and tangential speech. His memory for re-
> cent events is quite poor, and he is somewhat confused and disoriented
> as to person, place, and time. This is his first psychiatric hospitaliza-
> tion, but his history is rather sketchy with respect to his premorbid
> functioning. Indications are, however, that he performed at a near aver-
> age level in school. An intellectual evaluation now places him signifi-
> cantly below average in intelligence, and although he was admitted
> with the diagnosis of acute paranoid schizophrenia, the possibility of an
> organic brain syndrome is being explored. The Luria-Nebraska Neuro-
> psychological Battery is administered, and pathologic elevations are
> found on predominately the Rhythm, Receptive Speech, Memory, and
> Intelligence Scales.

This is a pattern of performance on the Luria-Nebraska that is
commonly found in schizophrenics and is not necessarily associated
with structural damage to the brain (Purisch et al., 1978). Here, the
neuropsychologic deficits in acoustic discrimination, language comprehension, memory, and complex intellectual operations are probably secondary to the disturbances in attention associated with
schizophrenia and tend to improve as psychotic symptoms are reduced. Although dysfunction is certainly present, it is not necessarily of the chronic nature that tends to exist with brain damage, and
may be reversible to the extent that improvement in the psychosis
can be achieved. Reexamination of the patient after a period of time
and upon clinical improvement may reveal an absence of neuropsychologic abnormality and a favorable prognosis, given appropriate
rehabilitation programming and follow-up. On the other hand, reexamination may reveal specific areas of dysfunction that are indeed

chronic and that must be taken into account as limiting factors in the patient's eventual adjustment. Either way, the appraisal is likely to be more favorable than what is found during a period of acute psychiatric disturbance. A neuropsychologic evaluation during a period of remission is thus one way of distinguishing the areas of dysfunctional performance that are more or less likely to persist despite improvement in psychiatric symptomatology.

Lastly, a highly important application of neuropsychologic assessment is in the early identification of individuals whose functional limitations place them at high risk for developing a psychiatric disorder. There is an unusually high incidence of cerebral impairment among children and adolescents with psychiatric disorders (Hertzig and Birch, 1968; Rutter, 1977). This, unfortunately, often goes undetected in the routine neurologic examinations conducted in psychiatric facilities (Hertzig and Birch, 1968; Tramontana et al., 1980). Although the precise mechanisms are unknown by which cerebral impairment during childhood or adolescence can lead to psychiatric disorder, the effects do seem to persist and influence many areas of adjustment and adaptability, including frustration tolerance and coping style, as well as intellectual development and school performance (Milman, 1979; Rutter, 1977). Similar factors probably account for the rather high incidence of psychiatric problems reported for retarded children (Chess and Hassibi, 1970; Menolascino, 1965; Philips and Williams, 1975). The functional limitations of the retarded or brain-damaged child may set the stage for increased exposure to stress and psychonoxious reactions from the environment, including parental reponses ranging from overprotection to scapegoating, and thus may predispose the child to psychiatric disturbance (Rutter, 1977). It is important that the functional limitations of the impaired child be comprehensively assessed, with early and accurate detection at least being the first step in reducing the risk for the later development of psychiatric disturbance.

The preceding examples should provide some idea of the relevance of neuropsychologic evaluation to diagnosis and treatment planning for the mentally retarded with psychiatric disturbance. As a comprehensive assessment of brain functions and adaptive abilities, a standardized neuropsychologic evaluation can be used: 1) to provide a direct and precise delineation of the effects of known brain damage; 2) to identify areas of impaired brain function that might otherwise go undetected; or 3) to reveal where there may actually be more ability and adjustment potential present than perhaps "meets the eye"; and 4) to help distinguish areas of impaired function and intellectual deficit that are more or less likely to be chronic, especially for the mentally retarded individual with psychiatric disturbance. As was indicated earlier, however, one may question the value of a *neuro*psychologic evaluation over a psychologic evaluation in meeting these ends. That is, apart from the merits of a comprehensive assessment of adaptive functions and abilities, what is gained by "neurologizing" the findings? What is the value of going "inside the head" and relating observable deficits in behavior and abilities to inferred disorders of the brain?

Of course one could instead proceed at a purely behavioral level performing a detailed assessment of all treatment-relevant behavior and abilities and formulating treatment plans in essentially a trial-and-error fashion. The trouble with such an approach is that it is inefficient. One can never measure all aspects of an individual's functioning that would be relevant to treatment; the possibilities are virtually infinite. Rather, one always obtains a selective sample of functioning and behavior that is hopefully representative of the individual and from which impressions and predictions about the individual are made. In a neuropsychologic evaluation, the selection is specifically grounded in a systematic appraisal of those aspects of an individual's capacity to adapt and perform successfully that depend upon intact brain function. Neuropsychologic diagnosis may thus be viewed as a *hypothetical construct* out of which testable predictions regarding prognosis and treatment can be derived. By relating behavioral and functional deficits to the brain, and by doing this in a way that draws upon the theory and science of brain-behavior relationships, one gains an integrated perspective that permits the tying together of otherwise discrete behavioral observations into clusters of related symptoms for which certain interventions are theoretically likely to be beneficial. Treatment planning need not proceed in a trial-and-error fashion because at least some basis exists at the outset for specifying conditions that may help maximize the individual's existing capabilities and potential for adjustment. These predictions can then be tested through programmatic implementation, and thereafter modified in relation to actual outcome. Thus, when incorporated into a more complete diagnostic evaluation of the mentally retarded and mentally ill individual—including medical, psychosocial, and educational assessments—the neuropsychologic evaluation can provide an important perspective in understanding the individual's limitations and in suggesting where and how intervention might most profitably proceed.

PROBLEMS AND PROSPECTS

Apart from the potential utility of neuropsychologic methods in the evaluation of coexisting mental retardation and mental illness, a more fundamental consideration has to do with the issue of validity. That is, do standardized neuropsychologic evaluations accurately diagnose brain impairment when applied to this population? Are differential treatment outcomes correctly predicted?

Much work is needed before questions such as these can be answered. Little attention has been given to the application of standardized neuropsychologic test batteries in the evaluation of mental retardation, but systematic investigations have begun. For example, Matthews and his colleagues (Matthews, 1974) have provided initial normative data on the Halstead-Reitan Neuropsychological Battery based on samples of institutionalized retardates consisting of 81 children and 286 adults subdivided into three IQ groups: 40–54, 55–69, and 70–84. Much more is known regarding the neuropsychologic performance of nonretarded psychiatric patients (Heaton et al., 1978), but even here comprehensive examinations of child and adolescent patients have only just begun (Tramontana et al., 1980). No study, however, has yet reported complete results on test batteries such as the Halstead-Reitan or Luria-Nebraska for a sample of subjects in whom mental retardation and psychiatric disturbance coexist.

Benton (1970) has discussed some of the methodologic problems involved in the neuropsychologic study of the mentally retarded, especially the difficulty in obtaining definitive criterion information as to the precise status of the brain, against which neuropsychologic findings could be validated. He proposed a research-by-analogy strategy whereby brain-behavior relationships derived from the study of neurologic patients with well defined lesions are extrapolated to the mentally retarded in evaluating their neuropsychologic performance. This was the implicit model of interpretation used in the case examples discussed in this chapter; that is, it was assumed that principles of neuropsychologic interpretation are not fundamentally different for psychiatrically disturbed retardates than for neurologic patients. One need not rely on assumption indefinitely, however. Recent technologic advances in noninvasive neurodiagnostic methods—including computed tomography and cerebral bloodflow analysis—now supplement the electroencephalogram, and together make it possible to gain more precise information on the neuroanatomical and neurophysiologic status of the brain. Brain-behavior relationships in psychiatric retardates can thus be directly appraised, with neuropsychologic norms and guidelines for inferring brain impairment developed specifically for this population.

Applications of existing norms and cutoff scores derived from comparisons of neurologic and control subjects would almost invariably result in impressions of impaired neuropsychologic functions in psychiatric retardates. Discriminative power would be reduced because of the overdetermining effects of nonspecific intellectual, attentional, and motivational deficits on the patient's performance. Specific normative data are thus needed that reflect performance variability within and across different psychometric, behavioral, and etiologic classifications of psychiatric retardates, and that provide a basis for diagnostic and prognostic differentiation within this broadly defined population. Moreover, it is probably a mistake to assume that a set of test procedures that works quite well with one population will also work well when applied to another. Although the Halstead-Reitan and Luria-Nebraska batteries are of demonstrated sensitivity in detecting brain impairment in neurologic patients, procedural modifications may be necessary to achieve this same goal with psychiatric retardates. This would certainly appear to be the case for the language impaired and for patients with moderate to severe retardation. Tests of higher cognitive functions and problem solving ability would probably provide little diagnostic yield in such cases, if indeed adequate samples of performance could even be obtained. As was seen in the case of L.H., asymmetries in motor and/or sensory-perceptual performance may provide the principle neuropsychologic basis on which brain impairment is discriminated in cases of this kind. Accordingly, research should explore the value of employing indirect measures of higher functions, such as the Developmental Profile (Alpern, Boll, and Shearer, 1980), combined with direct measures of fairly basic motor and sensory-perceptual functions in diagnosing brain impairment in patients whose level of functioning or clinical condition precludes a fuller direct assessment.

Lastly, research on outcome as a function of neuropsychologic diagnosis is largely lacking at this time. It will be important to determine how predictions derived from this particular diagnostic perspective actually correspond to the patient's eventual adjustment. A complex interaction of diverse contributing factors is most likely involved in producing the often perplexing clinical picture seen in patient's with coexisting mental retardation and mental illness. Neuropsychologic diagnosis provides only one perspective, but one that can perhaps have a powerful effect in guiding treatment selection and intervention in ways that are positively related to patient outcome. Further investigation is obviously needed to address issues such as this, and hopefully it will ensure the valid application of neuropsychologic methods in the evaluation of coexisting mental retardation and mental illness.

REFERENCES

Alpern, G. D., Boll, T. J., and Shearer, M. S. 1980. Developmental Profile II: Manual. Psychological Development Publications, Aspen.

Bender, L. 1938. A Visual Motor Gestalt Test and Its Clinical Use. Research Monographs, No. 3. American Orthopsychiatric Association, New York.

Benton, A. L. 1970. Neuropsychological aspects of mental retardation. J. Spec. Educ. 4:3–11.

Bruens, J. H., Gastaut, H., and Giove, G. 1960. Electroencephalographic study of the signs of chronic vascular insufficiency of the Sylvian region in aged people. EEG Clin. Neurophysiol. 12:283–295.

Carmon, A., Harishanu, Y., Lowinger, E., and Lavy, S. 1972. Asymmetries in hemispheric blood volume and cerebral dominance. Behav. Biol. 7:853–859.

Chess, S., and Hassibi, M. 1970. Behavior deviations in mentally retarded children. J. Am. Acad. Child Psychiatry, 9:282–297.

Gazzaniga, M. S. 1970. The Bisected Brain. Appleton-Century-Crofts, New York.

Golden, C. J. 1977. Validity of the Halstead-Reitan Neuropsychological Battery in a mixed psychiatric and brain-injured population. J. Consult. Clin. Psychol. 45:1043–1051.

Golden, C. J. 1978. Diagnosis and Rehabilitation in Clinical Neuropsychology. Charles C Thomas, Springfield, IL.

Golden, C. J., Hammeke, T. A., and Purisch, A. D. 1980. The Luria-Nebraska Neuropsychological Battery: A Manual for Clinical and Experimental Uses. Western Psychological Services, Los Angeles.

Heaton, R. K., Baade, L. E., and Johnson, K. L. 1978. Neuropsychological test results associated with psychiatric disorders in adults. Psychol. Bull. 85:141–162.

Hertzig, M. E., and Birch, H. G. 1968. Neurological organization in psychiatrically disturbed adolescents. Arch. Gen. Psychiatry 19:528–537.

LeMay, M., and Culebras, A. 1972. Human brain-morphologic differences in the hemispheres demonstrable by carotid arteriography. N. Engl. J. Med. 287:168–170.

Luria, A. R. 1966. Higher Cognitive Functions in Man. Basic Books, New York.

Luria, A. R. 1973. The Working Brain. Basic Books, New York.

Matthews, C. G. 1974. Applications of neuropsychological test methods in mentally retarded subjects. In: R. M. Reitan and L. A. Davison (eds.), Clinical Neuropsychology: Current Status and Applications. John Wiley & Sons, New York.

Menolascino, F. 1965. Psychiatric aspects of mental retardation in children under eight. Am. J. Orthopsychiatry 5:852–861.

Milman, D. H. 1979. Minimal brain dysfunction in childhood: Outcome in late adolescence and early adult years. J. Clin. Psychiatry 40:371–380.

Milner, B. 1964. Some effects of frontal lobectomy in man. In: J. M. Warren and K. Akert (eds.), The Frontal Granular Cortex and Behavior. McGraw-Hill Book Company, New York.

Moses, J., and Golden, C. J. 1980. Cross validation of the effectiveness of the Luria-Nebraska Neuropsychological Battery in discriminating between schizophrenic and neurological populations. Int. J. Neurosci. 10:121–128.

Newlin, D. B., and Tramontana, M. G. 1980. Neuropsychological findings in a hyperactive adolescent with subcortical brain pathology. Clin. Neuropsychol. 2:178–183.

Philips, I., and Williams, N. 1975. Psychopathology and mental retardation: A study of 100 mentally retarded children. Am. J. Psychiatry 132:1265–1271.

Purisch, A. D., Golden, C. J., and Hammeke, T. A. 1978. Discrimination of schizophrenic and brain-injured patients by a standardized version of Luria's neuropsychological tests. J. Consult. Clin. Psychol. 46:1266–1273.

Quay, H. C., and Werry, J. S. 1979. Psychopathological Disorders of Childhood. 2nd Ed. John Wiley & Sons, New York.

Reitan, R. M. 1974. Methodological problems in clinical neuropsychology. In: R. M. Reitan and L. A. Davison (eds.), Clinical Neuropsychology: Current Status and Applications. John Wiley & Sons, New York.

Reitan, R. M., and Davison, L. A. 1974. Clinical Neuropsychology: Current Status and Applications. John Wiley & Sons, New York.

Rutter, M. 1977. Brain damage syndromes in childhood: Concepts and findings. J. Child Psychol. Psychiatry 18:1–21.

Schain, R. J. 1977. Neurology of Childhood Learning Disorders. 2nd Ed. Williams & Wilkins, Baltimore.

Tramontana, M. G., and Wilkening, G. 1980. Detection of left hemispheric cerebral impairment in a childhood schizophrenic. Paper presented at the 88th Annual Convention of the American Psychological Association, September, Montreal.

Tramontana, M. G., Sherrets, S. D., and Golden, C. J. 1980. Brain dysfunction in youngsters with psychiatric disorders: Application of Selz-Reitan rules for neuropsychological diagnosis. Clin. Neuropsychol. 2:118–123.

Tucker, D. M. 1981. Lateral brain function, emotion, and conceptualization. Psychol. Bull. 89:19–46.

Chapter 3

The Handling and Mishandling of Parents of Mentally Retarded Persons

Philip Roos

In a society that cherishes intelligence, learning that one's child is mentally retarded can be an extraordinarily painful experience. It is unfortunate, therefore, that mental health services to families of mentally retarded people have traditionally failed to meet their needs (e.g., National Association for Retarded Citizens, 1974; Roos, 1963, 1970, 1975, 1977a, 1977b). This tragic neglect may reflect the reluctance of many mental health professionals to work with mentally retarded clients.

Typically, psychotherapists and counselors have selected clients that reflect their own self-image (e.g., Fenichel, 1945; McKinney, 1958). That is, they have selected people who are intelligent, highly verbal, introspective, and capable of a high level of abstract thinking. Favorable prognostic indicators for psychotherapy have typically included such dimensions as "ego strength" and "freedom from intracranial organic psychopathology." Mentally retarded people, by definition, are lacking in these attributes. Indeed, the presence of mental retardation has often been listed as contraindicative for psychologic forms of treatment. Consequently, retarded people in mental health facilities have traditionally been assigned to the chronic back wards and provided custodial care.

PROFESSIONAL NEGLECT

Mental health professionals' negative attitudes toward mentally retarded people have often been generalized to the parents of such persons as well. Negative stereotypes of these parents are reflected by such labels as *disturbed, overemotional, neurotic,* or *rejecting.* Some of the emotional "problems" frequently attributed to them include the following:

> "Denying reality" by failing to "accept" the fact that a child is mentally retarded. The parent's search for an informed and sympathetic professional may thus be interpreted as refusal to "accept" a diagnosis of mental retardation.

> Chronic depression, resulting from "internalization of unacceptable death wishes" toward the mentally retarded child. The normal reaction of "chronic sorrow" (Olshansky, 1966) may thus be interpreted as symptomatic of unresolved emotional conflicts.

> Overprotectiveness of the handicapped child, sometimes attributed to a "reaction formation" to latent hostility toward the child. The parent's realistic apprehension about a handicapped child's vulnerability may thus be discounted as a sign of pathology.

> Irrational hostility inappropriately displaced from the child to others, particularly members of the health professions. Hence, a parent's legitimate anger resulting from professional mishandling may be rationalized as a manifestation of his or her own unresolved problems.

> Chaotic marital relationships, resulting from displaced and/or projected hostility. Although divorce and marital conflict is undoubtedly more prevalent among parents of retarded children than in the general population, it would be naive to assume this is uniformly the case (e.g., Gath, 1977; Holt, 1958).

In view of these negative stereotypes of mentally retarded people and their parents, it is not surprising that mental health professionals have tended to neglect such parents and in some cases to mistreat them (Ingalls, 1978; McWilliams, 1976; Menolascino, 1977; Menolascino and Michael, 1978; Murray, 1959; Roos, 1975, 1976, 1977a, 1977b; Turnbull and Turnbull, 1978).

Not infrequently, mental health professionals possess little understanding of mental retardation, and consequently they are prone to disseminate misinformation (McWilliams, 1976) and to give parents erroneous recommendations, such as institutionalizing the mentally retarded individual (Ingalls, 1978; Murray, 1959). Conversely, some professionals fail to recognize mental retardation and attribute parental concern about their child to the parents' own emotional disturbance (e.g, Roos, 1978).

Likewise, some mental health professionals tend to assume that parents of mentally retarded children are emotionally disturbed and in need of "treatment" (Menolascino, 1977; Menolascino and Michael, 1978). The Freudian tradition of tracing psychologic problems to early parent-child relationships may have contributed to this orientation in mental health professionals (e.g., Fenichel, 1945); for example, autism was attributed to parental influences on the affected child (e.g, Bettleheim, 1967; Kanner, 1944).

PARENTAL REACTIONS

Although most parents of mentally retarded people are not suffering from serious psychologic disturbances, having a mentally retarded child is nonetheless a highly painful emotional experience for most people. Such great value is placed on intelligence that "humanhood" tends to be equated with this attribute (e.g., Fletcher, 1972). Hence, a mentally retarded child is likely to be experienced as less than fully human and as a major disappointment. Considerable research supports the assumption that a mentally retarded child provides significant family stress (e.g., Holt, 1958; Gath, 1977; Kramm, 1963).

Typical parental emotional reactions have been described in the literature in considerable detail. They usually reflect reactions to frustration, stress, and crisis (McWilliams, 1976; Menolascino, 1977; Menolascino and Michael, 1978; Murray, 1959; Roos, 1963, 1977a, 1978; Schild, 1964). Common reactions include shame, guilt, ambivalence, depression, sorrow, defensiveness, self-sacrifice (martyr posture), denial, reaction formation (typically manifested in overprotectiveness of the child), and mourning. These reactions are not necessarily pathologic, unless they are unusually severe or become chronic.

Some authors have described characteristic patterns of parental reactions to a retarded child. Farber (1972), for example, noted two kinds of crises. First, the tragic crisis results from frustration of aspirations and expectations for the retarded child and the parents themselves. He found this reaction typical of middle-class, achievement-oriented parents. Second, the role organization crisis is characterized by concern with day-to-day reality problems and is typically found in low-income groups. Menolascino (1977) described three common crisis patterns: 1) novelty shock crisis, referring to the shock at the initial diagnosis and the resulting "demolition of expectations"; 2) crisis of personal values, resulting from the symbolic value assigned to the child and the difficulty of fitting the child into the parents' personal value system; and 3) reality crisis, resulting from practical day-to-day problems and associated frustrations.

Roos (1977a, 1977b, 1978) stressed the intensification or exacerbation of existential anxieties characteristic of the human condition. Emphasizing that these reactions are not necessarily pathologic, he described the following sources of existential anxiety:

Disillusionment   Most people experience considerable discrepancy between myths and expectations prevalent in culture and reality. Children are taught to anticipate success, achievement, status, fame, wealth, and love. They learn to expect wise parents, loving and lovable mates, and perfect children. These expectations are constantly reinforced by parents, schools, books, and the media; yet experience gradually erodes these myths, leading to a long series of disappointments in oneself, in others, and in life in general.

A common pattern is for parents to channel their frustrated yearning for perfection into their children. Parents thus vicariously hope to realize their own thwarted dreams of success and happiness. A retarded child, unfortunately, is not a suitable vehicle for fulfilling these dreams. Such a child may represent a major disillusionment—often the culmination of a long sequence of disappointments.

Aloneness   Most people suffer from the inability to transcend their personal boundaries and to achieve true intimacy. The parent-child relationship provides a rare opportunity for parents to develop a deeply intimate contact. In many cases of mental retardation, such intimacy may be much more difficult to achieve than with a nonretarded child. This is particularly likely if the child is seriously limited in capacity to introspect or communicate. Hence, parents may feel that they have lost their final chance for achieving true intimacy and become overwhelmed with feelings of aloneness.

Vulnerability   Having a mentally retarded child can be a painful reminder of one's relative helplessness and vulnerability to a merciless fate. Although most people abandon the myth of omnipotence characteristic of early childhood, few events are more dramatic in challenging this myth than having a retarded child. It is a cruel reminder of the tenuousness of one's control over the world and, indeed, the fragile nature of life itself.

Inequity   Having a mentally retarded child threatens the cultural myth of fairness and justice. When learning of mental retardation in his or her child, the parent is likely to ask, "Why me?" The inevitable conclusion is that either the punishment is deserved because of grievous sins or that the world is neither fair nor just. The first conclusion leads to guilt and self-depreciation; the second may challenge fundamental religious and ethical beliefs (Murray, 1959).

Insignificance   Parenthood provides for many people an important *raison d'être*. The role of being a parent contributes to the meaning of life. Parents strive to achieve unfulfilled aspirations through their children. They may gain self-esteem from perceiving themselves as good providers and sage guides for their children; but the limitations imposed by mental retardation may often preclude these parental reactions. Parents may then consider themselves without purpose or meaning.

Past Orientation   Whereas most people anticipate the future as a source of potential gratification, parents of a mentally retarded child tend to view the future as a source of anxiety and potential threat. For parents of nonhandicapped children, the future typically holds the promise of such gratifying events as their child's scholastic achievements, success in sports, graduation, marriage, promising careers, and birth of grandchildren. In contrast, parents of a retarded child can anticipate the child's scholastic failure, exclusion from services (educational, social, recreational, etc.), inability to work or menial employment, sexual problems, difficulty in living independently, and a life of loneliness and isolation. Realistically, services tend to become less adequate as a retarded person ages, contributing to the parents' frustrations. As a result, whereas most parents tend to be future oriented, there is a decrease in future orientation for parents of a retarded child as a function of impaired hope, trust, and faith (Murphy, 1976).

Loss of Immortality   Because symbolic immortality is achieved for many people through their children and grandchildren, this avenue may be blocked in the event of a mentally retarded child (particularly if it is the only child), thereby exacerbating anxieties relating to death and ultimate loss of personal identity.

COUNSELING PARENTS

Recognizing, then, that most parents of mentally retarded children are not emotionally disturbed or mentally ill but relatively normal people facing a life crisis, some basic principles of successful parent counseling can be identified. Perhaps the most useful principle in providing mental health services to parents of mentally retarded people is to approach them as basically healthy persons who can be helped to deal even more effectively with a difficult situation. Thus, emphasis is placed on fostering mental health rather than on treating mental illness (Menolascino, 1977; Olshansky, 1966; Schild, 1964).

Another important principle is to adopt a parent-centered approach, recognizing that parents will manifest a diversity of needs. It is naive and potentially destructive to consider parents of retarded children as if they were a homogeneous group. Individual parents will often pass through a series of phases (McWilliams, 1976;

Menolascino, 1977; Menolascino and Michael, 1978; Murphy, 1976; Roos, 1963). Thus, the parents' needs and objectives are likely to change over time. It is essential, therefore, that the mental health professional not discount the parent, and that he or she listen attentively and with respect (McWilliams, 1976; Murphy, 1976; Roos, 1963). Menolascino (1977) and Menolascino and Michael (1978) have recommended different counseling approaches for specific types of parental crises. Thus, they feel that the novelty shock crisis should be met with emotional support, factual information, and life planning arrangements; the crisis of personal values should be handled with extensive family counseling or formal individual psychotherapy; and the reality crisis should lead to practical, down-to-earth help and guidance or training.

Establishing effective communications is, as in all counseling, a critical ingredient. Attending to nonverbal communication can be particularly useful (Murphy, 1976). Likewise, communicating in the parents' preferred representational perceptual system can foster good contact between counselor and client. This approach has been carefully described as a key element of neurolinguistic programming (e.g., Bandler and Grinder, 1975b). Communication problems tend to occur, according to this theory, when people use language based on different perceptual systems (e.g., visual, auditory, or kinesthetic).

To avoid falling in the trap of assuming a posture of professional omnipotence, it is important for the counselor to recognize that decision making is ultimately the parents' responsibility (Murray, 1959; Roos, 1963). Professionals can assist the parents in making decisions by providing full disclosure, including practical information and facts regarding mental retardation (McWilliams, 1976; Menolascino, 1977; Menolascino and Michael, 1978; Roos, 1963). Thus, bibliotherapy can be a valuable adjunct (McWilliams, 1976). The counselor can also assist the parents to become more skilled in making decisions. It is particularly useful to emphasize that deciding is an active process (e.g., Bandler and Grinder, 1975b), and that the parent can periodically reevaluate any situation and redecide (Menolascino, 1977; Schild, 1964).

Counseling approaches that provide opportunities for dealing with the parents' existential conflicts are particularly appropriate (Ingalls, 1978; McWilliams, 1976; Menolascino, 1977; Menolascino and Michael, 1978; Murphy, 1976; Murray, 1959; Roos, 1977a, 1977b, 1978). To deal effectively with such conflicts, it is essential that the counselor feels comfortable with whatever anxiety he or she may experience. Experiential approaches, such as those developed by Gestalt therapists (e.g., Perls, 1973; Satir, 1972) can be particularly useful in helping parents deal with existential conflicts. A key element in these approaches is to foster full self-awareness and acceptance of personal responsibility for one's feelings. A wide variety of nonverbal techniques has also been used effectively, including drawings, still pictures, body sculpture, writing, and sociodrama (Ferber, Mendelsohn, and Napier, 1973; Murphy, 1976).

GROUP APPROACHES

Group counseling with parents of mentally retarded people is particularly advantageous in that it provides opportunities for mutual support, sharing of information and feelings, and modeling (Ingalls, 1978; McWilliams, 1976; Sternlight and Sullivan, 1974). Group meetings have proven to be an effective tool in parent education. Some experts report that providing parents factual information about mental retardation is the most effective contributor to parental acceptance of their mentally retarded child (Ingalls, 1978). Wolfensberger (1967) has developed a compendium of specific topics suitable for educating groups of parents of retarded children.

A variety of different types of parent groups have been found successful (McWilliams, 1976). Parent-established groups, using professional advisors, have been particularly useful in fostering the sharing of information. Group counseling by professional clinicians has likewise been helpful. Some groups have been successfully run by trained parents with primary focus on the provision of mutual help (Irwin and McWilliams, 1973). Other groups have been designed to focus specifically on the problems of parenting, using such approaches as parent effectiveness training (Gordon, 1972).

Barsh (1961) has identified five levels of goals typically found in parent groups, progressing from those found in the early group sessions to those occurring after the group has reached considerable sophistication:

Information seeking
Sharing of information, opinions, and suggestions
Exposure and acceptance of feelings and emotions
Generalization, consisting of application of group experiences to other behaviors
Maturity, described as "insightful ability to effect change for better in one's life"

Parent-to-parent services have been particularly successful in helping parents who have a mentally retarded child. A number of effective prototypes have appeared; for example, the St. Louis Association for Retarded Citizens has developed an outreach program to parents of newly diagnosed mentally retarded children (Bassin and Kreeb, 1978). This program is similar to the pilot parents outreach program operated by the Omaha Association for Retarded Citizens (Nebraska Association for Retarded Citizens, 1974). The Allegheny County Association for Retarded Citizens (Pennsylvania) has reported a parent-to-parent program designed to provide new parents with strong emotional support. The Parent Helper Service of Wisconsin (Wittenmeyer and Nesbitt, 1971) has provided self-help and crisis intervention-oriented approaches for new parents.

Typical ingredients of these parent-to-parent services include training of parent helpers (parents of retarded individuals who have adjusted successfully), establishment of a formal training curriculum and information referral service, group meetings providing support and sharing, and an outreach component. The programs seem particularly useful in that the parent helpers are able to empathize with the new parents as well as furnish models of successful coping. In some cases, parents learning of mental retardation in their child might find it easier to relate to other parents who have successfully weathered this situation than they would to professionals.

Parents have increasingly adopted active, constructive roles. It has been repeatedly demonstrated, for example, that parents can successfully function as extensions of professional educators (e.g., Bijou, 1968; Ingalls, 1978; Luterman, 1971; NARC, 1978). Data indicate they are successful in raising the level of their child's performance, including significant increases in measured IQ (Caldwell, Bradley, and Elardo, 1975; Shearer and Shearer, 1976). Parents have demonstrated proficiency in implementing behavior modification programs, thereby fostering generalization from formal training and habilitation settings (Ingalls, 1978). A wide variety of curricula and training materials suitable for use by parents have been available for some time (e.g., Bijou, 1968; Ferritor, 1970; Gray and Klaus, 1965; Wahler; 1969; Wildman, 1965).

PROMISING APPROACHES

Although mental health professionals have paid little attention to parents of severely handicapped children, developments in counseling and psychotherapy suggest that approaches now exist that could be extremely helpful to such parents. These approaches have not, however, been systematically focused on helping parents of handicapped children. Their success is predicated on helping parents cope more successfully with a painful situation rather than on treatment of pathology. The following mental health approaches are illustrative of avenues that seem particularly promising for helping parents deal with a severe handicap in their child.

Stress Management Approaches

A severely handicapped child often produces chronic distress in his or her parents (Selye, 1974), a situation that is likely to produce serious physiologic damage (Pelletier, 1977). Providing these parents with tools that would improve their reaction to stressors could, therefore, be highly beneficial. Specific approaches that have been found successful in improving reactions to stressors include biofeedback (e.g., Brown, 1974; Green and Green, 1977; Pelletier, 1977), meditation (e.g., Benson, 1975; Benson, Beary, and Carol, 1974; Bloomfield et al, 1975), autogenic training (e.g., Schultz, 1953; Schultz and Luthe, 1959), and hypnosis (e.g., Kroger and Fezler, 1976; Spiegle and Spiegle, 1978; Wolpe, 1958).

Teaching these approaches to parents of retarded children would provide them with a simple means of reducing potentially destructive reactions to stress. In addition, these techniques have been successfully combined with cognitive therapy to eliminate or reduce stress resulting from specific situations. In systematic desensitization, for example, the parent would develop a hierarchy of actual situations that he or she experiences as stressful (Wolpe, 1958). After inducing deep relaxation (using hypnosis, deep muscle relaxation, or a similar approach), the parent would then imagine the least stressful item in the hierarchy while remaining free of anxiety. Increasingly stressful items would gradually be introduced as each item is imagined without anxiety. This procedure can be taught so that it can be self-administered (McKay, Davis, and Fanning, 1981). Successful desensitization to imagined situations tends to generalize to the actual situations. In addition, the individual is taught to become sensitive to the signs of anxiety and to induce relaxation on first detecting them as he or she experiences real situations.

Cognitive Therapy

A major focus of cognitive therapy techniques (e.g., McKay et al. 1981; Mahoney, 1974; Meichenbaum, 1977; Wolpe, 1958) is to increase people's control of their own behavior. For example, parents could be helped to reduce their anxiety regarding their retarded child or to develop new skills to cope with frustrating situations. Likewise, they could be provided with tactics to reduce obsessive rumination (worrying) or depressive ideation.

Parents of retarded children often dread such situations as being in public places with their child or meeting with professionals. When they experience such situations as stressful, they are likely to avoid them or to deal with them ineffectively. Stress inoculation is one of several available techniques for helping parents cope with such situations without undue stress (Meichenbaum, 1977). This approach involves learning to relax and developing a hierarchy of stressful situations, much as in systematic desensitization. In addition, however, the individual is taught to develop a private series of stress coping thoughts designed to counteract habitual automatic thoughts that lead to anxiety or anger. Four steps have been identified as effective in using stress coping thoughts for dealing with situations: 1) preparing (e.g., "I know exactly what to do," "Tomorrow it'll be over," "I'm going to be all right"); 2) confronting the stressful situation (e.g., "Stay organized," "Be systematic," "It's OK to make errors"); 3) coping with emotional arousal (e.g., "Calm, calm," "Relax now," "Breathe deeply"); and 4) reinforcing success (e.g., "I did great," "I felt relaxed," "Next time it'll be easier") (Meichenbaum and Cameron, 1974). The final stage of the stress inoculation program is practicing the use of relaxation and stress coping thoughts in actual situations.

Thought stopping is another technique that could be useful to parents of retarded children. (Davis, Eshelman, and McKay, 1980). This simple procedure is particularly effective in eliminating ruminative obsessing, common in some parents preoccupied with the "tragedy" of having a retarded child. Some parents also ruminate on imagined past misdeeds or on traumatic interactions with other people. These parents would be taught to make a list of those stressful thoughts and identify disturbing and unproductive thoughts that they want to eliminate. They would then be taught to imagine the situation in which the stressful thought is likely to occur and to focus on the thought. The next and crucial step in the procedure is to interrupt the thought with a "startler" technique (an external stimulus such as an alarm clock or a loud shout of "stop"). This startler can later be replaced by a silent shout of "stop." The final step in this procedure is substituting a positive thought for the disturbing thought. If the individual has learned to induce relaxation by using a specific word, such as *calm,* he or she can substitute that word and replace the tension associated with the obsessive thought by relaxation.

Rational Emotive Therapy

Rational emotive therapy (RET) (e.g., Ellis, 1971, 1977) emphasizes that the source of psychologic disturbance lies not in events, but in people's interpretation of and irrational beliefs about events. Ellis argues that when an event (A) is followed by an emotional reaction (C), the latter results not from the event, but from beliefs (B) about the event. These beliefs often include irrational as well as rational elements. These irrational beliefs lead to undesirable emotional reactions. A common pattern is to interpret events as being awful and catastrophic. People then typically conclude that they are worthless and deserving of awful consequences. Ellis' therapy focuses on teaching the client to recognize and to dispute (D) his irrational beliefs.

Maultzby (1975) has proposed five specific criteria for establishing the irrationality of beliefs, and Ellis has developed lists of common irrational beliefs.

This approach could be readily applied to parents of retarded children by helping them identify and then dispute their irrational beliefs about the child, as well as about themselves. As a result, they would modify their emotional responses and develop more positive behaviors. Common irrational beliefs of parents of handicapped children could readily be identified and disputations developed for each to assist counselors as well as parents in applying RET. Once introduced to the system, parents could be taught to continue using it on their own, applying Maultzby's (1975) Rational Self-Analysis.

Hypnotherapeutic Restructuring

Parents of retarded children may feel trapped and helpless to cope with what they perceive to be an intolerable situation. Hypnotic restructuring (e.g., Spiegle and Spiegle, 1978) provides a technique to help the client place an old problem in a new perspective. Spiegle and Spiegle (1978) define the process as "... formulating a problem in dialectical terms as a conflict of oppositions which can then be integrated in a variety of ways, giving the person a choice" (p. 206).

This approach could be useful, for example, in helping parents adopt a constructive attitude toward their retarded child and in modifying their perception of the child from that of a pitiful individual to that of a fully human person with potential to grow and develop.

Neurolinguistic Programming

By analyzing the work of renowned psychotherapists in terms of communications patterns, Bandler, Grinder, and their associates have developed a new model of psychotherapy: neurolinguistic programming (NLP) (Bandler and Grinder, 1975a, 1975b, 1979; Cameron-Bandler, 1978; Grinder and Bandler, 1976; Grinder, DeLozier, and Bandler, 1977). It includes a number of elements that could be particularly useful to parents of retarded children. For example, NLP provides specific tactics that could help members of families of retarded people to communicate more effectively with each other. These tactics could be of special value in reducing destructive patterns of communication, such as reaching unwarranted inferences from ambiguous statements. Parents who have mastered these techniques would also be better equipped to extract information from professionals.

NLP has also been applied to provide people with new options for dealing with anxiety and stress. A procedure known as reframing is designed to identify maladaptive behaviors or symptoms and to assess the client's own creativity to generate constructive alternatives that will better serve the individual's needs (e.g., Lankton, Lankton, and Brown, 1981). Another procedure, known as editing experience or change history, allows people to eliminate negative consequences of painful past experiences. Thus, parents of retarded children who continue to be influenced by past trauma (e.g., first learning of their child's retardation) could be freed from the destructive emotions still generated by these past experiences.

Gestalt Approaches

Derived from psychoanalysis, Gestalt therapy (e.g., Perls, 1973; Polster and Polster, 1973; Satir, 1972) emphasizes experiential techniques focusing on clients' current awareness and dealing with conflicts and unresolved problems in terms of here-and-now experiences. Past experiences and trauma can, according to this formulation, continue to influence current feelings, attitudes, and behaviors. Specific techniques have been developed to help people bring closure to this unfinished business from the past. Thus, parents of retarded children could be provided opportunities to resolve painful past events that might otherwise continue to influence their lives negatively.

Gestalt techniques are also effective in helping people come to terms with unexpressed feelings. For example, using the so-called empty chair technique, parents of a retarded child could express their ambivalence toward the child. In one approach, they might be instructed to imagine the child sitting in the empty chair facing them and then to express directly to the fantasized child their appreciations, their resentments, their regrets, their hopes, and what they are willing to do.

A similar approach uses two chairs to represent the polarities involved in internal conflict. In this technique, the client first speaks from one chair as one of his or her polarities, then shifts to the other chair and responds as the opposite polarity. This approach helps people become fully aware of internal conflicts and resolve them. Parents of retarded children could thus be helped to recognize, accept, and reconcile conflicting feelings regarding themselves as well as mates, parents, and the retarded child. This and similar approaches are also useful in dealing with existential conflicts.

Most Gestalt approaches are designed for group work and incorporate group support. Hence, they would be well suited for parent groups.

CONCLUSION

Parents of mentally retarded children have demonstrated effectiveness and power. United in advocacy groups, they have been potent social change agents and have, indeed, helped to reshape the field of mental retardation (e.g., Roos, 1977a). Unfortunately, they have often been misunderstood and neglected by mental health professionals.

Successful counseling and other mental health approaches have already been demonstrated in a variety of settings; but other potentially useful approaches have not yet been applied to parents of retarded children. Development of prototypes using these approaches in a systematic manner would be highly desirable. Such prototypes could incorporate evaluation components to identify those specific elements that contribute to success. Associations for retarded citizens seem particularly well suited to develop, pilot, and evaluate such prototypical services.

This publication is symptomatic of the growing recognition of the need to bridge the long existing gap between the fields of mental retardation and mental health. Mental health professionals have resources that could be extremely helpful to families of mentally retarded people. It is more than time to start applying these resources appropriately and to bridge the gap.

REFERENCES

Bandler, R., and Grinder, J. 1975a. Patterns of the Hypnotic Techniques of Milton H. Erickson, M.D.I., Meta Publications, Cupertino, CA.

Bandler, R., and Grinder, J. 1975b. The Structure of Magic I. Science and Behavior Books, Palo Alto, CA.

Bandler, R., and Grinder, J. 1979. Frogs Into Princes. Real People Press, Moab, UT.

Barsh, R. H. 1961. Counseling the parent of the brain-damaged child. J. Rehabil. 27:26–42.

Bassin, J., and Kreeb, D. D. 1978. Reaching Out to Parents of Newly Diagnosed Retarded Children. St. Louis Association for Retarded Children, St. Louis.

Benson, H. 1975. The Relaxation Response. William Morrow and Company, Inc., New York.

Benson, H., Beary, J. F., and Carol, M. P. 1974. The relaxation response. Psychiatry 37:37–46.

Bettleheim, B. 1967. The Empty Fortress: Infantile Autism and the Birth of the Self. Collier-Macmillan, London.

Bijou, S. W. 1968. Research in remedial guidance of young retarded children with behavior problems which interfere with academic learning and adjustment. Office of Education, Bureau of Research, E.D. 024-196. U.S. Government Printing Office, Washington DC.

Bloomfield, P. C., Cain, M. P., Jaffe, D. T., and Kory, R. B. 1975. TM: Discovering Inner Energy and Overcoming Stress. Dell Publishing Co., Inc., New York.

Brown, B. B., 1974. New Mind, New Body. Harper & Row, New York.

Caldwell, B. M., Bradley, R. H., and Elardo, R. 1975. Early stimulation. In: J. Wortis (ed.), Mental Retardation. Vol. 7. Grune & Stratton, New York.

Cameron-Bandler, L. 1978. They Lived Happily Ever After. Meta Publications, Cupertino, CA.

Davis, M., Eshelman, E., and McKay, M. 1980. Relaxation & Stress Reduction Workbook. New Harlinger Publications, Richmond, CA.

Ellis, A. 1971. Growth Through Reason. Science and Behavior Books, Palo Alto, CA.

Ellis, A., and Grieger, R. 1977. Handbook of Rational-Emotive Therapy. Springer Publishing Co., New York.

Farber, B. 1972. Effects of a severely retarded child on the family. In: E. P. Trapp and P. Himelstein (eds.), Readings on the Exceptional Child. 2nd Ed. Appleton-Century-Crofts, New York.

Fenichel, O. 1945. The Psychoanalytic Theory of Neurosis. W. W. Norton & Co., New York.

Ferber, A., Mendelsohn, M., and Napier, A. 1973. The Book of Family Therapy. Houghton-Mifflin, Boston.

Ferritor, D. E. 1970. Modifying interaction patterns: An experimental training program for parents of autistic children. Diss. Abstr. 30:3114–3115.

Fletcher, J. 1972. Indicators of humanhood: A tentative profile of man. Hastings Center Rep. 2(5):1–4.

Gath A. 1977. The impact of an abnormal child upon the parents. Brit. J. Psychiatry 130:405–410.

Gordon, T. 1972. Parent Effectiveness Training. Wyden, New York.

Gray, S. W., and Klaus, R. A. 1965. An experimental preschool program for culturally deprived children. Child Dev. 36:887–898.

Green, E., and Green, A. 1977. Beyond Biofeedback. Dell Publishing Co., New York.

Grinder, J., and Bandler, R. 1976. The Structure of Magic II. Science and Behavior Books, Palo Alto, CA.

Grinder, J., DeLozier, J., and Bandler, R. 1977. Patterns of the Hypnotic Techniques of Milton H. Erickson, M.D. II. Meta Publications, Cupertino, CA.

Holt, K. S. 1958. Home care of severely retarded children. Pediatrics 22:744–755.

Ingalls, R. P. 1978. Mental Retardation—The Changing Outlook. John Wiley & Sons, New York.

Irwin, E. C., and McWilliams, B. J. 1973. Parents working with parents: The cleft palate program. Cleft Palate J. 10:360.

Kanner, L. 1944. Early infantile autism. J. Pediatr. 25:211–217.

Kramm, E. R. 1963. Families of Mongoloid Children. U.S. Government Printing Office, Washington, DC.

Kroger, W., and Fezler, W. 1976. Hypnosis and Behavior Modification: Imagery Conditioning. J. B. Lippincott Company, Philadephia.

Lankton, S., Lankton, C., and Brown, M. 1981. Psychological level communication in transactional analysis. Transactional Anal. J. 11(4):287–299.

Luterman, D. M. 1971. A parent-oriented nursery program for preschool deaf children. Volta Rev. 73:106–112.

Mahoney, M. J. 1974. Cognitive Behavior Modification. Ballinger Publishing Co., Cambridge, MA.

Maultzby, M. 1975. Help Yourself to Happiness. Institute for Rational Living, New York.

McKay, M., Davis, M., and Fanning, P. 1981. Thoughts & Feelings. New Harlinger Publications, Richmond, CA.

McKinney, F., 1958. Counseling for Personal Adjustment. The Riverside Press, Cambridge, MA.

McWilliams, B. J. 1976. Various aspects of parent counseling. In: E. J. Webster (ed.), Professional Approaches with Parents of Handicapped Children. pp. 27–64. Charles C Thomas, Springfield, IL.

Meichenbaum, D. 1977. Cognitive-Behavior Modification, An Integrative Approach. Plenum Press, New York.

Meichenbaum, D., and Cameron, R. 1974. The clinical potential of modifying what clients say to themselves. In: M. J. Mahoney and C. E. Thorensen (eds.), Self-Control: Power to the Person. Brooks/Cole, Monterey, CA.

Menolascino, F. J. 1977. Challenges in Mental Retardation: Progressive Ideology and Services. Human Services Press, New York.

Menolascino, F. J., and Michael, L. E. 1978. Medical Dimensions of Mental Retardation. University of Nebraska Press, Lincoln.

Murphy, A.T. 1976. Counseling as a process of creating self in helping relationship with others. In: E. J. Webster (ed.), Professional Approaches with Parents of Handicapped Children. pp. 3-25. Charles C Thomas, Springfield, IL.

Murray, M. A. 1959. Needs of parents of mentally retarded children. Am. J. Ment. Def. 63(6):1084-1099.

National Association for Retarded Citizens. 1974. Avenues to Change. National Association for Retarded Citizens, Arlington, TX.

National Association for Retarded Citizens. 1978. The Partnership. How to Make it Work. National Association for Retarded Citizens, Arlington, TX.

Nebraska Association for Retarded Citizens. 1974. Pilot parents defined. Focus, September.

Olshansky, S. 1966. Parent responses to a mentally defective child. Ment. Retard. 4:21-23.

Pelletier, K. R. 1977. Mind as Healer, Mind as Slayer. Dell Publishing Co., New York.

Perls, F. S. 1973. The Gestalt Approach and Eye Witness Therapy. Science and Behavior Books, Palo Alto, CA.

Polster, E., and Polster, M. 1973. Gestalt Therapy Integrated. Vintage Books, New York.

Roos, P. 1963. Psychological counseling with parents of retarded children. Ment. Retard. 1:345-350.

Roos, P. 1970. Parent organizations. In: J. Wortis (ed.), Mental Retardation, An Annual Review, II. Grune & Stratton, New York.

Roos, P., 1975. Parents and families of the mentally retarded. In: J. M. Kauffman and J. S. Payne (eds.), Mental Retardation: Introduction and Personal Perspectives. Charles E. Merrill, New York.

Roos, P. 1976. Action implications of the developmental model. In: Symposium on Early Intervention: Steps in the Prevention of Developmental Handicaps. Parsons State Hospital and Training Center, Parsons, KS.

Roos, P. 1977a. Parents of mentally retarded persons. Int. J. Ment. Health 6(1):3-20.

Roos, P. 1977b. NARC view of parent involvement: A parent's view of what public education should accomplish. Educ. Train. Ment. Retard. 12(4).

Roos, P. 1978. Parents of mentally retarded children: Misunderstood and mistreated. In: A. P. Turnbull and H. R. Turnbull (eds.), Parents Speak Out: Views from the Other Side of the Two Way Mirror. Charles E. Merrill, New York.

Satir, V. 1972. Peoplemaking. Science and Behavior Books, Inc., Palo Alto, CA.

Schild, S. 1964. Counseling with parents of retarded children living at home. Social Work January:86-91.

Schultz, J. 1953. Das Autogene Training. Geoerg Thieme, Stuttgart.

Shultz, J., and Luthe, W. 1959. Autogenic Training: A Psychophysiologic Approach in Psychotherapy. Grune & Stratton, New York.

Selye, H. 1974. Stress Without Distress. J. B. Lippincott Company, Philadelphia.

Shearer, D. E., and Shearer, M. S. 1976. The portage project: A model for early childhood intervention. In: T. D. Tjossem (ed.), Intervention Strategies for High Risk Infants and Young Children. University Park Press, Baltimore.

Spiegle, H., and Spiegle, D. 1978. Trance and Treatment: Clinical Uses of Hypnosis. Basic Books, New York.

Sternlight, M., and Sullivan, I. 1974. Group counseling with parents of the MR: Leadership selection and functioning. Ment. Retard. 12(5):11–13.

Turnbull, A. P., and Turnbull, H. R. (eds.) 1978. Parents Speak Out: Views from the Other Side of the Two Way Mirror. Charles E. Merrill, New York.

Wahler, R. G. 1969. Setting generality: Some specific and general effects of child behavior therapy, J. Appl. Behav. Anal. 4:239–246.

Wildman, P. R., 1965. A parent education program for parents of mentally retarded children. Ment. Retard. 3:17–19.

Wittenmeyer, J. J., and Nesbitt, N. J. 1971. Parent helper service, a self-help program for ARCs. Paper presented at meeting of American Association on Mental Deficiency. June, Houston.

Wolfensberger, W. 1967. Counseling the parents of the retarded. In: A. A. Baumeister (ed.), Mental Retardation: Appraisal, Education, and Rehabilitation. Aldine, Chicago.

Wolpe, J. 1958. Psychotherapy by Reciprocal Inhibition. Stanford University Press. Stanford, CA.

Chapter 4

The Effects of Law Reform on the Mental Health of Retarded Citizens and Their Families

H. Rutherford Turnbull, III

It is often useful to discuss this topic and others like it by referring to data-based research and then identifying some implications of the research for various programs or policies. In this chapter, however, I wish to bring a different perspective to the topic than a clinician might.

I am a lawyer whose 13-year-old son is low-moderately mentally retarded. As an attorney, I have been a consultant to national, state, and local mental health, mental retardation, and special education agencies. It is from the perspective of a father-attorney that I wish to speculate about the legal changes on retarded citizens' mental health and the mental health of their families.

Lest my speculation be interpreted as calling for a slowdown or retrenchment in the movement to bring retarded citizens to fuller citizenship by establishing and enforcing their basic rights, let me disclaim any such intent or effect. Instead, let me say that my sole purpose is to stimulate research and thought about the effect of recent law reform on retarded people and their families.

THE PRESIDENT'S COMMISSION ON MENTAL HEALTH REPORT

It may be useful to begin by reviewing the 1978 Report of the President's Commission on Mental Health, particularly its conclusions concerning retarded people and their families. The report points out the obvious: the effect of a mentally retarded child on his or her parents is to exacerbate their existential anxieties. The obvious, however, frequently is overlooked. This point commands particular attention if we are to think profitably about the law's effects on retarded people and their parents. Recent law reform establishing and enforcing retarded citizens' rights has indeed had the same effect the child has: it has exacerbated the parents' existential concerns. One might ask whether this is a good, benign, or bad result, or simply an inevitable one, and whether, without regard to how we characterize the result, there might have been ways to mitigate any bad results. These are issues that mental health professionals should address.

The report points out that mentally retarded people can suffer from mental illness and need treatment for it but that treatment rarely is available. Mental health systems pay inadequate attention to the mental health needs of retarded people; mental health services are not easily accessible to retarded people, and such services frequently are inappropriate to retarded people's needs even when they are available. The causes of these shortcomings are the tendency among some professionals and many funding agencies to confuse mental retardation and mental illness and the failure of mental health training systems to train mental health professionals to work with retarded people.

The report also points out that parents are a vital resource for a retarded person, that parents often are mishandled by mental health and mental retardation professionals (they are miscast as emotionally disturbed when they react to their child's disability, their "chronic sorrow" is characterized as psychopathologic, and their sometimes militant demands for services are called misplaced hostility). Indeed, said the commission, parents' fortitude and dedication to their children and their efforts to secure services for their children are only belatedly being recognized, yet parents still face hard and disturbing prospects: their retarded children often lack mental health services, sometimes they are institutionalized because appropriate community facilities do not exist, and, more often than not, retarded residents of state mental health facilities are the lowest claimants for mental health services and care.

THE ORIGIN OF MENTAL
RETARDATION LAW: CHILDREN'S RIGHTS CASES

Recent case law affecting mentally retarded people has its origins in the original abortion cases—*Doe v. Wade* (1973) and *Doe v. Bolton*

(1973). Briefly stated, the Supreme Court recognized in those cases that an adult woman has a right to an abortion because the Constitution creates a zone of privacy into which the state may not intrude. In later cases—*Planned Parenthood v. Danforth* (1976) and *Bellotti v. Baird* (1979)—the Supreme Court held that a minor may obtain an abortion without having to secure her parents' prior approval. The Court acknowledged that the minor has a right to privacy, that the right is independent of her parents' right to control her, and that the state may not condition her right to an abortion on her parents' approval. It also recognized that a minor and her parents have concurrent interests, namely to maintain as much family integrity and unity as possible. The Court candidly acknowledged that the independent rights of the minor and the concurrent rights of the minor and her parents create a potential for conflict between those interests. Indeed, the Court's efforts in Danforth and Bellotti were directed at balancing the parents' and child's interests, without diminishing the minor's independent constitutional interests in privacy and the independent right to make an abortion decision.

THE EFFECTS OF THE CHILDREN'S RIGHTS CASES ON MENTALLY RETARDED PEOPLE AND THEIR FAMILIES

The Supreme Court's decision in Danforth was to prove critical in its 1979 decision, *Parham v. J. R. and J. L.* In that case, the issue was whether a minor is entitled to judicial review of his or her parents' decision to place him or her in a state mental health or mental retardation facility. The Court held that although judicial review could be required by state law, it was not required by the Constitution, which mandates only a "neutral" review of the institutionalization decision. Such a review can be accomplished by an independent mental health professional.

The Court's reasoning is important and clearly relies on its assumptions in Danforth. In Parham, the Court recognized the potential for conflict between the independent rights of the minor (the rights to be free from erroneous placement in institutions and from erroneous labeling as "retarded" or "emotionally disturbed" as a consequence of institutionalization) and of the parents (to control and raise their children without undue state interference). The Court did not assume that there will be a conflict in every case; it said only that the child's independent rights require a neutral review of the institutionalization decision, a bare minimum of due process. The Court's effort clearly was directed at harmonizing the minor's and the parents' rights; the effort of law, indeed of social policy, in the

Court's view should be directed at maintaining family integrity and unity. When the rights cannot be harmonized, however, the minor's independent rights—based on his or her rights to freedom from mistaken judgments (much like a minor's rights to freedom from the mistaken judgment of the state or her parents in the abortion cases)—must prevail.

By recognizing that there are analogies between the minor's rights to abortions (Danforth) and freedom from erroneous institutionalization, the Parham Court runs at least three risks. First, it runs the risk of attenuating the family ties between mentally retarded children and their families. Whether constitutionally required or not, the neutral review of the institutionalization decision may drive a wedge between children and their families, especially at a time when the relationship is strained. Interestingly, the neutral review requirement reflects a different view than the President's Commission; the Constitution, as the Court interprets it, may prevent families from performing the services that the commission recognizes they must perform, namely to care for and obtain services for their retarded children. It is not that the Court is unaware of the families' efforts to care for and obtain services, but rather that the Constitution requires institutional care and services be given only under reviewed conditions.

The second risk is that Parham will give renewed credence to the notion that mentally retarded people, whatever their age, are "permanent children." True, the case itself involved only minors, but the analogies on which the decision rested—Danforth analogies—were established in children's rights cases. It would not be farfetched for the Court to accept an argument that all retarded people should be given the "protection" of Parham whenever their liberties are at issue because they are mentally incapable of asserting their own rights and are "children" in a developmental sense. This risk, however minimal, must be resisted because it flies in the face of the developmental model and the normalization principle.

Third, the Parham decision creates a risk of adding to the confusion concerning which legal or social principles should apply to the relationships between children and families. The Court was unclear whether Parham was a "kid lib" case (freeing children or other dependent citizens from legal disabilities by granting them the right to treatment (*Wyatt v. Stickney*, 1972), protecting them from unnecessary involuntary sterilization (*Relf v. Weinberg*, 1974), or granting them the right to education (*PARC v. Commonwealth of Pennsylvania*, 1972)), a "kid saver" case (protecting children from the potentially adverse consequences of decisions made by others (Danforth (1976)), or a *parens patriae* case (limiting the extent of governmental intervention into the family (*Wisconsin v. Yoder*, 1972)). Careful analysis suggests that Parham partially rejected the "kid lib" line of cases because it refused to recognize that children's liberty interests are entitled to a generous dose of due process (Teitlebaum and Ellis, 1978); by the same token, Parham asserted the traditional power of parents over children (Burt, 1979), borrowing from the "kid saver" cases and the *parens patriae* cases.

Parham nonetheless helps focus attention on some of the unanswered issues that arise from the concern with the liberty of retarded people (whether to be free of erroneous placements and labeling, as in Parham, or of legal disabilities, as in the other cases cited above). To be specific, what is the nature of liberty for retarded people? What does liberty mean to them? Does it mean something different than it means to nonretarded people? Something different than it means to mentally ill people?

The liberty that the Constitution protects necessarily includes the right to make choices (for example, to have an abortion or not); but what is the nature of choice for retarded people? What is the role of choice for retarded people? What does "having a choice" mean to retarded people? Does it mean something different than it means to nonhandicapped people? To mentally ill people?

For nonhandicapped people, being free (having liberty) and having a choice are essential ingredients to good mental health. Indeed, free choice is important in sustaining life and hope in persons of any age, and the special need for the experience of freedom, within certain limits, is a prerequisite for growth and development, especially in the young.

The principles of liberty and choice and their important role in mental health, not to mention constitutional law, are necessarily related to another important relevant legal doctrine, one that appears in the children's rights law as well as in mental health and mental retardation law, namely "least restriction."

As has been noted with respect to the doctrine of least restriction and freedom of choice, the ultimate benefit from providing the least restrictive appropriate alternative should lie in assuring to the retarded people a feeling of having greater control over their lives (AAMD, 1981). This sense of control or dominance has manifestations that have been linked to mental health and even survival.

Having choice, however, is not necessarily the same thing as experiencing choice. There is a complex relationship between the availability of freedom of choice and what is best for an individual. Experiencing real choice, choice within capacity, is essential to child development, and offering appropriate intellectual and practical choices is an essential component of education. The provision of choices, however, is not in and of itself an enhancing condition. The sense of control arises from meaningful choice. Thus, the provision of choices is helpful only under certain conditions.

The first of these conditions is the quantity of choice (AAMD, 1981). There is a likelihood that having too many choices can deter maturation and slow down the growth process with a lot of "shopping" behavior and failure to commit oneself to a way of life or to the tasks of life. Similarly, one would predict that many choices suddenly open to a retarded person, as in sudden deinstitutionalization or with respect to educational settings, would not be beneficial to that person's development or adjustment to the community or to school; but the opposite condition—no choices—also has been shown to be detrimental to growth, and the phenomenon of "learned helplessness" has been observed in retarded people. The absence of choice makes the person inordinately slow to learn, feel and act helpless, and fail to thrive.

A second ingredient in choice is the quality of choice. Choices may be too important or too trivial to be beneficial to an individual. Many choices that seem trivial to a competent or experienced person may give a sense of mastery to a child or retarded person. Too difficult a problem, particularly one involving poorly understood prospects, may seem overwhelming and hence does not enhance well being.

A third ingredient in choice, as noted in the AAMD volume on this topic (1981), is that there is not a perfect correlation between the choices available to people and the choices they feel they have (i.e., those that enhance one's feeling of self-control). The critical variable in mental health is more a sense of having understandable choices than the actual options.

Finally, the shaping of choices can determine behavior. Strict emphasis in schools on learning the Three R's can have a devastating consequence for retarded students, who will perceive that there is no way by which they could choose success. By the same token, education or other developmental activity that shields a child or a retarded adult from experiencing failure causes the person to lose one's sense of dominance, one's sense that voluntary choices of behavior can control what happens. Neither extreme is beneficial to a person's mental health, much less a retarded person's mental health.

There is a real need to take what is known about child development and the development of retarded people, as summarized above,
and recognize that liberty implicates another important notion,
namely that of responsibility.

One is not accustomed these days to hearing someone say that
"rights imply duties" or that "privilege implies responsibility." Indeed, I have yet to read a case outside the area of criminal law, torts,
or contracts in which a court grants rights to retarded people and
also addresses their responsibilities. Usually, retarded people's
rights evoke duties only on the part of others, namely caregivers (institutional, parental, educational, etc.).

It is critical that we address the rights-responsibilities issue in
light of what is known about development, for it seems clear that
mental health depends on having both liberty and choices and on the
imposition of consequences for the exercise of liberty and choice;
that is, a mentally sound person is one who has or feels he or she has
liberty and choice and who also appreciates the consequences of exer-
cising those rights, that he or she has responsibilities to both himself
or herself and others as a result of his or her exercise of rights.

What, then, are the responsibilities that accompany or should
accompany the rights that retarded people have been granted
through recent law reform? What responsibilities should or can a
retarded child or adult be asked to assume?

Mental health considerations aside, one might inquire whether a
retarded person should be asked to be responsible. It is perfectly
clear that this must be done, for failure to impose responsibilities
where there are rights flies in the face of not only the developmental
model but also the normalization principle (at the very least, it is
hypocritical about both principles). Moreover, it is a subtle way of
saying that we do not really believe that adult retarded people—or at
least some of them—are competent; it is a way of *de facto* rebutting
the legal presumption in favor of competence. One result of our turning our backs on the presumption of competence is to focus on a person's disability, not on his or her ability. This in turn may make it
easier for us and others to be persuaded that retarded people should
be easily—and in most cases—adjudicated incompetent or committed to institutional care.

To require retarded people to be responsible in the exercise of
their rights may cause us some mental health problems of our own.
First, it may require us to adjust our natural protectionistic instincts about our retarded children or retarded clients. We quite
properly recognize that they need special protection, over and above

what we accord to our nonretarded children and clients; but we may be unwilling to pay the price of surrendering our protection in order for them to have both rights and concomitant responsibilities.

Second, to require retarded children and adults to be responsible for the consequences of their rights is to be quite out of sync with how the present generation of young people (those aged 15 to 30) were raised; our permissiveness in child rearing affects our very notion of the relationship of rights and responsibilities, for we tend to say that our children should have the rights but not the accompanying responsibilities.

Nonetheless, out of consideration of the mental health needs of retarded people, we must be willing to impose responsibilities if we grant rights. We will do them a great disservice if we fail to impose responsibilities when we grant rights. The problem that the law has failed to address is, what are the responsibilities of retarded people that their freedom and free choice entail? This question is one of the more important ones that we must consider in the next several years.

LIBERTY, CHOICE, AND CONSENT

When a retarded adult gives consent to something, he or she exercises liberty and makes choices. The capacity to consent is therefore an important matter for consideration, especially as it relates to a person's mental health and the role of choice and liberty in mental health.

Every adult, retarded or not, is legally presumed to be competent; only upon an adjudication of incompetence and the appointment of a guardian is that presumption set aside. In fact, however, the presumption of competence does not attach to many retarded adults; too many people presume that the retarded adult is incompetent or at least not as competent as nonhandicapped people. When the *de jure* and *de facto* presumptions are at odds, any hesitation on our part to consider imposing responsibilities as the trade-off for rights of a retarded person simply feeds into the *de facto* presumption, underscoring the prejudice that retarded people are incompetent.

Indeed, even the *de jure* presumption of competence is troublesome, for it can imply that there is either total competence or no competence at all. In some people's minds, adult retarded people are wholly incompetent; such people do not even consider the fact that a retarded adult can be partially competent or that his or her competence may be situationally specific. Again, any hesitation on our part to consider asking that a retarded person be responsible for his actions—even in a limited way—underscores the notion that retardation is wholly incapacitating.

GUARDIANSHIP AND INCOMPETENCE

Although guardianship properly tailored to the capacity of the retarded adult and imposed only after extensive due process safeguards have been observed is seen by some as a right of a retarded adult, and although limited guardianship is increasingly available at law in many states, there is a strong reluctance on the part of the parents of mentally retarded people to have their adult retarded child adjudicated imcompetent (Turnbull, 1979). One cannot help but note the irony: parents who generally favor creating rights for retarded children hesitate to assert one of their children's rights. Surely this is an existential issue for parents, one that can be highly dilemma creating and anxiety producing.

Parents fail to exercise the right of guardianship on behalf of their retarded adult child for several reasons, many of which may relate to how parents feel about their children and the law (Turnbull, 1979).

1. They fear that they will lose control of their child if they have been giving legally questionable consent to services and think they have no legal or practical needs for legal guardianship of their child. I use the word *control* in both its affirmative and its negative sense; affirmative in the sense that control enables a person to protect those of one's own flesh, and negative in the sense that control entitles one to maneuver another person.
2. There are costs involved in guardianship—attorneys, expert witnesses, and even the psychic cost that any litigation extracts. Judicial procedures are traumatic; one does not need to represent many people in a commitment or guardianship hearing to understand that trauma is part of litigation, especially if it involves one's own child.
3. Parents and the professionals on whom they rely are unclear about who is an appropriate "candidate" for guardianship. They are especially uncertain whether the retarded person merits limited guardianship and how the guardianship should be limited.
4. They hesistate to use guardianship because it entails a formal recognition that their child is incompetent, a recognition that

they shy away from because it may add injury to their already wounded concepts of themselves and their child.

5. Finally, they recognize the need for guardianship after they die, but would rather have guardianship postponed than deal with it presently.

Mental health professionals working with parents of retarded children or treating their emotional disabilities must recognize that parents are likely to be highly anxious about guardianship for their retarded adult children, that these types of reactions are valid, and that they must be addressed. The professionals also must come to grips with the ineluctable fact that without formal adjudication and appointment of a guardian, there may be important unresolved questions about the legal effectiveness of the retarded person's consent; persons dealing with the retarded adult, including mental retardation and mental health professionals themselves, will be in a state of anxiety concerning the retarded person's consent, asking themselves, "When will consent be challenged, by whom, and why?" To take one very dramatic example, treatment professionals may legitimately be anxious over whether the retarded person's consent to medical procedures—especially such optional surgery as tendon lengthening, cosmetic repair or, even more dramatically, sterilization—is legally effective or not. In some cases, mental health or other professionals themselves raise the concerns about guardianship; in a sense, they trigger the parents' anxiety and have a special duty to treat it.

Often because state law does not allow families to consent for retarded adult members without an adjudication of incompetence and sometimes because treatment professionals and their legal counsel wish to resolve all legal and other doubts about the effectiveness of consent by a nonadjudicated adult retarded person by having him or her adjudicated to be incompetent, there is an almost irresistible impulse toward adjudication. Given that the legal procedures themselves can be traumatic and the results can be even more traumatic for the retarded person if he or she is found incompetent and for the parents if they or someone in whom they have great faith are not appointed to be the guardian, one must acknowledge that legal adjudication and guardianship may have the effect of increasing the retarded person's sense of helplessness and of "divorcing" himself or herself from his or her parents, of relieving them of any sense of responsibility, or of submerging their natural protective instincts to the rather cold and formalistic legal requirements for effective consent. More than that, guardianship entails a loss of rights by the retarded person and a transfer of them to a third party, the guardian. The transfer may be debilitating both legally (the loss of legal freedom and the right to choose) and otherwise (the loss of the sense of dominance).

PLACEMENT AND COMPETENCE

One origin of the legal rights of retarded people is the law granting rights to minors, and Parham was linked to the minors' rights cases involving abortion. The Parham case, although it may satisfy the constitutional interests of retarded children in not being erroneously placed or labeled, is another example of the effect that mental retardation law has in "divorcing" parents from their retarded minor children and in interposing a legal obstacle between the parents' natural instincts to provide treatment for their child and to achieve somewhat more normalized lives for themselves. Boggs (1978) has argued that parents of retarded children have the right to normalization. In recognizing the concurrent interests of parents and retarded children and that the child's independent interests must prevail (because of the Constitution) over the parent's rights, the Court not only may have attenuated the natural instincts of parents toward their children but also have made it legally more difficult for parents to voluntarily admit their children to a residential facility.

THE EFFECT OF THE GUARDIANSHIP AND
PLACEMENT LAW ON THE MENTAL HEALTH
OF MENTALLY RETARDED PEOPLE AND THEIR FAMILIES

Research must be undertaken to document the effects of law reform on retarded people and their families, if not just to help them cope with the effects but also to point the way to how law can be more useful to retarded people and their families. With respect to retarded people themselves, the issue is how to minimize some of the traumatic effects of being a respondent in a guardianship or placement case. What might those effects be? If they are adjudicated incompetent, for example, their rights are transferred to their guardians; in a very real sense, their liberty and freedom of choice are taken away. Yet we know that liberty and freedom of choice are important ingredients of sound mental health; at least, a person's belief that he has liberty and freedom of choice are important ingredients. In the deprivation of rights, have we also put his mental health at greater risk? Even after adjudication, is there enough latitude—

practically, not legally—for the guardian to allow his or her ward to experience some liberty and choice?

The loss of liberty may have other nonlegal consequences for the retarded person. One can begin to think about a person without rights learning to be dependent. The phenomenon of learned dependency, learned helplessness is not unknown, and those who have the behavior of learned dependency must experience adverse effects (AAMD, 1981). The primary effects are that they fail to thrive and they lose hope; those consequences have very real implications for sound mental health. Liberty and choice are important ingredients of a person's mental health; at the very least, the person's belief that he has liberty and can exercise some choice are important, whether in fact he can or not. In depriving retarded people of their rights through guardianship, judicially reviewed parental placement, or commitment, action is being taken that may impair their sense of self. That is an issue to which the mental health profession needs to address itself seriously.

Also with respect to retarded people, what is the effect on their mental health of participation in court or other safeguard proceedings to adjudicate them incompetent or to rule on the appropriateness of placement outside their parents' home? Do they see themselves as chessboards on which others are the real players (parents, treatment professionals, lawyers, and judges)? If they see that they are mere agents of others' maneuverings, is their self-concept apt to be injured and emotional stability jeopardized? Is their sense of dependency and helplessness increased? Is their mental health put at risk? Do they see that they are "victims" of their rights? Do they think that although having legal rights dignifies them and proclaims them worthy of legal protection, they would just as well forego their rights in order to spare themselves the trauma of being the focal point of legal jousting? Do they see themselves as people who are forced by the logic of the Constitution to be alienated, even if only briefly, from their families? Or do they even have the capacity to think on these terms? These are questions that deserve attention.

Another question that deserves attention is, after we interpose legal hurdles and then take away the rights, how much residual freedom, how much residual choice can we give (not necessarily legally but practically) to the person who is under guardianship, has been involuntarily commited, or has been voluntarily placed? Even after a person's rights are taken away, what can be done to prevent or ameliorate his or her sense of deprivation, sense of helplessness, feelings of dependency?

With respect to the retarded person's family, one can postulate some of their reactions to legal requirements that, as in the case of guardianship and placement, interpose the Constitution between their child and their protective (or less worthy) instincts. They may feel anger that someone would question their motives and decisions; that kind of questioning is inevitable in guardianship and placement hearings. They may feel frustrated on at least two accounts. First, that legal proceedings, for which they sometimes do not see the need, cost them money, time, and anxiety, and may even result in outcomes that they do not want (for example, the child is adjudicated competent or is not allowed to be placed in the institution). Second, they may feel frustrated that they were forced to engage in proceedings that simply confirmed their own instincts and decisions (i.e., the outcome is the one they sought).

They may in fact express their frustrations by rejecting law reform in part or altogether, forgetting that the law grants rights to their retarded child, dignifying him or her and thus reflecting well on them. Or they may become resigned to the legal process, acknowledging that they are powerless to influence it. They may question the worth of any system that causes further alienation of the governed from their government, especially if it impairs their own sense of dominance over their children's lives. Or they may acknowledge that, in any event, the law's price on their relationship with their child is worth paying, for the child's sake and for others' as well.

Finally, they may welcome the legal process because it affirms that their child has rights and because it is a neutral arbiter that resolves whose rights should prevail if there is a conflict of interests. They also may recognize their loss of control, however; they may see some evidence in these proceedings of their child's failure (he or she has been sent to an institution) and they may see some evidence of themselves as failures: "We are the parents of a child who has been institutionalized." They may be especially troubled that they will share the stigma (indeed, parents do share the stigma of their handicapped child), but the stigma may be increased by institutionalization or commitment. Indeed, there may be in their minds a welcome or unwelcome shift of responsibility from themselves to the state because the state has acted to remove or has at least interposed a legal objection between them and their child.

CONCLUSION: A ROLE FOR THE MENTAL HEALTH PROFESSION

An important effect of mental health law, especially when it is seen as derived from "children's rights" law, is to interpose legal considerations between the natural relationships of parents to children, especially of parents to their mentally retarded children.

Many parents of mentally retarded children are not wholly and unquestionably free from suspicion with respect to their motives and actions concerning their children; but I have yet to be satisfied that parents of mentally retarded children are inherently untrustworthy; indeed, my experience has persuaded me that parents are loyal, steadfast, and trustworthy allies of and advocates for their children.

Thus, I cannot help but be concerned about the effects on parents and mentally retarded people of law that interposes barriers between parents and children (Turnbull and Turnbull, 1978). As one who recognizes, along with the President's Commission on Mental Health, that mental retardation is a problem that affects entire families, that families have been an important source of aid for mentally retarded people, that the mental health profession is not performing at an acceptable standard in treating the emotional needs of the parents of mentally retarded people and retarded people themselves, and that the emotional effects of guardianship and placement hearings may be adverse for the retarded person as well as the family, I make the following concluding observations.

There is a crucial need for more research and better treatment of the emotional needs of retarded people and their families (especially as those needs are highlighted by the guardianship or placement hearings). A duty of mental health and mental retardation professionals is to resort to guardianship and institutional placement only as a last resort and then only in accordance with the principle of least restriction so that retarded people preserve, if only for their mental health needs, as much liberty and freedom of choice as possible. Finally, incompetency and placement hearings invariably estrange retarded people from their families and thereby impose additional emotional burdens. Whether good law or bad, the law's consequences for the mental health of retarded people and their families must soon be addressed by the mental health profession.

REFERENCES

American Association on Mental Deficiency. 1981. The Least Restrictive Alternative: Principles and Practices. Washington, DC.
Bellotti v. Baird. 1979. US 47 USLW 4969.
Burt, R. 1979. The Constitution of the Family. The Supreme Court Review, University of Chicago Law School, Chicago.
Doe v. Bolton. 1973. 410 US 179.
Parham v. J. R. and J. L. 1979. 442 US 584.
Pennsylvania Association for Retarded Citizens v. Commonwealth of Pennsylvania. 1972. 343 F. Suppl. 279, ED Pa.

Planned Parenthood v. Danforth. 1976. 428 US 52.

Relf v. Weinberg. 1974. 372 F. Suppl. 1196 DDC.

Roe v. Wade. 1973. 410 US 13.

Teitlebaum, I., and Ellis, J. 1978. The liberty interest of children. Family Law Q. 12:153.

Turnbull, H. R. 1979. Law and the mentally retarded citizen. Syracuse Law Rev. 30:1093.

Turnbull, A., and Turnbull, H. R., (eds.). 1978. Parents Speak Out: Views from the Other Side of the Two-Way Mirror. Charles E. Merrill, Columbus, Ohio.

Wisconsin v. Yoder. 1972. 406 US 205.

Wyatt v. Stickney. 1974. 344 F. Suppl. 387.

PART II

TREATMENT AND MANAGEMENT CONSIDERATIONS

Chapter **5**

Bridging the Gap through Individual Counseling and Psychotherapy with Mentally Retarded People

Richard L. Rubin

MODERN PRINCIPLES AND DEFINITIONS AS THE BRIDGE

The gaps often appear as chasms in bringing mental health services to mentally retarded people. Efforts to help mental health problems through therapy and counseling frequently flounder between the two service systems and different approaches in educational and medical models. In mental retardation programs, the practice of counseling is often acceptable, but not psychotherapy. Many parents and mental retardation professionals view psychotherapy with unrealistic and archaic attitudes of menace or mystery. Many psychotherapists consider counseling of the mentally retarded as an inferior form of practice and neglect retarded people themselves out of exaggerated pessimism and ignorance. Dybawd (1970) compared these assumptions that psychotherapy could not benefit retarded people with earlier erroneous judgments about their lack of educability.

The girders of a bridge can be built from modern mental health approaches and mental retardation normalization principles. Mental health disorders can be defined as problems in thoughts or emotions that have sufficient severity or duration to cause significant distress or problem behavior. In retarded people, such problems must be distinguished from the cognitive, adaptive, and developmental deficits of their primary handicap. A mental health problem in a mentally retarded person can be transient and reversible, not necessarily a permanent aspect of the retardation. Too often in the past a disorder in thoughts or emotions that led to behavior problems was managed by efforts at placement rather than temporary treatment with goals of improved functioning. When the differences are clearly defined, concurrent mental health and mental retardation services are compatible. Mental health disorders can be helped by psychotherapy or counseling/therapy as an addition to the other valuable services required by retarded people and their families, such as education, training, and casework. Similarly, individual counseling/therapy has value in addition to other mental health treatments such as group therapy, psychotropic medicine, and hospital care.

The gap between mental retardation counselors and mental health psychotherapists can be bridged by emphasizing the common areas of agreement and practice. Sufficient consensus exists in the major recent literature reviews from both psychotherapy and counseling perspectives to derive a working definition of *counseling/ therapy* (Jakab, 1970; Katz, 1972; LaVietes, 1978; Menolascino, 1970, 1971, 1977; Robinson and Robinson, 1976; Steward, 1978; Szymanski, 1980). Counseling-therapy consists of a professionally trained practitioner who uses a systematic method and a cooperative relationship to achieve goals of change in another person's emotions, thoughts, or behavior. Differing therapy approaches and psychologic theories fit under this definition. The literature reviews tend to not advocate any particular viewpoint, but rather describe benefits observed from multiple forms of clinical experience. Conventional psychiatric and psychologic practitioners commonly divide individual approaches into psychodynamic psychotherapy, supportive psychotherapy, and counseling. A psychodynamic approach may use psychoanalytic, ego psychology, object relations, or interpersonal theories and techniques such as Gestalt, and focuses on changing abnormalities within the individual's personality that cause problems in effective living and subjective distress. Supportive therapy attempts to strengthen a person's existing personality skills for managing life problems. In counseling, more direction and practice are provided in solving living problems, accomplishing social tasks, and developing coping skills. These are methods that fit a modern counseling/therapy definition and are applicable to a modern definition of mental health problems that focuses on the individual's thoughts and emotions, as distinguished from education and training modalities for learning and adaptive problems.

Which retarded people can benefit from counseling/therapy? Four considerations (Figure 5.1) are: 1) intellectual aptitude; 2) personality capacity for relationships; 3) organic brain integrity; and 4) communication skills. First, change through counseling/therapy depends on learning. The mildly retarded definitely have sufficient aptitude for all approaches. When the ability to learn drops into the moderate range, however, the potential for counseling/therapy benefit diminishes. Family or social group management training and behavior therapy are usually more effective.

Second, because the person needs to engage in a working relationship for counseling/therapy to be effective, sufficient capacity for interpersonal relating is necessary. This excludes retarded persons who are psychotic and accordingly have grossly disturbed object relations. However, after symptom reduction has been obtained with psychotropic medications and the psychosis is in remission, the counseling/therapy will be effective. Similar considerations apply to retarded people who have suffered extensive early childhood emotional trauma or deprivation of important relationships, such as through parent abuse or institutional neglect. These individuals are often incapable of establishing a working therapeutic relationship. Such deficits in personality development are commonly mistaken for

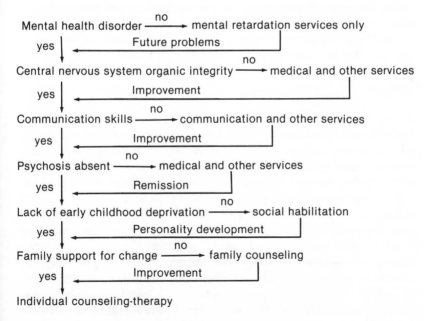

Figure 5.1   Criteria for selecting counseling-therapy patients.

retardation handicap problems, and their implications for counseling/therapy are overlooked.

Third, effects of organic brain impairment commonly extend beyond retardation to cause problems in attention, integration of emotions and thoughts, and response capacity that would interfere with the counseling/therapy process. These deficits occur along a spectrum of severity and present relative rather than absolute contraindications to counseling/therapy. Similarly, communication skills must be sufficiently effective to manage complex problems and flexible to allow change. Severe language disorders at worst prevent counseling/therapy, and at best require development of alternative communication modes. In a climate of limited mental health services for the retarded in public facilities and the significant cost of private treatment, these limiting characteristics must be considered seriously.

Additional criteria for applying counseling/therapy to retarded people involve the family and social living circumstances. The family needs to support and promote mental health change; this can be prevented by attitudes of overprotection, overemphasis on a fixed handicap, or hostile and neglectful parents. Family living in which the parents and habilitation program foster goals of development, normalization, and maximizing independence provides the best milieu for counseling/therapy. It is a normalizing point of view, consistent with community living goals, to consider that a retarded person can have a temporary mental health problem that can be treated and improve like anyone else.

SELECTION OF COUNSELING/THERAPY METHOD

The choice among psychodynamic therapy, supportive therapy, and counseling depends on the type of mental illness needing treatment, the retarded person's capacities, and decisions about feasible and desirable goals. For example, an internalized anxiety (neurotic) disorder needs a dynamic therapy approach, whereas a conduct or reactive disorder usually improves with supportive therapy or counseling. Affective disorders, particularly forms of depression, are commonly seen. Whether neurotransmitter abnormalities, early deprivation experiences, chronic social or parental rejection, or acute losses are contributory, counseling/therapy is useful. Generally, the more chronic and fixed the depression, the less psychotherapy is feasible, and counseling/therapy is more useful. Similarly, lower intelligence, relating strengths, and impaired organic integrity require more directive counseling. The degree of dependency as a personality trait must be considered. Retarded people are forced by their handicap into extended dependent realtionships. If present to a lesser degree, this can facilitate willingness to work with a dynamic therapist. If the dependency is more rigidly fixed and extensive, directive counseling is a better choice. The choice among counseling/therapy approaches is not clear-cut, and all therapy courses include dynamic, supportive, and directive elements. The differences are in relative emphasis and depend on multiple factors (Figure 5.2).

Although the overall purpose of these counseling/therapy methods is similar with the retarded to any person's mental health problems, certain differences influence the choice of goals and method. In considering goals for counseling/therapy of a mental health disorder, the retardation developmental level must be considered as the baseline to measure improvement, rather than a normal, nonretarded level. The benefits from counseling/therapy should not be expected to extend beyond the level of underlying adaptive handicap. This has been called the "postulate of limited goals" (Jakab, 1970). The mental health treatment goals influence the choice of counseling/therapy method. As in all people, personality functioning and growth in the retarded depend on an interplay of physical brain ability, internal (in-

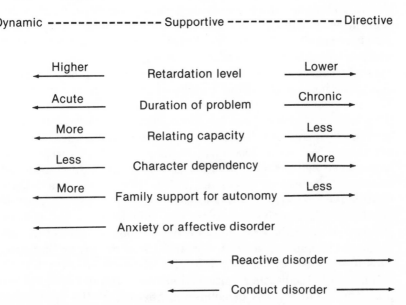

Figure 5.2   Criteria for selecting counseling-therapy methods.

trapsychic) psychologic functions, family relationships, and social experiences. Given a sufficient level of physical brain integrity, the counselor/therapist decides where emotional trauma, distortions, or deficient experiences have occurred in the other three areas and what changes may be achieved through treatment. Dynamic psychotherapy approaches help intrapsychic problems, such as immature and maladaptive defenses. Traumatic or deficient parent relationships often need dynamic or supportive therapy with goals of improving inappropriate and distressing internal reactions and providing a corrective relationship. Disorders from adverse social experiences need a supportive therapy or counseling approach to develop compensatory personality strengths and practical skills.

TECHNIQUE

In general, counseling/therapy techniques with retarded people are similar to conventional approaches with any patient and do not need extensively different methods. Techniques for counseling/therapy cannot be reduced to explicit steps that fit in all cases. The process in each case is individual and consists of a counselor/therapist applying knowledge through the vehicle of his or her own personality in a fluid relationship with a fragile and impaired person. Therefore, discussion of technique can only provide general guidelines. Appropriate adaptations and modifications of common counseling/therapy methods should begin with clarifying the person's developmental level. In addition to intellectual and adaptive levels, the counselor/therapist's dynamic framework for emotional and social development is applicable, whether psychosocial, psychosexual, object relations, etc. These develomental data are used to choose therapy techniques appropriate for that level, not the chronologic age. Therapy obstacles attributed to the retarded, such as problems in abstract thinking, impulse control, self-reflection, attention, and social awareness, can be managed well if compared to characteristics of all children and adolescents in treatment (LaVietes, 1978). Because of these deficits, more active executive skills are needed in the initial phase of counseling/therapy. The active promotion of a safe, low-key, and pleasant atmosphere must be provided in order to counter fears of punishment, abandonment, or confusion regarding the presenting problems. The counselor/therapist must also take more intiative in structuring and facilitating interaction and communicating the procedures and process of counseling/therapy at the appropriate level of intellectual and interpersonal development. Confidentiality rules require adequate explanation to be effective. Guidance toward the goals requires more therapist direction.

In addition to factors of retardation and developmental level, the techniques chosen for working with problems will depend on the type of counseling/therapy method. A dynamic psychotherapy approach can use techniques ranging from projective, expressive play with children to verbal interaction with mildly handicapped adolescents and adults. In general, dynamic therapy with the retarded, while still working with material about defensive operations and transference, should focus more on immediate life experiences rather than historical review. Self-reflection occurs better with fresh observations and reactions than with recall. In a psychodynamic approach, excessive dependency is a common transference problem. Symptoms and defenses related to this trait should not be confused with diminished functioning from the primary handicap. Similarly, the frequent experience of social failure and rejection can inhibit therapeutic trust and verbal sharing of problems at the initiation of treatment (Szymanski, 1980). Therefore, the therapist may need to begin with a supportive approach and progress to dynamic methods when sufficient ego strengths are developed.

Supportive psychotherapy and counseling approaches differ with the retarded in greater use of concrete demonstration rather than verbal techniques. Play modeling, role playing, and corrective practice are used and adapted to the level of needs and goals, whether child, adolescent, or adult. These two methods differ in their content; psychotherapy focuses on internal personality strengths and counseling on practical living problems. In supportive psychotherapy, modeling and role playing can be used to label emotions, clarify psychologic processes, and illustrate more adaptive defenses. In counseling, the content would consist of demonstrating and practicing interpersonal skills through more directive techniques.

The duration and frequency of sessions may be adjusted to suit retarded people. Shorter sessions, such as ½ hour, are useful when the patient may be overwhelmed by anxiety. This occurs in those with fragile integrity due to either psychologic or organic weaknesses. It also occurs in mildly retarded children who are fearful in the early stages of counseling/therapy. Beginning with ½-hour sessions two or three times a week helps pace the development of a secure working relationship. When anxiety over being with the therapist diminishes and continuity between sessions occurs, the schedule can be changed to hourly sessions weekly to allow more thorough development of material and opportunity for therapeutic interventions. With moderate level or more organically impaired people, attention span and fatigue limits may require continuing shorter sessions in the directive counseling appropriate to this type of patient. The overall length of treatment expressed in sessions or months is highly variable. Often less time is spent with that group than the nonretarded in practice because of more specific, less comprehensive goals.

APPLYING COUNSELING/THERAPY IN A FAMILY AND MULTIDISCIPLINARY SETTING

Successful counseling/therapy with retarded people requires building collaboration with the family and other helping services in a comprehensive habilitation program. The retarded individual has greater emotional and practical dependency on family. The demands imposed by retardation have profound effects on the family's emotions, values, and practical resources. Problems in the family can adversely affect the retarded person as the most vulnerable member to stress. The family is dependent on multiple professional services, usually with strong involvement in a mental retardation system. Credibility and coordination are needed for their acceptance of mental health services.

The *first step,* after a diagnostic evaluation has indicated the need for individual counseling/therapy, is to schedule a few clarifying sessions with the family. These sessions should include the retarded person and significant others, such as siblings and grandparents in the home, as much as possible, as opposed to counseling with the parents separately. The topics to cover with the family should begin with the mental health professional showing respect for and gathering information to develop a liaison with the other services, such as special education, home management training, parent organizations and support groups, social casework, medical care, and financial programs.

Step two is to educate the family about distinctions between mental health disorders and problems from the mental retardation handicap. Emphasize the role of thoughts and emotions, and attempt to foster their and understanding for the inner psychologic life of the handicapped person, rather than the usual focus on surface behavior, intelligence, and social adjustment. Explain the principle that mental health problems can be ameliorated and are not always an irreversible result of retardation. Encourage recognition of family relationships with the retarded person for promoting mental health improvement and personality development.

Step three is education of the family about the counseling/therapy method indicated. Explain the definition and distinguish the process from other helping services, with particular emphasis on the therapeutic relationship and the efforts expected of the patient as the major vehicles for progress. As with other efforts to promote development, this is best viewed as an active process for the patient. Clarify differences between mental health counseling/ therapy and the multiple types of counseling by professionals in vocational, medical, educational, and other services.

Step four is to address the dynamics in the family that contribute to the patient's mental health the dynamics. A family systems evaluation approach can be useful (Serrano, 1979). Such problems may be harmful attitudes, inappropriate performance of parent roles, or distorted interaction patterns resulting from emotional stresses. Concurrent family counseling/ therapy may be indicated. Stress from critical phases in a family's evolution with a retarded child may contribute to mental health problems. These include anniversary reactions, unresolved diagnostic questions and doubts, disappointed expectations at plateaus in progress, sexual and aggressive changes at puberty, early adult separation and independence struggles, residential placement pressures, and parent aging concerns. Assistance for these problems may require collaboration with other helping services.

After completion of these four steps, individual counseling/therapy can more optimally proceed. Interference from reality needs will have been minimized, whereas credibility and accurate empathy with the family are maximized.

The use of individual counseling/therapy with the retarded and their families often requires more professional flexibility. As the mental health problems change and family events progress, changes in modality are useful, possibly to a family approach, to transition from mental health to habilitation services for social development, or to provide for individual mental health needs of other family members. Because mental retardation is a chronic condition for the person and family, with a constantly high risk for mental health problems, the mental health practitioner can maintain a long-term working relationship with the family as counselor/therapist when problems are acute, and provide continuing availability as consultant for future problems and periodic intervention.

REFERENCES

Dybwad, G. 1970. Psychiatry's role in mental retardation. In: N. Bernstein (ed.), Diminished People. Little, Brown & Co., Boston.

Jakab, I. 1970. Psychotherapy of the mentally retarded child. In: N. Bernstein (ed.), Diminished People. Little, Brown & Co., Boston.

Katz, E. (ed.), 1972. Mental Health Services for the Mentally Retarded. Charles C Thomas, Springfield, IL.

LaVietes, R. 1978. Mental retardation: Psychological treatment. In: B. Wolman et al. (ed.), Handbook of Mental Disorders in Childhood and Adolescence. Prentice-Hall, Englewood Cliffs, NJ.

Menolascino, F. (ed.). 1970. Psychiatric Approaches to Mental Retardation. Basic Books, New York.

Menolascino, F. (ed.). 1971. Psychiatric Aspects of the Diagnosis and Treatment of Mental Retardation. Special Child Publications, Seattle.

Menolascino, F. 1977. Challenges in Mental Retardation: Progressive Ideology and Services. Human Sciences Press, New York.

Robinson, N., and Robinson, H. 1976. The Mentally Retarded Child. McGraw-Hill Book Company, New York.

Serrano, A. 1979. A Child-centered family interview. In: J. Noshpitz (ed.), Basic Handbook of Child Psychiatry, Vol. I. Basic Books, New York.

Steward, J. 1978. Counseling Parents of Exceptional Children. Charles E. Merrill, Columbus.

Szymanski, L. 1980. Individual psychotherapy with retarded persons. In: L. Szymanski and P. Tanquey (eds.), Emotional Disorders of Mentally Retarded Persons. University Park Press, Baltimore.

Chapter 6

Managing the Disruptive Behavior of the Mentally Retarded

Luke S. Watson, Jr.

It is extremely difficult to operate educational or habilitation programs for the mentally retarded without using behavior management techniques. Although most retarded persons are reasonably cooperative, a minority can become extremely difficult to handle from time to time. Some become aggressive toward peers, teachers, and/or staff members; others become aggressive toward themselves; and still others may engage in destruction of property, such as breaking windows. A fourth group may simply exhibit extremely bizarre behavior which can be very disconcerting. All four categories of behavior problems can be extremely disruptive and should be dealt with for the sake of other persons who may be adversely affected (Watson, Owen, and Uzzell, 1980).

Before one can deal with these kinds of behavior problems, however, a humane, effective, and economical treatment strategy should be selected. In the process of developing a treatment strategy, the human rights and legal rights of the client should be carefully considered (Martin, 1975; Stolz, 1978). Each treatment procedure considered should be examined in light of the type of behavior problem it is designed to manage and the personal discomfort and inconvenience it can create for the recipient. The problem should justify the treatment procedure used. In addition, if a more comfortable or a more convenient (from the standpoint of the client) procedure is available than the one under consideration, it should be the preferred alternative (Watson et al., 1980).

Ideally, any procedure selected should be reviewed and approved by a Client Human Legal Rights Committee or a Programming Committee that is relatively impartial and independent of the treatment staff (Watson, 1978a). They should determine whether the procedure is safe, reasonable for the type of behavior problem under consideration, and effective. With regard to safeguarding the physical welfare of the client, physical therapists, physicians, and registered nurses are highly qualified to determine that a particular procedure is safe and should not cause any type of physical injury if used correctly. Ideally, such persons should be members of Human and Legal Rights or Programming Committees.

A THREE-ALTERNATIVE APPROACH
TO MANAGING DISRUPTIVE BEHAVIOR

In an attempt to develop a treatment strategy that is humane, effective, and economical, a three-alternative approach to managing disruptive behavior was created (Watson et al., 1980). It was designed to deal with aggressive behavior, self-destructive behavior, destruction of property, and bizarre behavior, such as temper tantrums. The approach is summarized below:

Alternative I
Schedule therapeutic programs and interesting activities
Alternative II
Interrupt the chain, prevent the response from occurring, fines (loss of points or tokens), loss of privileges, and required relaxation (without holding)
Alternative III
Required relaxation (with holding), overcorrection, positive practice, time out from reinforcement, and physical restraint

Alternative I consists of scheduling programs and activities that keep the client interested and involved throughout his or her waking hours, as much as possible. This alternative is designed to eliminate the conditions that cause disruptive behavior. If the client does not respond to Alternative I (i.e., his or her disruptive behavior still continues), then Alternative II is introduced. Such procedures as required relaxation, fines, and loss of privileges are introduced to deal with the disruptive behavior. In addition, Alternative I is still continued because it is designed to improve the client's mental health and should make Alternative II more effective. If the client still does not respond to this alternative, then Alternative III is introduced.

Such procedures as forced required relaxation, time out, overcorrection, and positive practice are used. Again, Alternative I is still continued. Notice the progression of treatment procedures. They move from the most comfortable to more uncomfortable, from the least restrictive alternatives to more and even more restrictive alternatives. This approach is intended to be as humane as possible (meaning as comfortable and as least restrictive as possible), effective, and economical.

Alternative I

Alternative I is designed to eliminate the *causes* of disruptive behavior. This usually solves around 75% of the behavior problems that exist. The remaining 25% of the behavior problems can be dealt with using Alternatives II and III (see Figure 6.1). If the causes of undesirable behavior are to be eliminated, those things that cause undesirable behavior to occur need to be known (see list on p. 133). Causes of undesirable behavior come from two sources: *outside* the person and *inside* the person. As indicated in the list, there are at least six outside causes of undesirable behavior. First, tasks that are too difficult can be a source of frustration and can make a person both angry and discouraged. The person may get upset and attack someone or destroy property, become self-destructive, or simply withdraw. Second, interrupting a compulsive client when he or she is trying to complete an activity also can be very upsetting and can cause the client to become disruptive. This is particularly true of autistic kinds of clients. The client may have a violent temper tantrum as a result of this interruption. Third, bullying and teasing is something that goes on in institutions, schools, and homes. Observations have shown that it is a common cause of window breaking. An aggressive client begins to scream and yell and hits another client, who in turn hits a third client, who runs over and breaks out windows. Fourth, excessive heat or cold can cause disruptive behavior, especially in the case of young profoundly retarded or psychotic children. Fifth, a lack of something to do, such as sitting around idle, can be a major source of behavior problems. This is one of the greatest problems to contend with when working with the mentally retarded. Sixth, too much stimulation, too much going on with too many people, and too much noise also can be very disturbing and make the client disruptive. In residential facilities, such events as mealtimes, getting up in the morning, and getting ready to go to bed at night often are extremely frustrating to clients due to the "hassles" concerned with these activities. Some clients react to this frus-

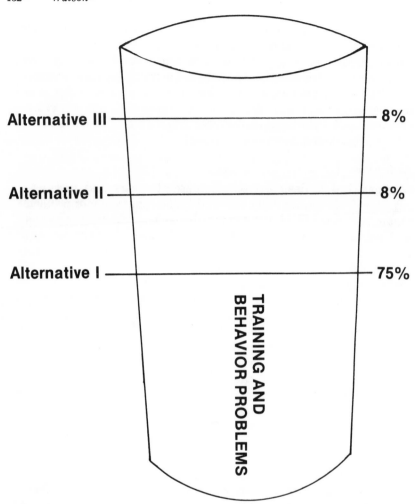

Figure 6.1.   Relative effectiveness of the three BMT treatment techniques.

tration by attacking another client or staff member or they engage in self-destructive behavior.

As already mentioned, there are also things going on inside the person that cause disruptive behavior. First, there is a need for attention. Everyone needs attention. If this cannot be attained by appropriate behavior, then inappropriate behavior is used to get it. The old adage, "the squeaky wheel gets the oil," certainly fits here. Most people would rather be scolded than be ignored. Second, curiosity seems to be a characteristic of all individuals to some extent. Experience has shown that certain children labeled hyperactive get into mischief at least partially because of curiosity. Third, everyone needs vigorous physical activity; one tends to become irritable and even aggressive without it. One way to improve the disposition of everyone, especially small hyperactive children, is to schedule vigorous physical activity twice a day. Fourth, the sex drive develops in everyone when they reach puberty. Much of the disruptive sexual behavior witnessed from retarded people is the result of this powerful sex urge. They typically have no reasonable sexual outlet. Fifth, hunger and thirst can be a problem, especially with profoundly retarded clients and small psychotic children. When they get too hungry or too thirsty, they become irritable. Lastly, fatigue can be a problem, particularly with profoundly retarded clients and small psychotic children. Whey they get too tired, they become very irritable, and may then attack someone, destroy furniture, or injure themselves.

Conditions that Cause Undesirable Behavior

Outside the person	Inside the person
1. Difficult tasks	1. Need for attention
2. Interrupting activity	2. Curiosity
3. Bullying or teasing	3. Need for physical activity
4. Excessive heat or cold	4. Sex drive
5. Lack of visual, auditory, or tactile stimulation (boredom)	5. Hunger and thirst
6. Excessive visual, auditory, or tactile stimulation	6. Fatigue

The main way the various causes of undesirable behavior are eliminated (summarized above) is to schedule activities for clients that will eliminate these conditions. Set up a full day's activities for each client that are interesting and stimulating. Find worthwhile things for the client to do, at which he or she can succeed, so that the client's craving for attention will be satisfied normally. Then the client will no longer be bored—a real problem in most residential facilities. He or she also will feel worthwhile and develop a more positive attitude about getting involved in things. In addition, see that the client has frequently scheduled vigorous physical activity, is warm or cool enough, is not too tired nor too hungry or thirsty, and is not being bullied.

An example of such a schedule for a moderately mentally retarded teenage male in a residential facility might go as follows. He gets up in the morning and gets himself ready for breakfast. The staff on his unit reinforce him with praise for his appearance and may give him privilege points, which he can use for recreational activities in the afternoon, and in the evening too. The client comes back from breakfast and makes his bed and picks up his room before he goes to school. Again, a staff member comes by to check his room and praises him for a job well done, and perhaps gives him more privilege points. Then the client goes to school, which is set up to be interesting and challenging. The client may be learning academic skills that will be needed in order for him to develop a vocational skill. Good performance in class gives him still more privilege points.

After classes are over, the client comes back to his living unit, gets a snack with some of his privilege points, and there are interesting recreational activities for him to get involved in during the afternoon. If he has the privilege points, he can play softball, basketball, or tennis, or go swimming, or do something that allows him to use up considerable energy before the evening meal.

By now, it is time for the evening meal. After dinner, there are other recreational activities for the client if he has the privilege points. He may watch television, see a movie, go to the arts and crafts building, or go bowling. Then it is bedtime. The client has a snack and gets ready for bed.

Staff needs to have a good relationship with their clients. If the clients are all teenagers, staff would develop a sort of friendly big brother—surrogate parent relationship with them. They would give clients recognition frequently for their good behavior. The program would be designed so that clients earned enough privilege points to buy snacks and the opportunity to participate in the recreational activities they like. With this type of schedule, much of the undesirable behavior exhibited by most clients in institutions would disappear. Ideally, such a schedule would operate 7 days a week. On weekends, clients would go on special outings. They might go fishing, hiking, camping, or go on picnics. Sometimes they would go on short trips, such as to the beach or to an amusement park. They also would go bowling, play miniature golf, go to the YMCA, or attend movies. The point is, they would be kept active during the weekends, as well as during the week.

If the clients were severely or profoundly retarded or severely disturbed autistic children, programs and activities would be somewhat different. If they were living in a residential facility—either a large, long-term care facility or a group home—the daily routine would consist of self-help skill training in the living area. Initially, clients would receive basic self-feeding, toileting, and dressing skills training, as well as training in compliance. As these basic skills were acquired, clients would be enrolled in a special educational day school program from 3 to 6 hours a day where they would learn preacademic and academic skills. While in school, they would be taught how to come into the class, hang up a hat and coat, use the bathroom, and take a seat at a preassigned place at a table or desk. They also would learn to follow the teacher's instructions and carry out simply preacademic tasks to completion without interfering with others.

After 4 to 6 months of this special educational program, clients would be completing more complex and time-consuming tasks, as well as learning certain preacademic skills preparatory to academic skills needed later to enroll in a vocational workshop or work activity program. In addition, they would be taught to play a series of games, either individually or in groups, that could be played during leisure time. Such activities can be incompatible with self-stimulatory or other bizarre activities. Back in the living unit, clients would learn to shower and bathe, brush their teeth, comb their hair, and learn more advanced dressing skills. In addition, they would be taught to make their beds, pick up their rooms, hang up their clothes, sweep, and mop. There would be vigorous physical activities scheduled each day, either on regular playground equipment, such as swings and sliding boards, or in a swimming pool or on a trampoline. On weekends, there would be special activities, such as field trips, picnicking, or hiking. The main point, again, is that this type of client would be kept as active as possible and would not be allowed to sit around any more than necessary.

Activities Can Be Incompatible with Disruptive Behavior   Programs and activities can be used to compete directly with disruptive behavior. For example, if a number of moderately retarded teenage clients routinely became disruptive on Friday nights (usually between the hours of 8 p.m. and 10 p.m.), such as fighting, breaking furniture, and yelling and screaming at one another and using abusive language (this is a fairly common disruptive behavior pattern with some moderately retarded teenage males), this problem could be managed by scheduling activities off the unit for the evening. A staff member could take these same clients to a movie from 7 p.m. to 10 p.m., or take them out to play putt-putt golf or maybe take them shopping. The point is that during these hours when the residents are usually disruptive in their residence, they would not be present in the residence and would be actively involved doing something they enjoyed.

Eighty Percent Positive Reinforcement   Happiness is having 80% of one's daily experiences or consequences come out positive. This is an oversimplified interpretation of good mental health, but if clients have their daily routines scheduled so that a minimum of 80% of the experiences they have or the consequences that they receive are positive, they should be much happier, have a better outlook on life, and be more cooperative. Most of the consequences that a retarded person receives come from staff or parents, i.e., social reinforcement. So, the key to providing 80% positive reinforcement in a client's daily routine is for staff or parents to program this reinforcement ratio into their daily interaction pattern. For example, if the client exhibits disruptive behavior and a treatment program is designed to deal with it, staff should plan on no more than 20% of the consequences or the experiences of the client's day to be negative. Clients who operate under this formula should be more cooperative, and Alternatives II and III should be more effective as a result. One simple way to apply the 80% rule is to keep Alternative I going on all the time, and when programming decelerator procedures, ensure that no more than 20% of the consequences that the client receives are negative.

In order to give clients negative feedback using this positive approach, staff should use a simple formula: $+4/-1 +$ positive. This means that when giving feedback to a client, staff should on the average make four positive comments followed by a negative comment in the form of a polite suggestion with an explanation that provides the reason why things would be better if the suggestion was followed, followed by another positive comment. For example, if there is a disruptive client in a group home, the disruptive client might receive negative feedback in the following way. Imagine the client has been assigned to wash the supper dishes. At the end of the meal, she washes the dishes, but she does not rinse them off. Using the positive approach, the staff member would say, "Hey Rita, I see you got all the dishes washed. We had spaghetti and meatballs for supper and you got all the spaghetti and all the meat sauce off those dishes. They sure do look good. Wow!" And the staff member adds, "But I wonder what would happen if we took the dishes and rinsed them off in hot water?" Then the staff member rinses the dishes off in hot water and explains, "Wow, you can see clean down to the shine. Look, you can see your face in them now. They are a lot cleaner when they have been rinsed off. And I bet they won't taste like soap when we eat breakfast off of them in the morning either." Then the staff member rinses one or two more dishes to model what he or she wants the client to do and also demonstrates the influence of rinsing them in hot water. Finally, the staff person adds, "Why don't you go ahead and finish getting all those dishes rinsed off, and then we will all go bowling. After all, we can't go without you. You are one of the best bowlers we have." Under these conditions, a client who would ordinarily be negativistic about being told she did not do a satisfactory job of washing the dishes is much more likely to complete the job without any unpleasant repercussions.

Alternative II

Alternative II involves the use of the following procedures: interrupt the chain, prevent the response from occurring, fines (loss of points or tokens), loss of privileges, and required relaxation without holding. This alternative should not be used until Alternative I has been implemented. When attempting to use Alternative II, Alternative I should still be continued. Alternative I provides the 80% positive environment the client needs to maintain his or her mental health. In addition, continuation of the Alternative I approach should make Alternative II more effective. Staff also should employ the +4/-1 + positive feedback procedure with clients to make them more cooperative.

Interrupt the Chain   This procedure is used to stop violent or explosive outbursts of anger. This kind of behavior is often exhibited by individuals labeled emotionally disturbed or psychotic as well as mentally retarded. They quickly become very angry and begin destroying things, and they may attack people. One way to stop this behavior is by interrupting the chain of events that lead to the actual outburst of anger. If intervention occurs early enough, the undesirable behavior can be prevented from occurring.

A typical example of this type of problem is a youth (in this example a male) living in a group home, who is identified as predelinquent and/or emotionally disturbed. He comes home from school with a "bad note" from his teacher. Perhaps he badmouthed the teacher. A group home staff member senses trouble by the look on the youth's face and his general posture as he walks into the house. The staff member asks the client for the card the teacher fills out each day that describes how he behaved in class. The client replies that he lost it, so the staff member telephones the teacher to get the correct story. The client is then told that because of the bad incident in school that day he will lose 10,000 points, and he is asked to give his point card to the staff member so that the point fine can be marked on the card. By now, the youth is standing there with his fists clenched and with an angry look on his face. He reaches in his pocket, takes out the point card, rips it up, and throws it at the staff member. As he storms out of the room, the staff member yells, "That just cost you 10,000 more points, mister!".

The client goes up the stairs to his room, picks up a lamp from his desk and throws it through the window. Then he kicks a hole in the wall of his room as he shouts obscenities. Next he storms back out of the room and encounters another smaller, more timid client. He hits the smaller client and storms out of the house.

The client now has accumulated fines of approximately 50,000 points, which will take him about 3 weeks to work off and which will deny him most privileges for that period. Unfortunately, it will be almost impossible to get him to work off the fine. Valuable gains made in the treatment program have been lost.

To interrupt the chain of events that led to this situation, each staff member in the home would become an *advocate* for one or two clients so that each client has someone to be his or her friend. The advocate should be someone the client naturally is attracted to. The advocate would spend some time privately each day with the client doing something that would help to develop a closer or warmer friendship.

Next, the staff would identify those times of day when clients are most likely to explode in anger. One such time is after school. If they run into trouble with a teacher or classmate, clients often come home angry. If they can be identified as angry or upset as they come in the door—by the look on their faces or the way they walk in—there still may be time to stop the anger from building. The staff member who is a particular client's advocate should be alerted. Then the advocate can take the client for a walk to get him out of the house and to let the client talk it out and tell what went wrong at school. As the client talks, the staff member can listen sympathetically and let the client know he or she understands how the client feels. It does not mean that the staff member wants to take sides against the teacher or make the client feel it is okay to break school rules. The objective is to let the client know that the staff member knows how he feels and that as a friend he or she is sorry that the unfortunate situation occurred. Perhaps the incident concerned an argument that the client was having with a classmate, and the teacher interceded and accused him of causing it when the client felt that he did not.

Once the client has "talked himself out" and has settled down, the staff member then could say, "Well, I understand how you feel, but talking to the teacher like that is going to cost you 10,000 points. If you keep talking to teachers and police like this, you're going to continue to get into trouble with them." There is a risk, of course, that the loss of points can cause the client to become very angry and start acting out, so the staff member could add, "If you role play with me a better way to deal with the teacher in a situation like you got into today, I'll give you 5,000 points." The client and staff member role play an appropriate way for the client to talk to the teacher in that type of situation. The staff member praises the client for working out a better alternative to dealing with the teacher and awards him 5,000 points. Then the staff member tells the client that if he will role play the same situation with another client in the group home, an additional 5,000 points will be given, and the fine will be eliminated. To increase the chance that the client will use the newly acquired techniques with the teacher, he also should role play this procedure with the teacher, if possible. This role playing technique serves two important purposes: it stops the client from exploding in anger, and it provides a valuable opportunity to teach the client an important social skill he evidently lacks, i.e., diplomatically handling a difficult situation that ordinarily makes him angry and invariably gets him into trouble. The staff member is able to succeed because he or she approaches the client as a friend.

Prevent the Response from Occurring This procedure is administered during skill training sessions and requires two trainers, a primary trainer and a backup trainer. The purpose of the procedure is to make clients more cooperative during skill training sessions by preventing disruptive behavior. It also may make clients more cooperative in other situations. It is designed primarily for severely and profoundly mentally retarded clients and for autistic children. Once the client becomes cooperative, the backup trainer is faded.

The backup trainer is employed in the following way. The client sits at a table with the primary trainer sitting across and in front of him (assuming the client is male) and the backup trainer stands just behind the client, as illustrated in Figure 6.2. From this position, the backup trainer can control the client's arms or head, or keep him seated in the chair throughout the training session. Ideally, the table should be approximately 20 inches wide (between the client and the primary trainer), thus allowing the primary trainer to maintain control over the client's legs by holding them between his or hers. Not only does the backup trainer prevent unwanted behavior from occurring, but he or she also serves as an additional source of reinforcement. Whenever the client responds correctly, the backup trainer gives verbal praise and pats the client on the arms or shoulders. At the same time, the primary trainer also gives the client praise, primary or token reinforcement, and pats him on the arms. Sometimes the presence of the backup trainer standing behind the client is enough to ensure cooperation. When this happens, the backup trainer merely stands behind the client for several training sessions and then gradually fades out. If the presence of the backup trainer fails to elicit the client's cooperation, the backup trainer can provide physical guidance.

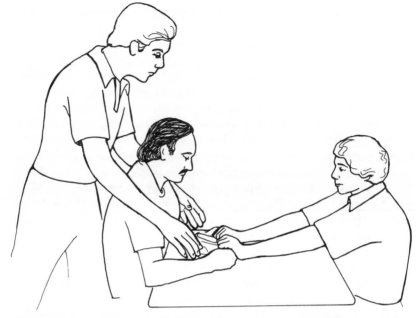

Figure 6.2.. The backup trainer stands with one thigh placed firmly against the back of the client's chair while the other leg is extended backward.

There are 11 disruptive behavior problems that can be managed with the backup trainer procedure:

1. Eye contact
2. Looking at the task
3. Muscular rigidity
4. Getting up from the chair
5. Throwing objects
6. Yelling and screaming
7. Headbanging
8. Headslapping
9. Hitting the trainer
10. Biting the trainer
11. Self-injurious biting

The stance and the arm and head holds used by the backup trainer are extremely important and are described in detail.

A basic problem encountered when training severely and profoundly retarded persons and psychotic children is that they often will not give the trainer *eye contact*. This may indicate that the client is negativistic, and elimination of this problem may promote increased cooperation during training. Obtaining the client's eye contact tells the trainer that he or she has the client's attention. In addition, the client will look more normal if he or she looks at someone when his or her name is called.

To deal with this problem, the backup trainer stands directly behind the client (who is seated) and assumes the basic stance employed for handling most of the disruptive behavior problems listed on p. 140. One thigh is placed firmly against the back of the client's chair while the other leg is extended backward with the knee in a locked position, as illustrated in Figure 6.2. While standing behind the client in this manner, the backup trainer shadows his shoulders with his hands. From this position, the backup trainer is able to deal with a variety of behavior problems through the combined use of weight, body leverage, and locked joints. One advantage of this position is that the backup trainer avoids becoming involved in a struggle that pits brute strength against brute strength—something that quickly fatigues the trainer.

Once the backup trainer has assumed this stance, the primary trainer calls the client's name. If the client fails to respond, the primary trainer holds the reinforcement by his or her eye and calls the name again, adding, "Look at me." If this fails to get the client's eye contact, the primary trainer calls the client's name and says, "Look at me" firmly, takes the client's chin in his or her hand and gently orients the client's face toward his or her own while bringing his or her own face closer to the client's face. If the client still fails to look, the primary trainer says, "No!" firmly, and the backup trainer orients the client's head so that it faces directly toward the primary trainer's face (see Figure 6.3).

To control the client's head without risk of injury, the backup trainer places his or her hands on either side of the client's head, as shown in Figure 6.3. The thumbs of both hands are positioned together just behind the bony protrusion on the back of the client's head. The index finger of each hand is extended along the side of the lower jaw, and the middle two fingers of each hand are placed under the jaw against the soft fleshy portion just inside the bony ridge. Care should be taken not to apply pressure in the direction of the client's throat because this can interfere with breathing.

To bring the client's head forward or downward, the backup trainer gradually pushes the client's head forward with his thumbs. To bring the head up, upward pressure is gradually applied with the middle and ring fingers. To move the head to the right, the backup trainer uses the left forefinger; to move the client's head to the left, pressure is applied with the right forefinger.

Figure 6.3. The backup trainer orients the client's head so that he is directly facing the trainer.

If the client resists the backup trainer's attempt to control his head, the backup trainer does not force the head movement. Instead, the backup trainer meets force with force and immobilizes the client's head by locking his elbows and using his thumbs to prevent backward movement of the head, while using the middle and ring fingers to prevent the head from moving downward and the fore-fingers to prevent head movement to the right or left. Fatigue from muscle tension will gradually cause the client to stop resisting. As the resistance decreases, the backup trainer provides physical guidance to orient the client's head in the desired position. As the client's resistance subsides and eye contact is established, the primary trainer and backup trainer reinforce the client. Both are very enthusiastic in the manner in which they give verbal and physical reinforcement. In addition, the primary trainer gives the client an edible reinforcement or a token.

The backup trainer and primary trainer continue using this technique with the client until he reliably will give eye contact when his name is called. After a session in which the client gives eye contact without physical guidance, the backup trainer begins to fade the guidance. There are four steps to this fading approach:

1. The backup trainer maintains the hand position on the head and face but does not apply any resistance or physical guidance.
2. The backup trainer stands behind the client with his or her hands on the client's shoulders.
3. The backup trainer stands behind the client with his or her arms to his side.
4. The backup trainer fades out of the room (by standing increasingly further away from the client).

One training session should be devoted to each fading step. If the client stops cooperating with the primary trainer during any stage of fading the backup trainer should move back to the previous step to regain the client's cooperation and then fade back to the next step at the next session. For example, if the backup trainer had faded to step three, standing with arms at the side, and the client stops cooperating with the primary trainer, the backup trainer should back up to step two, standing behind the client with hands on the client's shoulders for the remainder of the session. If the client's cooperation is obtained in step two, the backup trainer should go back to step three at the beginning of the next session. If the client's cooperation is not regained within two or three trials at step two of fading, the backup trainer should back up to step one. If the client's cooperation is regained at this point, the backup trainer should stay at that fading step for the remainder of the session and resume the fading procedure at the next session (i.e., go to step two).

It is extremely important that the client *look at the task* in which he is engaged. Otherwise, many skills probably will not be learned successfully, such as shoe tying or bed making. If the primary trainer is unable to get the client to look at the task at hand, the backup trainer can be employed to obtain cooperation, assuming the same position behind the client's chair that was used to obtain eye contact.

The procedure would begin with the primary trainer calling the client's name and giving a command such as, "Billy, tie the shoe." If the client does not look at the shoe as he attempts to tie it or if he begins to look away after initially looking at the shoe, the primary trainer would tap the table beside the shoe and firmly say, "Billy, look!" If the client still does not look or continues looking away after initially looking at the task, the backup trainer would give a firm negative bridging signal and establish the same head holding position used to obtain eye contact. The primary trainer would control the client's hands and the backup trainer would block the client's inappropriate head movements by meeting force with force until the head position was stablized. The backup trainer then would use physical guidance to orient the client's head so that he is looking at the task. As before, when the client complies and looks at the task, both primary trainer and backup trainer would enthusiastically praise and pat him on the arms and shoulders, and the primary trainer also would give either tokens or edible reinforcement. Once the client begins to cooperate, the backup trainer is faded in the same manner described for eye contact.

Some clients *will not allow trainers to use physical prompts.* If the trainer attempts to manipulate the client's hands for guidance in the training process, the client may either hold them rigid or pull them back. This problem can be managed by using a backup trainer to control the client's forearms. If the client pulls his arms back when the primary trainer attempts to initiate a physical prompt, the backup trainer reaches forward over the shoulders and grasps the client's wrists. At the same time, the primary trainer reaches across the table and grasps the hands. Using weight and leverage, the backup trainer locks his or her elbows and gently leans forward against the client's efforts to hold his arms rigid. The primary trainer also locks his arms and uses his weight by leaning back in the chair; so together and with little exertion, the backup trainer and the primary trainer move the client's arms gradually back on task as the client tires from attempts to hold the rigid posture. Physical guidance, not brute force, is used by the two trainers to gradually move the client's arms from the rigid position to getting him back on task. As the client tires and begins to ease his resistance, both primary trainer and backup trainer verbally reinforce this movement in the direction of compliance. When the client actually begins to allow the primary trainer to use a physical prompt, the primary trainer and backup trainer praise him with great enthusiasm. As soon as the task is completed, both trainers give the client more enthusiastic praise as well as physical reinforcement, and the primary trainer also provides a token or edible reinforcement. After the client's cooperation is obtained, the backup trainer is faded.

Some clients *refuse to sit in a chair* throughout a training session. They frequently get up and walk around the room. This is not only disconcerting to the trainer, but it also interferes with the training process itself. The backup trainer's stance becomes extremely important in attempts to prevent a client from getting up out of a chair. It also helps if the table is narrow enough (ideally 20 inches) for the primary trainer to pin the client's legs between his or her own under the table. This added stability helps the backup trainer to control the backward thrust of the chair as the client attempts to stand up. The client is placed as close as possible to the table. If the client attempts to push the chair backward to stand up, the backup trainer immediately gives a firm negative bridging signal, "No!" while simultaneously preventing the chair from moving backward with his or her legs and pulling the client's back against the back of the chair by gripping his shoulders in the front under the armpits, locking his arms, and leaning back. At the same time, the primary trainer holds the client's legs between his or her own, grasps the client's hands and pulls backward. With both the backup trainer and primary trainer working together in this manner, the client can use only the stomach muscles in an attempt to stand up and is usually unsuccessful. As soon as the client begins to tire and stops resisting, the primary trainer and backup trainer move to get him back on task and immediately begin to reinforce any cooperative efforts exhibited by the client.

Another problem frequently encountered in training situations is that the *client throws the training materials.* This not only disrupts training, but it also may cause a painful injury if someone is hit by a shoe or some other hard flying object. The backup trainer can be used effectively to prevent this type of disruptive behavior by assuming the same stance described earlier and standing ready to anticipate the possibility that the client might attempt at any time to throw an object used in training. Using shoe tying as an example, should the client try to grab the shoe and pull it away from the primary trainer to throw it, the backup trainer would quickly grasp each of the client's wrists while the primary trainer would grab the shoe. Thus, the backup trainer would attempt to control the client's arms while the primary trainer would attempt to control the object the client was trying to throw. Once control was established, the backup trainer and primary trainer would again use physical guidance to resume the training process. As the client began to cooperate, the backup trainer and the primary trainer would give verbal reinforcement. When the client completed the trial, both trainers would reinforce him with enthusiastic praise, pat him on the arms or shoulders, and rub his back, and the primary trainer would give a token or edible reinforcement. As the client became more cooperative, the backup trainer would be faded.

When clients become frustrated in a training situation, they frequently *yell and scream.* There are two ways to deal with this problem. The first approach is for both the primary trainer and backup trainer to give a firm negative bridging signal followed by the primary trainer grasping the client's hands to control them, while the backup trainer places one hand behind the client's neck and at the same time places the other hand rigidly cupped over the client's mouth, as illustrated in Figure 6.4. To prevent the backup trainer from being bitten on the hand, it is essential that he or she cups the hand placed over the client's mouth so that the thumb rests along the jawline and the index finger is in a similar position on the other cheek. The hand should not touch the lips as this can increase the risk of being bitten. The backup trainer should cover the mouth immediately after saying "No!" and should move quickly, because the element of surprise seems to be one of the factors that causes the client to stop yelling or screaming. The backup trainer should maintain this hand position for approximately 15 seconds, then remove the hand; if the client continues to yell and scream, the negative bridging signal should be repeated and the backup trainer should cup his hand over the client's mouth for an additional 15 seconds. The procedure should be repeated several times, if necessary.

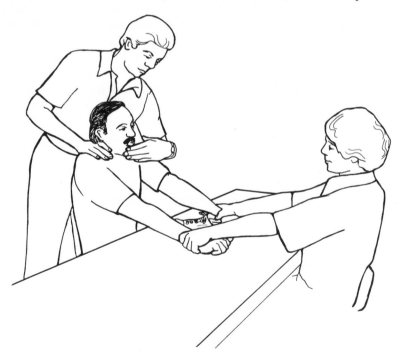

Figure 6.4.   The backup trainer placed his hand over the client's mouth to stop him from screaming.

The second way to stop yelling and screaming is for the backup trainer to employ a basket hold, dropping down to firmly control the client's position in the chair (as described earlier). Once the backup trainer has restrained the client, the primary trainer cups a hand and places it over the client's mouth. In this case, the side portion of the primary trainer's hand is used and is placed just under the client's nose along the upper lips in an effort to quickly muffle the scream. This maneuver also would be preceded by a firm negative bridging signal from both the primary trainer and the backup trainer. As soon as the client stops screaming, both the backup trainer and the primary trainer would use graduated guidance to bring the client back on task, and both would enthusiastically reinforce any cooperative behavior. When the client becomes cooperative, the backup trainer is faded.

Head banging is often associated with yelling and screaming. In a training situation, the client may bring his head down to the table surface or attempt to turn and beat it against the chair in which he is sitting. A backup trainer can easily prevent this from occurring. With a primary trainer controlling the client's hands, the backup trainer would quickly grasp the front portion of the client's shoulders and bring the client back against the back surface of the chair, simultaneously giving a firm bridging signal. The backup trainer would then lean back with his arms locked, using his weight to control the client. Then the client would be unable to lean forward and bring his head down in contact with the table surface. Similarly, the client would be unable to turn and strike the back of the chair with his head. Once the client stops attempting to bang his head, the primary trainer and backup trainer would use graduated guidance to get him back on task. As the client begins to engage in the task again, he would receive appropriate reinforcement. The same fading procedure would be used as described earlier.

Sometimes when a client is unsuccessful in an attempt to bang his head, he begin *head slapping,* i.e., he hits the side of his head or face with his hands. This, of course, completely disrupts the training process, and it also can result in an injury to the client. To control this type of disruptive behavior, the backup trainer would attempt to block the upward movement of the client's hands by catching the wrists in his open hands with the hands positioned just in front of and to either side of the client's head. At the same time, the primary trainer would use his or her hands, with arms locked at the elbow, to block the client's blows, as shown in Figure 6.5. In addition, both trainers would give negative bridging signals. Using this technique,

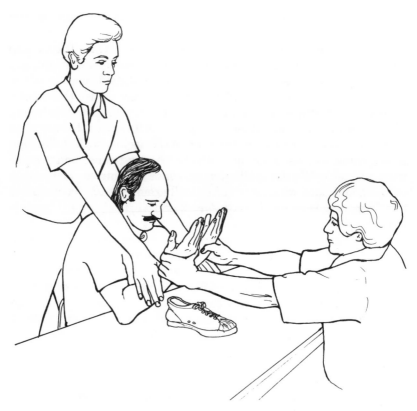

Figure 6.5. The backup trainer and the primary trainer prevent the client from slapping his own head.

a direct blow can be effectively blocked. Should the client bring his hands around to the outside to strike the head (rather than bringing the hands straight up from the table surface), the backup trainer can move his arms outward to block the blows. Once the attempted blows are blocked, the backup trainer and primary trainer use graduated guidance to bring the client's arms back down and to get him back on task. As the client resumes a particular training sequence, both trainers provide reinforcement. The backup trainer would be faded after cooperation was established.

Sometimes clients deal with their frustration by *striking a trainer,* who is a readily accessible target sitting just across the table. Bringing the backup trainer into this situation provides the primary trainer with added security. As a preliminary precaution, the primary trainer should be positioned across the table so that his or her face is just out of arm's reach from the client. This makes it easier for the backup trainer to prevent the client from striking the primary trainer. The backup trainer deals with this problem in the same way a client is prevented from getting up from the chair. If the client attempts to hit the primary trainer, the backup trainer quickly grasps the client under the arms over the front of the shoulders, hooks his or her fingers, and brings the client back against the back of the chair. The primary trainer controls the client's hands, bringing them down to the surface of the table. As the client's resistance decreases, both trainers use physical guidance to get him back on task to complete the training trial. As the two trainers get the client back on task, they reinforce him for cooperation and for completing the task. The backup trainer is faded as described earlier.

There are some *clients who bite themselves* when they become frustrated during training sessions. Others may bite the trainer. Both problems can be managed effectively by using the backup trainer approach. If a client attempts to bite his own arm or hand during training, the backup trainer reaches over the shoulder with his or her arm locked at the elbow and blocks the client's upcoming hand, as shown in Figure 6.6. He then moves quickly to establish control over the client's other hand to prevent it from being brought up to the mouth. If the client attempts to bring his head down to bite one of his own hands, the primary trainer should control the client's hands while the backup trainer grasps the client's shoulders and brings him back against the chair. This maneuver effectively keeps the client's mouth away from his own arms or hands.

If the client attempts to *bite the primary trainer*, the backup trainer again grasps the client by the shoulders and pulls him to the back of the chair while the primary trainer controls his hands. If the client should attempt to bite the backup trainer, the backup trainer should quickly immobilize the client's head while the primary trainer continues to control the client's hands. The backup trainer can accomplish this transfer to head immobilization by pulling the client's arms straight back and placing one hand firmly on top of the other on top of the client's head, while holding his inner forearms around the sides of the client's head over the ears. Then the backup trainer simply uses his or her weight, pushing his or her chest against the back of the client's head, completely preventing any further biting. After the client is brought under control and brought back to task, cooperative efforts are reinforced. Once cooperation is reliably established, the backup trainer is faded.

A number of disruptive behaviors can be managed in training situations using the backup trainer approach. The backup trainer and the primary trainer act to prevent the client from making any in-

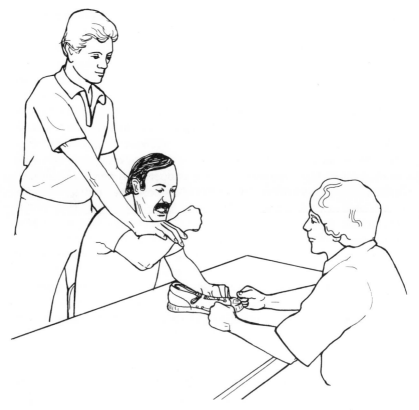

Figure 6.6.   The backup trainer prevents the client from biting himself.

appropriate responses while saturating him with reinforcement whenever he cooperates during training sessions or makes desirable responses. This approach can produce successful training in clients who otherwise would not benefit appreciably from training when only one trainer is employed. Once a client is cooperating in training, the backup trainer is faded, leaving only the primary trainer. Thus, the purpose of the technique is to make the client cooperative so one trainer can work with him effectively. This procedure would be used primarily with severely and profoundly retarded clients and with autistic children.

Fines   One technique that is useful when clients are given points or tokens is to use a *fine system*. This is the same kind of system used on the general public by traffic courts when someone is caught speeding or running a stop sign. In this procedure, the client pays a fine in the form of losing points, tokens, or privileges. The same precautions mentioned previously should be used here; that is, the client should receive, if at all possible, *four accelerators for every decelerator*—80% positive. The fine, however, should be substantial to be effective.

If the client loses points or tokens, he or she should be given an opportunity to earn them back as soon as possible. Otherwise the client may become discouraged and angry and violate a series of rules that could result in the loss of even more tokens or privileges. It is helpful if the person fining the client has a friendly relationship with him or her. When the client is fined, it should be done politely and with an explanation of why the fine is being applied. The client should also be given an opportunity—ideally immediately—to work off the fine and earn back the tokens so that he or she does not walk away and develop a high state of anger. It is helpful if there are some special jobs kept in reserve for clients to work off fines. Finally, if the client is being fined because he or she lacked a social skill needed to handle an emotional situation appropriately, this is an excellent opportunity to teach the appropriate way to act in that situation by having the client go through a role playing sequence to work off the fine. If the client becomes skillful at role playing the appropriate way to behave in the same kind of situation for which he is fined, he may behave appropriately in the same situation in the future.

Many times clients must be fined because they do not cooperate. One way to avoid giving them so many fines is to approach them in such a way that they will want to cooperate. First of all, it helps if staff members have a friendly relationship with clients, as mentioned previously, and if staff spend a little time with them each day making small talk or "horsing around" to develop a good relationship. Then when their cooperation is sought, the +4/-1 + positive approach is used.

Loss of Privileges   This is handled in a manner similar to fines. There are two ways to take privileges from clients. The more positive approach interfaces nicely with a point or token system. If clients lost their points or tokens, they cannot buy the privileges at that time. As more privileges are added that must be purchased, the motivation to earn points or tokens is increased. Thus, disruptive behavior is managed by the client losing points or tokens exclusively; as the client loses them, privileges are lost because they cannot be purchased. The other alternative is for clients to lose privileges directly in attempts to control disruptive behavior.

Required Relaxation (without Holding)   The final Alternative II procedure to be considered is required relaxation (without holding).

Basically, the client is told to lie down. He or she may be required to lie down for ½ hour or up to 2 hours. Many clients will lie down when told to, particularly if a staff member remains close beside them where he or she can be seen. If the clients will lie down and remain there without being held for the full interval of time, then required relaxation will qualify as an Alternative II procedure. If they have to be held on a bed to keep them there, that is classified as an Alternative III technique.

Required relaxation can be used for a variety of disruptive behaviors, such as verbal abuse, physical aggression, temper tantrums, and destruction of property. If a particular form of disruptive behavior occurs, the staff member should call the client's name and give a negative bridging signal ("No!"). If the client is still engaged in the disruptive behavior, the staff member should tell her (assuming the client in this example is female) to go lie down. The client may lie down on her own bed if in her residence, or on a bed set aside for the purpose in an out-of-the-way area if at school or a vocational workshop. The client is then required to remain lying down for ½ or up to 2 hours, depending on how long it may take her to settle down. The client will tend to be more cooperative if someone stays and observes her and if that person can be seen by the client.

One useful application of the required relaxation procedure is to have a client lie down before she gets upset to the point where she actually engages in some form of disruptive behavior. Clients who have a history of being disruptive often signal that they are becoming upset prior to actual disruptive behavior episodes. If they are required to lie down for 1 or 2 hours when they become agitated, the disruptive behavior may be prevented.

Alternative III

Alternative III includes overcorrection, positive practice, required relaxation (with holding), time out from reinforcement, and physical restraint. Before this alternative is introduced, Alternatives I and II should have been attempted and found to be ineffective. In addition, Alternative I should be continued, because it presumably will maintain the client's appropriate ratio of positive to negative consequences and make Alternative III more effective.

Overcorrection   Overcorrection can be a very useful technique for eliminating undesirable behavior. When the overcorrection procedure is used, the client is made to correct an error he made (assuming the client is a male). Then he must *overcorrect*. For example, a client may wet the bed, a frequent occurrence with the mentally retarded. The client might be required to correct the situation by taking off his pajamas and the sheets and the mattress cover on the bed and rinsing them out in a sink with detergent in it. The client has to *correct* the error. *Overcorrection* would involve scrubbing the clothing for around 15 minutes, then rinsing them out, and hanging everything on a line, and rinsing out the sink. Then the client would have to come back to his room, wipe off the mattress cover, and make the bed with clean sheets and mattress cover. All of this would require about 20 minutes. Because of the extreme amount of time and effort involved, the client is discouraged from wetting the bed again (this procedure would only be used if the client had bladder control). This technique can be used to stop a variety of behaviors, such as wetting, soiling and smearing, temper tantrums, attacking other clients, destroying property, and obscene language. It is ideally suited for the severely and profoundly mentally retarded and for autistic clients.

When using the overcorrection procedure, the total treatment period may be reduced if the disruptive behavior in question can be made to occur at a higher rate. For example, if a client spits on people when they approach him, the staff member who is going to use overcorrection to eliminate this behavior can shorten the total treatment time by approaching the client, inducing spitting, overcorrecting it, approaching him or her again, inducing spitting, and overcorrecting, to the point where spitting is occurring approximately 12 to 16 times a day or even more. By providing a large number of treatment sessions each day, the total number of days required to complete treatment should be decreased.

To carry out overcorrection correctly and to avoid physical injury or excessive stress to either the staff or the client, certain precautions should be taken. The staff member should learn to use his or her weight rather than muscle to control the client physically, and he or she should not use undue force to get the client to go through the overcorrection procedure. When a client is being overcorrected, the staff member should use his or her body weight, if at all possible, to keep the client in a position that allows cleanup or correction of the problem. Also, the staff member should not force a client who is actively resisting movement of his or her limbs. Rather, the staff member should immobilize the limb that holds the cloth, brush, mop, and as the client's arms relax, guidance can then be applied by beginning to move the client's arms through the motion of cleaning up or correcting the situation. When overcorrection is used, we recommend that it be carried out until the client stops struggling or resisting, and then it should be continued for 5 more minutes. The total interval usually ranges from 15 to 30 minutes. The procedure used to carry out overcorrection goes as follows. If the client spills something on the floor or wets herself (assuming the client in this example is a female), the trainer says, "No!" firmly, then promptly walks over to the client and says (for example), "You wet, now you clean it up." A gestural prompt is used with the statement to emphasize the error. With one hand, the trainer grasps the client firmly just about the elbow, while placing the other hand on the shoulder of the arm opposite the one he or she is holding. Then the client is guided to the place where cleaning materials are stored. The next step is to get the client into the "cleanup position." The trainer attempts to do this first by using a verbal prompt. If the client does not respond, a gestural prompt is used. If the gestural prompt fails, the trainer uses a physical prompt. If the client is right-handed, the trainer grasps the client's left wrist with his or her left hand and places the right hand on the client's right shoulder. The trainer pushes down on the client's shoulder while placing his or her left hand on the client's waist (still holding the client's left wrist) and bends the client over, putting his or her chest weight on the client's back and placing his or her left knee under the client's upper abdomen to prevent a fall. The trainer continues to guide the client down to the floor and into a position on her knees and elbows, keeping the left hand on the client's forearms approximately 1 inch below the elbow. The trainer leans over, placing his or her chest on the client's upper back and shoulders, with the trainer's head just over and outside the client's shoulder (to avoid being butted in the face), takes the client's right wrist in his or her right hand and says, "Clean it up," while using graduated guidance with his or her right hand. If the client cooperates, graduated guidance is faded by the trainer moving his or her hand up the client's arm toward the shoulder and reducing the force or firmness of the grasps. The verbal prompt is repeated periodically. The trainer does not force the client to scrub if she actively resists. Instead, the client's arm is held immobilized until it relaxes, the verbal prompt is repeated, and guidance is again applied.

If the client spills something on a table and is right-handed, the trainer grasps the left elbow with his left hand and the client's right shoulder with his right hand and walks the client to the table. The trainer then places his left hand on the client's waist and pushes down on the client's right shoulder to bend her over the table. Next, the trainer holds the client's left forearm and elbow down on the table with his left hand and manipulates the client's right hand, always protecting his head by keeping it just over and outside the client's shoulder, as shown in Figure 6.7.

The procedure just described will work well if the client is small enough to be managed by one staff member; however, in cases when the client is too large or too strong to be managed by a single person, two staff members will be needed to administer overcorrection. Overcorrection for window breaking provides a good example of the two-person procedure. When a client is overcorrected for breaking a window, a push broom is used, and the client is required to sweep. One person stands on each side of the client. The client should hold the top of the broom handle with the right hand and the middle of the broom handle with the left, as illustrated in Figure 6.8. To accomplish this, physical guidance is required. The person standing to the client's right holds the client's right arm on the top of the broom by grasping the client's thumb and forefinger and the broom handle with his or her right hand while grasping the client's right elbow with the left hand. The person standing to the left of the client holds

Figure 6.7.   The trainer uses the weight of his body, not his muscle, to carry out overcorrection.

Figure 6.8.   Positions used by two trainers to physically prompt a client to sweep or mop.

the client's thumb and forefinger in his or her left hand and maintains control of the broom with this same hand. He or she holds the client's wrist with the thumb of the right hand and grasps the broom handle in the center with the fingers of the right hand. Notice in Figure 6.8 that the right hand is inside the client's elbow to catch him if he falls to the floor.

The staff member to the client's right provides guidance for pushing the broom forward by pushing on the client's right elbow. The staff member to the client's left provides guidance for pulling the broom backward by pulling back on the client's wrist and the broom. If the client resists guidance from the staff, the staff member to the client's left holds the broom down so the client cannot lift it from the floor. This is done by locking both elbows and using his or her weight to hold the broom down. At the same time, the person to the client's right lifts up on the top of the broom to assist the other staff member in keeping the bristles of the broom on the floor.

When a client breaks a window, the staff member who observed the incident says firmly, "No, Billy! You don't break windows. Now you are going to have to clean it up!" The second person comes in with the push broom; together they lead the client to the broken window and assume the positions just described. One staff member says, "Billy, sweep it up," and they begin the physical guidance. If the client resists, both staff members hold the broom to the floor and keep it immobilized until the client begins to relax. Then the command to sweep is repeated, and the two staff members resume the physical guidance. If the client begins to initiate sweeping himself, the staff members reduce their physical guidance and allow him to take greater responsibility for sweeping. If he will sweep independently, they should allow him to sweep but stay close to him. The client should be required to sweep for approximately 20 minutes. It is not necessary for him to actually sweep up the glass.

Positive Practice   Positive practice is the other restitution procedure. One way positive practice can be used is to have the client practice the correct behavior after a rule is broken. In the case of a toileting accident, the client would be required to walk to the bathroom from the place the accident occurred, go over to the toilet, take down his or her pants, sit, get up, flush the toilet, and leave.

Another way positive practice is used is to have the client practice a behavior that is incompatible with the undesirable behavior. For example, if a client engages in self-stimulatory behavior, such as turning his or her head back and forth or repeatedly gesturing with fingers in front of his or her face, he or she would be required to do positive practice—either arm or head exercises. In the case of arm exercises, the client would have to hold his or her arms straight out to the side for 15 to 20 seconds, in front for 15 to 20 seconds, straight out again for 15 to 20 seconds, straight up for 15 to 20, back out to the side for 15 to 20 seconds, and so on for three to 5 minutes. This frequently stops self-stimulatory behavior.

Staff who are taught to use this procedure are first taught the correct holding positions. If they are going to do arm exercises, the client is seated in a chair. Then the staff member holds the client's arms at the elbows so that the thumbs are at the juncture of the elbow, if he or she is given upward guidance, or so the palms of the hands are on the juncture of the elbow, if downward guidance is being applied. Staff always give the command for the arm movement about 2 seconds prior to applying physical guidance. For example, the trainer would say, "Arms up," approximately 2 seconds prior to lifting the arms upward. If the client voluntarily lifted the arms, the trainer would only touch the arms slightly or shadow them as they were raised. The trainer would ensure that the client held that position for 15 to 20 seconds and then would give the command for the next movement, "Arms out." When the arms had been out for 15 to 20 seconds, the next command would be, "Arm forward," followed by arms out, followed by arms down, then arms out, and the cycle would be repeated. If the client slapped his or her own head, the procedure should be carried out for approximately 20 minutes.

In the case of stereotyped activity or self-stimulatory behavior involving the head, chronic refusal to give eye contact, or banging the head on the floor, walls, or on furniture, positive practice would be carried out using head exercises. The head movements used are head down, head straight, and head back. Again, the command is given about 2 seconds prior to applying the guidance. To move the head downward, the trainer pushes gently but firmly with his or her thumbs on the back of the head. To bring the head up to the head straight position, the trainer applies upward pressure under the chin using the middle and ring fingers, taking care not to interfere with the client's breathing (see Figure 6.3). To move the head to the head back position, the trainer again applies upward pressure with the ring and middle fingers but does not bring the head so far back or up that it will cause the client discomfort. Staff should role play these procedures to understand the problems that can occur with breathing when the head is moved too far back. Head movement should not be forced. If the client resists having his or her head moved, it should be immobilized until the trainer feels it relax, then the command should be repeated and guidance should be applied again. The client should hold his or her head in each position for 15 to 20 seconds. The exercise should be used for approximately 5 minutes for refusal to give eye contact or stereotyped behavior involving the head and for 20 minutes in the case of head banging. This procedure can be used to eliminate head banging, head slapping, chronic scratching, and self-stimulatory behavior involving the arms or hands. It too is quite effective with severely and profoundly retarded clients and with autistic children.

Required Relaxation (with Holding)   There are some persons for whom required relaxation will not work unless they are held in a prone position. They either will not lie down when they are told to or if they do lie down, they will get up again before the end of the time they are supposed to lie down is completed. For these kinds of clients, a double holding procedure by two staff members can be implemented.

To correctly carry out required relaxation with holding, the client should be placed face down on a bed with the arms at his or her sides. To prevent the client from getting up, the staff members should position themselves in the following manner:

1. Facing the client's head, each staff member should place an inside knee adjacent to and just outside the client's upper thigh on the edge of the bed. The staff members then can control the client's legs by bringing their feet inside the legs so that the ankles are locked across the back of the client's knees.
2. To gain control of the client's arms, the staff members should simply lean forward and, with their arms locked at the elbow, grasp the client's wrists with their inside hands while applying a gentle to moderate pressure downward on the client's elbows with their other hands. Under no circumstances should the client's wrists be pulled up into the small of his back; the wrists and elbows should be pressed simultaneously into the surface of the bed. In this position, with the pressure applied correctly, the staff members should be able to hold the client until he relaxes, at which time they can begin gradually fading their physical control.

The purpose of this procedure is to provide an opportunity for the client to learn to relax for a period of time following or just preceding a disruptive episode. If the client becomes so disruptive that the implementation of this procedure is compromised, another alternative should be sought to deal with the client's behavior. Whenever a procedure requires this type of physical guidance, range of motion limitations should be carefully considered. Finally, as with any other procedure of this kind, staff should be properly trained and certified before attempting to use it in a real confrontation.

Time Out from Reinforcement   Another technique that is similar to loss of privileges is time out from reinforcement. The client is deprived of the opportunity to obtain reinforcement, usually by placing him or her in a small, bare room or by having him or her sit in a chair in a corner. A small child may be placed in time out for as little as 5 minutes, a 6 to 12 year old from 15 to 30 minutes, and a teenager or adult from 30 minutes to an hour.

Time out probably works best if the client can do nothing else during that time. If the client can wiggle and fidget, walk around, scream and yell, injure himself or herself, or even read a book or watch television, time out will not work as well or may not work at all. Also, it is not very effective if the client is not being deprived of something he or she likes, such as some favorite game or activity. If the client sits around all day with nothing to do and is placed in time out, it probably will not be very effective.

Physical Restraint   Sometimes clients have to be restrained if time out is to be effective. There are two ways to physically restrict a younger client (age 10 or younger), both involving holds. The client can be immobilized by being placed in a chair with the front of the chair close to the wall to keep him or her from sliding out of it. The client's arms are crossed in a basket hold and held in this position for approximately 15 minutes, if he or she is quiet and cooperative. The time should be extended 5 minutes for each episode of crying, screaming, kicking, or other forms of tantrums. The client should be held firmly in this position but not so tightly that the arms can be injured.

An alternative hold is the one shown in Figure 6.9. The trainer stands behind and over the client and holds one of the client's hands on each of his or her legs. The client is held in this position for 15 minutes. The advantage of this procedure is that if the client yells or screams, the trainer can place a hand over his or her mouth and say firmly, "No yelling!" The hands should be cupped so that there is no opportunity for the client to bite the trainer.

Time out can be used for temper tantrums, general negativism, aggressive behavior, or destruction of property. It should not be used for self-destructive behavior. The first holding procedure should be used for classroom teachers and mothers who work with their own children. The second holding procedure (Figure 6.9) is used for children who are disruptive in classrooms.

MAKING THE SYSTEM WORK

In order for a behavior management program to be effective, seven additional problems (or factors) should be considered. These are: 1) weak reinforcement systems; 2) staff training problems; 3) lack of accountability for staff; 4) absence of reinforcement for staff; 5) inconsistent treatment of clients when they exhibit disruptive behav-

Figure 6.9.   Alternate hold used to keep a younger client in a chair.

ior; 6) generalization training; and 7) maintenance. If any of these factors do occur, the effectiveness of a behavior management program can be reduced.

Weak Reinforcement System

A major reason why behavior management programs fail is because of weak reinforcement systems. There are not enough items and/or activities that can be purchased with tokens or points, or the client does not like much of anything, so virtually no reinforcers can be found. If at all possible, a token or point system should be used with mentally retarded clients. It is potentially the most powerful type of reinforcement system (Ferster and DeMyer, 1962). If the system is properly designed, the client should always be able to find something he or she would like to exchange points or tokens for, such as things to eat or drink, clothes, jewelry, watches, and radios, or special activities such as movies, field trips, shopping trips, or trips to the beach, etc. If there is a reasonable number of reinforcers that a client can purchase with points or tokens, such a system can be extremely effective for maintaining appropriate behavior. Below is a list of items and activities that severely and moderately mentally retarded clients like and that can be used for purchase in a token store.

Snacks	Radios
Coffee	Rent a bike
Soft drinks	Rent a tape player
Cigarettes	Rent a stereo
Cigars	Fishing tackle
Pipes	Sports equipment
Smoking tobacco	basketball
Snuff	football
Foot lockers	baseball
Trinket boxes	baseball glove
Locks	Fishing trips
Jewelry	Watches
bracelets	Alarm clocks
necklaces	Purses
rings	Billfolds
earrings	Hats
Clothes	Wigs
Cosmetics	Monogrammed T-shirts
Special trips and outings	Sunglasses
Opryland	Games

Gulf Shores   puzzles
Six Flags   cards
New Orleans   checkerboard
Zoo
Holiday on Ice

Unfortunately, these reinforcers are not usually available. The client has little to buy if he or she is operating under a token or point system or receiving no reinforcement of any kind for appropriate behavior. Consequently, the client has little or no incentive to be cooperative. In fact, if the client wants recognition under these kinds of circumstances, the main way to get it is by being disruptive.

There are some mentally retarded persons who do not respond to token or point systems. These are certain severely mentally retarded individuals and many profoundly retarded clients. For these kinds of persons, primary reinforcement or activities must be provided directly. Unfortunately, a minority of these persons does not seem to like much of anything. Experience has shown that if the client does not like at least five items or activities, it is difficult to provide sufficient incentive to carry out either a daily training program or a behavior management program (Watson, 1974).

One alternative to this problem is to condition items and activities as reinforcers. This can be done using a procedure based on the Premack Principle (Watson, 1978b). To condition edible items using the Premack Principle, the clients' relative food preferences need to be determined first. A cafeteria-style reinforcement preference sampling procedure can be used to accomplish this task. Five or six food items the client is known to accept should be laid side by side on a table, and the client given access to them. The item he or she eats the most of is, by definition, the most preferred item; the item the client eats the second greatest amount of is the second most preferred item, etc. This procedure can be used to determine the client's preferences for 10, 15, or more food items.

Once the client's relative reinforcement preferences have been determined, the conditioning procedure can begin. Perhaps the four most preferred items in order are milk, bread, vanilla custard, and hamburger. The trainer would begin with milk and bread. Because the client prefers milk to bread, he or she would have to eat a small bite of bread to get a drink of milk, that is, the client would have to eat a small amount of the less preferred item to get a "normal" amount of the more preferred item. It could take 2 to 3 weeks to increase substantially the reinforcement value of bread using this conditioning procedure.

Then milk and bread would be paired with vanilla custard and hamburger. The client would be required to eat a small bite of vanilla custard to get a drink of milk, and he or she also would have to eat a small bite of hamburger to get a normal size bite of bread. After 2 to 4 weeks of pairing these four items, the reinforcement value of vanilla custard and hamburger probably would be substantially greater. Then these four items could be used to condition other items. This kind of training could take place either at mealtime or between meals.

An alternative application of this same procedure would be to use edible reinforcement to shape a recreational activity. For example, an autistic or mentally retarded child might be taught to ride a tricycle or play a game using his or her favorite food or sweet (Watson, 1978b). Initially, food-type reinforcement would be used to get the child to participate in the training program; but once he or she learned to ride the tricycle or play the game, these activities would become reinforcing in and of themselves (in most cases), and the child no longer would require other kinds of reinforcement to get him or her to ride the tricycle or play the game. In turn, the tricycle or game could be used as reinforcement for other programs or activities.

Generalization Training and Maintenance

Once a disruptive behavior has been decelerated to some predetermined criterion by one or several staff members, *generalization training* should be carried out. Steps should be taken to ensure that the effects of the treatment program will generalize or transfer to all relevant persons and all relevant physical situations, such as the teacher, teacher's aide, mother, and bus driver in the classroom, at home, and on the bus. This procedure will be illustrated using a case study taken from a program at the Special Education District of Lake County in Illinois (Watson, 1978a). An 11-year-old moderately retarded girl had a history of being quite aggressive. She spit on and hit staff and pupils. To eliminate these problems, a *crisis team* person was used. A specially trained staff member was assigned to deal with the problem. After it was corrected, he taught all relevant people in all relevant physical locations how to manage this behavior problem, and the child then was placed on a *maintenance program.*

The crisis team person began treatment by dealing with spitting in the classroom. He brought this problem under control using an overcorrection procedure. Once he eliminated spitting, he showed the teacher and the aide how to control spitting using overcorrection and demonstrated with the child herself. When he completed the demonstration, the teacher and the aide showed the crisis team member how overcorrection should be used, again demonstrating with the same child. Not only was the crisis team person showing the teacher and the aide how to carry out overcorrection, but he also was carrying out generalization training as well.

When he completed generalization training in the classroom with the teacher and the aide, the crisis team person went to the child's home and showed the mother how to use overcorrection, employing the same procedure he used in the classroom.

Finally, the crisis team member carried out generalization training on the school bus. To accomplish this task, he used a *mediation* technique (Watson, 1978a). He boarded the bus prior to arriving at the child's house. When she got on the bus, the crisis team member told her that if she spit on anyone on the bus, he would overcorrect her. Once he had eliminated her spitting on the bus, the crisis team member faded himself from the bus. He told the child that rather than ride the bus the next day, he would be at the bus stop at school when the bus arrived. He said he would ask the bus driver if she had spit on anyone, and if the bus driver said yes, she would be overcorrected. Once spitting was brought under control at this stage of fading, the crisis team person told the child that he would no longer be at the bus stop when the bus arrived at school, but if she spit on anyone on the way to school, the bus driver would come to his office at school and report the incident to him, and he would then overcorrect her. This technique stopped spitting on the bus.

After generalization training was completed, the child was placed on maintenance. Everyone who was involved with her was instructed to overcorrect her whenever she spit on anyone. There was no more spitting for a year, and then it occurred only once.

Both time out using a holding technique (see Figure 6.9) and overcorrection were used to deal with hitting. Two years after these procedures were used to control spitting and hitting, the child continued to refrain from this kind of aggressive behavior. Prior to treatment, she was extremely negativistic. After treatment, she was cooperative with the teacher, teacher's aide, parents, and bus driver.

Staff Training Problems

Because an entire chapter in this volume is devoted to inservice training of paraprofessionals and professionals (McGee and Pearson, Chapter 11), only one point needs to be made here. Many behavior management programs fail because staff do not receive the proper training initially and because the quality of their behavior management skills is not maintained after they acquire them.

Staff Accountability Problems

The absence of an effective staff accountability system seems to be a major contributor to ineffective behavior management programs (Watson, 1978a). This problem probably is a significant factor in residential institutional programs. In many cases no individual is responsible for a specific client or a specific targeted behavior a particular client may exhibit. In such a situation, when a client exhibits the targeted behavior, no one steps in to deal with it, presumably because of the diffusion of accountability. Thus, treatment of the behavior problem is haphazard.

One solution to this accountability problem is a staff management system (Watson, 1978a). Staff are assigned specific clients to train or to manage when they are disruptive, and they are periodically monitored by a supervisor to determine whether they deal with the disruptive behavior as it occurs and manage it correctly. After the staff member is observed by the supervisor, he or she receives feedback using the +4/-1 + positive formula. When giving feedback, the supervisor makes, on the average, four positive comments to every negative comment, and a negative comment is followed by a positive comment. In addition, when giving negative feedback, the supervisor provides a rationale for why the negative feedback is being offered. Finally, the staff member is given the opportunity to ask questions at the end of the feedback session. All feedback is given politely and pleasantly. All of this is done by the supervisor in a very natural manner.

For example, the supervisor might observe a staff member carrying out an overcorrection procedure with a child who spit. Perhaps the consequence of spitting is to scrub the floor or rug with a brush for 15 to 20 minutes. The supervisor observes the staff member carrying out overcorrection. After overcorrection has been completed, the supervisor gives the staff member feedback. "Well Bill, that looked good. Your physical control over Mary was really great. Your commands were firm, polite, and you had no problem getting her to scrub, but you still did not look like you were exerting yourself too much. There were times when you could have faded your physical guidance more. She was cooperating after about 5 minutes, yet you still guided her hand. Why don't you try giving her less assistance next time as she becomes more cooperative. All in all though, I think you did a good job. Do you have any questions?"

Staff Reinforcement

It is extremely important that staff receive reinforcement for carrying out behavior management programs correctly. One reason why staff do not carry out treatment as they should probably is because they are unmotivated (Watson, 1978a). Dealing with behavior management problems can be tedious, and staff need recognition if they are to be expected to carry out treatment correctly.

A variety of items and events have been used as staff reinforcement. Staff have been given verbal recognition, awards, such as plaques, time off from work, the right to select their work schedule, and green stamps (Watson, Dix, and Owne, submitted for publication). To be most effective, staff probably should receive reinforcement daily. A staff reinforcement system in a large, residential facility was set up that utilized daily feedback in the form of recognition (Watson, 1978a). Staff were observed by supervisors on the average of twice a day as they either taught clients independent living skills or managed disruptive behavior problems. Supervisors used the +4/-1 + positive feedback approach. In addition, staff received other forms of reinforcement. Staff were selected as *trainer of the week* on each unit, *trainer of the month* on each unit, *trainer of the quarter* on each unit, and the *outstanding trainer for the quarter for the facility*. Outstanding trainers received plaques with their names engraved on them. The outstanding trainer of the quarter awardees were given a luncheon. In addition, the outstanding trainer of the facility received an engraved plaque plus a $25 savings bond at the luncheon.

Consistency of Treatment

Typically, when behavior management treatment programs are implemented, the interest and commitment that is necessary to make them work properly is short-lived. Staff may begin such programs with high levels of enthusiasm, and stay very involved for 30 to 120 days. This period may be characterized as the novelty effect period. After that, interest wanes. Whereas staff previously followed a client's treatment prescription very carefully during the novelty period, later on they either do not carry out treatment such as overcorrection every time they should, or if they do carry out treatment, it is not done correctly. Overcorrection, for example, may be carried out for only 5 or 6 minutes rather than for 15 or 20 minutes, as prescribed.

A solution to this problem may require two alternatives. First, a staff management system should be implemented like the one described in the section on staff accountability (Watson, 1978a). Second, a *crisis team* may be needed to reduce staff *burnout* (Watson et al., 1980). When a crisis team approach is used, certain staff are assigned to deal with behavior problems. For example, in a large residential facility, two staff members may be assigned to the crisis team for every 100 residents in the facility (on each of the day and afternoon shifts). Whenever a behavior problem occurs, staff alert the crisis team, usually by telephone, and let them deal with the behavior problem. Staff can use a mediation approach to bridge the time gap between the occurrence of the disruptive behavior and the arrival of the crisis team. If a client breaks a window, the staff member witnessing the event might say, "No Billy, you don't break windows. As soon as the crisis team gets here, you're going to have to clean that broken glass up."

To reduce staff burnout, a person could be assigned to the crisis team for 1 day or 1 week on a rotational basis, if the program is in a residential facility with a large number of staff. If the program is in a group home, school, or vocational workshop with only a few staff members, someone could be assigned to the crisis team for 6 months, 9 months, or 12 months, and then be replaced by someone else. Crisis team members typically have other duties, but must be available to intervene whenever they are called.

ACKNOWLEDGEMENT

A number of the procedures presented in this chapter were developed at Partlow State School and Hospital, Tuscaloosa, Alabama. I want to thank Robert Sanders, Superintendent, and the staff at Partlow for their participation and support during the development of these programs.

REFERENCES

Ferster, C. B., and DeMyer, M. K. 1962. A method for the experimental analysis of the behavior of autistic children. Am. J. Orthopsychiatry 32:89–98.
Martin, R. 1975. Legal Challenges to Behavior Modification. Research Press, Champaign, IL.
Stolz, S. B. 1978. Ethical Issues in Behavior Modification. Jossey-Bass, San Francisco.
Watson, L. S. 1974. A Manual for Teaching Behavior Modification Skills to Staff: An Inservice Training Program for Parents, Teachers, Nurses, and Relevant Direct Care Staff. Behavior Modification Technology, Inc., Libertyville, IL.
Watson, L. S. 1978a. A Management System Approach to Teaching Independent Living Skills and Managing Disruptive Behavior. Behavior Modification Technology, Inc., Tuscaloosa, AL.

Watson, L. S. 1978b. How to Teach Independent Living Skills and Manage Disruptive Behavior. Behavior Modification Technology, Inc., Tuscaloosa, AL.
Watson, L. S., Owen, J. R., and Uzzell, R. 1980. A Positive Approach to Managing Disruptive Behavior. Behavior Modification Technology, Inc., Tuscaloosa, AL.

Chapter **7**

Psychopharmacologic Agents in Mental Retardation

Issues and Challenges

James E. Wilson

The use of psychopharmalogic agents in the clinical management of mentally retarded citizens is a controversial issue. There is increasing concern over the potential effects of these agents as they affect impediments to personality growth and functioning (Rivinus, 1980).

This chapter presents an overview of the currently used psychopharmacologic agents and pertinent clinical research, as well as some pertinent findings concerning their effects. Guidelines for an approach to the use of psychopharmacologic agents in the mentally retarded person will be presented including clinical indications for the various psychopharmacologic agents, efficacy of these agents, dosage levels, and the appropriateness of these agents in the overall therapeutic regimes.

OVERVIEW

Psychopharmacologic agents have been utilized in the treatment and management of mental illness in the mentally retarded since the latter half of the century. The initial focus of utility was on sedative agents. Only since the advent of the psychoactive agents (i.e., tranquilizers, neuroleptics, psychotropic agents) in the fifth decade of this century has the control of specific aberrant behavior(s) through psychotropic intervention been addressed. These psychoactive drugs are administered for the explicit purpose of initiating beneficial alternations in aberrations of motor activity. Examples include hyperactivity and hypoactivity. These agents assist also in altering mood, abnormal thought processes, and overall modulation of behavior.

In the 1980s it is clear that the status of our knowledge concerning the efficacy of psychopharmacologic agents in aiding mentally ill-mentally retarded citizens remains inadequate. Although excellent reviews of the clinical utilization of psychopharmacologic agents in mentally ill-mentally retarded persons are available (e.g., Freeman, 1980; Lipman, 1970a; Lipman, DiMascio, Reatig, and Kirson, 1978; Sprague and Werry, 1971) the lack of extensive objective studies and the fact that the majority of studies were conducted among institutionalized populations (who represent less than 5% of the retarded population) seriously limit the data base.

Despite the limitations of these studies, some conclusions may be gleaned: 1) The major psychoactive agents (e.g., the phenothiazines such as chlorpromazine) seem to be effective in ameliorating hostile-aggressive behaviors, self-mutilization proclivities, and marked overactivity; 2) if the major psychoactive agents are prescribed in high dosages and for prolonged periods of time, there is noted serious interface with learning and performance abilities (Werry and Aman, 1975); 3) the minor psychoactive agents (e.g., the benzodiazepines such as diazepem), have not been adequately evaluated in the mentally retarded and thus a therapeutic opinion cannot be given; and 4) the level of mental retardation seems to have minimal if any effect on the response to psychoactive drugs (Freeman, 1970b; Werry and Sprague, 1972).

It is evident that psychopharmacologic agents can be utilized adjunctly to assist mentally retarded persons in alleviating certain symptoms or syndromes of mental illness. Alleviation of anxiety, schizophrenia, manic-depressive illness, depression, self-abusive behavior, and aggression can help the retarded person to achieve a more integrated level of cognitive functioning and to live in less restrictive residential or program environments.

Psychopharmacologic intervention has received a substantial amount of public attention both positive and negative. Some individuals are of the opinion that mentally retarded people are being seriously harmed with these agents. Advocates are convinced that some mentally ill-mentally retarded individuals are deliberately overdosed with drugs in order to reduce or minimize the amount of professional managerial time devoted to caregiving (Sprague, 1977; Tu, 1979). At the other end of the spectrum, fact indicates that a large number of mentally retarded people are underdosed with respect to psychotropic medications. It is this author's position that the judicious use of psychoactive agents as an adjunct to multidisciplinary team treatment and management can result in improved conditions for mentally ill-mentally retarded individuals. Specifically, the mentally ill-mentally retarded person cannot hope to improve maximally (and thus live in least restrictive environments) until such disturbing symptoms as delusions, hallucinations, withdrawal, loose associations, extreme anxiety, aggression, and other symptoms of mental illness are removed or reduced to a minimum. It follows that a rational utilization of these psychoactive agents is necessary to bring about these desired behavioral changes. The information summarized in Table 7.1 outlines available psychotropic medication dosages, the most frequent side effects, and the dosages listed in upper limit(s). It is necessary to stress that the dosage range of each of these agents must be individualized for each person to be treated according to his or her special mental status needs. Furthermore, there is no magical dosage for a given set of symptoms for persons with a given level of global intelligence range.

ANTIPSYCHOTICS

It must also be stressed that it may take from 7 to 60 days to adjust a dosage that obtains maximal clinical improvement with minimal, if any, side effects. For example, some symptoms such as hallucinations, delusions, and looseness of associations usually do not recede before 4 to 10 days of treatment with these agents. Indeed, some of these symptoms will not reverse completely, but will be reduced sufficiently so that the person will feel much more comfortable and be able to actively participate in ongoing treatment programs.

In case of the mentally ill-mentally retarded person, the use of antipsychotic agents may take some very special efforts, especially with nonverbal severely retarded persons. Dosage effectiveness and clinical progress may have to be assessed via visual observation of the patient, close assessment of nonverbal communications, and their increasingly more stable patterns of behavior. For example, attention must focus on assessing how well the patient reassumes his or her previously demonstrated repertoires of self-help skills or changes in the aggressive-impulsive behaviors with peers in occupational and recreational therapy situations. Assessments of these indices of improvement (and their objective recording) must be taught to and actively monitored by nursing and other personnel charged with the care and the treatment.

In Table 7.1 an extended classification of side effects is presented. The side effects of the major psychoactive agents are much more unpleasant than those of the antianxiety agents. The most severe include the extrapyramidal side affects wherein an area of the brain is medicated to the point where it affects muscle movements. It can lead to a devastating symptom complex: a syndrome called tardive dyskinesia. Tardive dyskinesia is currently thought to be an irreversible syndrome characterized by rapid movements of the tongue and lips, tics of the facial musculature, drooling, and a sucking or rooting motion of the mouth, as well as movements of other body parts. This syndrome is associated with long-term use of the neuroleptics at higher dosage levels. Tardive dyskinesia can be prevented by good medical management of the patient and periodic neurologic examinations (especially of the tongue and face) on a regular basis (Paulson, Rizvi, and Crance, 1975). Similarly, the extrapyramidal side effects must be evaluated on a regular basis. The need for

Table 7.1   Available psychotropic medication dosages[a]

I.   Antipsychotics
    A.   Phenothiazines
        Thorazine (chlorpromazine)
        2 g/day
        50 mg/injection
        Mellaril (thioridazine)
        800 mg/day
        Serentil (mesoridazine)
        500 mg/day
        25 mg/injection
        Stelazine (trifluoperazine)
        120 mg/day
        5 mg/injection
        Prolixin (fluphenazine)
        120 mg or 2.5 mg/day
        125 mg long-acting ester every 1–5 weeks
        5 mg/ml hydrochloride/injection
        Trilafon (perphenazine)
        64 mg/day
        5 mg/injection

    B.   Dibenzoxazepines
        Loxitane (loxapine)
        325 mg/day
        25 mg/injection

    C.   Indoles
        Moban (molindone)
        400 mg/day

[a]Doses indicated are listed as the upper limit for use as a neuroleptic.

D. Thioxanthines
   Taractan (chlorprothixene)
   600 mg/day
   25 mg/injection
   Navane (thiothixene)
   120 mg/day
   5-10 mg/injection

E. Butyrophenones
   Haldol (haloperidol)
   120 mg/day
   5 mg/injection

All of the neuroleptics listed in this table can produce the following side effects:

1. Sedation
2. Drowsiness
3. Reduction in learning ability
4. Extrapyramidal reactions, which include the following:
   a. Dystonias
   b. Dyskinesias
   c. Tremors
   d. Akinesia (stiffness)
   e. Akathesia (restlessness)
   f. Tardive dyskinesia
5. Constipation
6. Dry mouth
7. Hypotension
8. Impotence

II. Lithium
   A. Lithium carbonate capsules
   B. Lithium citrate liquid

   Monitoring is provided by therapeutic blood levels in both of the above.

   Side effects include:
   1. Tremor
   2. Nausea and vomiting
   3. Excessive thirst and urination
   4. CNS confusion

III. Antianxiety agents
   A. Glycerol derivatives
      Miltown (meprobamate)
      400-3000 mg/day
      Tybatran (tybamate)
      500-1200 mg/day

continued

B. Benzodiazepine derivatives
    Librium (chlordiazepoxide)
    15–100 mg/day
    Praxipam (halazepam)
    40–160 mg/day
    Valium (diazepam)
    5–40 mg/day
    Ativan (lorazepam)
    2–6 mg/day
    Serax (oxazepam)
    30–120 mg/day
    Xanax (alprazolam)
    0.5–4 mg/day
    Tranxene (chlorazepate)
    15–60 mg/day
    Centrax (prazepam)
    20–60 mg/day

C. Diphenylmethane derivatives
    Vistaril (hydroxyzine)
    75–300 mg/day

Side effects of the antianxiety agents include:
1. Drowsiness
2. Ataxia
3. Muscle weakness
4. General CNS depression

judicious monitoring is evident in the following clinical example. A young lady who was referred for evaluation because the house parents stated she displayed a "schizophrenic shuffle." The young lady presented with slow shuffling of the feet, interspersed with periods of being unable to sit, getting up and down frequently, and intermittently racing around the room. Is this clinical picture one of anxiety, psychosis, or akathesia (a form of extrapyramidal symptom)? After considerable evaluation the diagnosis was akathesia, and after the antipsychotic agent was reduced in dosage level, all of the schizophrenic shuffle symptoms disappeared. This case presents a graphic demonstration of the neurologic side effects of a major psychoactive agent—side effects that can masquerade as anxiety or other behavioral impairments.

As noted by Lippman (1970), Mellaril is a frequent drug of choice in treating mentally ill-mentally retarded persons, perhaps because it possesses as a side effect a high incidence of retrograde ejaculation and impotence. This agent seems to have the fewest side effects relevant to extrapyramidal phenomena. It is the case that these two reasons often suffice to make Mellaril the most frequently utilized psychoactive agent for this dual diagnosis population. It should also be noted that the other frequent side effects of Mellaril usage include a dry mouth, weight gain, and hypotension. Each of these particular side effects will need close medical monitoring to avoid the unnecessary induction of secondary medical disorders. They may be prevented in part by symptomatic adjuncts (e.g., sugarless candy for the dry mouth).

LITHIUM

Lithium is currently utilized in the treatment of manic-depressive illness in the mentally retarded. It has been increasingly utilized on an empirical basis to control symptomatically severe agression of unknown cause that does not respond to supportive treatment measures (Campbell, 1972; Dostal and Zvolsky, 1970; Grunberg, and Berkowitz, Goetzel, 1977; Lipman et al., 1978; Rivinus, 1980). There are three dosage forms available including tablets, capsules, and a liquid. The liquid form may have some advantages in ensuring that the mentally retarded person has ingested the drug. One of the clinical-management problems with lithium is the monitoring process which requires that Lithium be maintained in a therapeutic range in the blood. This can only be accomplished by withdrawing blood from the client. The lack of cooperation from the mentally ill-mentally retarded patient can make monitoring an extremely difficult undertaking for staff as well as the client.

The major side effects from the administration of lithium include tremor, excessive urination, and thirst. Attention to sodium in the diet is extremely important because changes of dietary sodium may alter the lithium levels. Furthermore, the medical status of the patient before and after the introduction of lithium therapy is of importance in excellent clinical management.

ANTIANXIETY AGENTS

Antianxiety agents such as the benzodiazapines for low to moderate anxiety are useful, especially if they are utilized for short periods of time (Greenblatt and Shader, 1974). There are psychologic and physiologic addictive qualities to these agents and these can occur in the mentally retarded patient. Several reports have documented that the use of Valium or Librium on a long-term basis especially in low to moderate anxiety syndromes, can actually induce high levels of anxiety, and precipitate hostility, anger, or rage (DiMascio, 1969). Thus, psychologic and physiologic addiction, plus a tolerance for these drugs may exacerbate the cluster of symptoms one is attempting to alleviate. Antianxiety agents are effective in a short-term trial for the relief of mild to moderate anxiety.

CHOICE OF PSYCHOACTIVE AGENT

As noted by other contributors to this volume, mentally retarded persons are more likely to have an acute psychotic episode than nonretarded persons especially if the interpersonal stress factors in a given setting are high. The antianxiety agents can be considered if the anxiety level is severe enough; however, the antianxiety agents may not control the psychosis. At that point in treatment the antipsychotic agent will be required. In these instances, many prescribing errors are perpetuated, and these agents become substitutes for active interpersonal counseling and modifications in ongoing program efforts. This trade-off of drug overutilization in lieu of programmatic treatment is also noted in the care of other dependent populations such as the elderly.

The psychoactive agents listed are effective *only* in terms of a specific person's reaction(s) to them, especially in regard to observed reduction of specific symptoms. This finding stresses the point that it takes time and a realistic individual tailoring of these agents to each individual and his or her specific signs or symptoms of mental illness. For example, a patient who presents with hostile, homicidal-aggressive, or agitated schizophrenic behavior may respond more rapidly to psychoactive agents which have a sedative action as part of their psychoactive properties. Rather than overstressing the sedative dimension, it should be noted that the decrease in agitation, via motor slowing, allows the patient to become less disorganized, and thus function more appropriately.

It is extremely important to note that symptomatic behavior can be misleading. An individual with an impacted molar for example, can present a clinical picture marked by hostile and aggressive activities. Such a client may even appear to be psychotic to such a degree that professional treaters may wish to place the individual on a psychoactive agent. In other words, the effects of a toxic disorder can present as a mental illness (e.g., an acute toxic psychosis which has disorganized the personality). Accordingly, before any psychotropic agents are prescribed, the patient should be initially observed carefully and provided with thorough physical, neurologic, and laboratory examinations to determine if the behavior may in fact be secondary to a physical illness. If it is determined that there is no physical basis for the observed behavior pattern, then one should closely examine the previous interpersonal and living situations to determine if there had been recent crisis situations that precipitated or produced the observed abnormal behavioral patterns. A case in point: two retarded young ladies in a group home engage in a vigorous fight over a male coresident. They had been vying as to which would be the steady girlfriend of this particular young man. It was then recommended by their group staff that the more aggressive girl be placed on Thorazine, so that she would " . . .not be so demanding or mean to the other girl." Medication is *not* an appropriate resolution for this type of problem. Staff in care facilities must be sensitized to methods for alleviating crisis situations other than requesting for inappropriate medications. There has been a dichotomy between advocates of the medical model and advocates of the behavioral analysis model relative to the management of persons with mental retardation and allied mental illness. The one side had argued that drugs are the cure, whereas the other side has argued that behavioral management is the cure. Frequently, the mentally ill-mentally retarded individual has been left in the middle of this ideologic dispute, buffeted about by an extreme of one or the other treatment approach. Both of these therapeutic tools can be subjected to abuse because neither has a broad enough vision of the afflicted person's right to receive and participate in programs that meet his or her total needs in the most individualized and sensitive manner possible. There needs to be a balanced approach between the use of psychotropic medications and behavioral analysis-based programming because *both* are valid tools for assisting a dual diagnosis person to overcome or control his or her mental illness and develop more fully toward independence. Each has a legitimate place in the treatment and management of this population if used in an individualized and balanced manner.

Perhaps the most reasoned way to reach this balance is first to examine the following precipitating reasons for the use of psychoactive agents.

1. The patient displays marked motor overactivity (i.e., persistent agitation).
2. The patient displays marked motor underactivity (i.e., withdrawal).
3. There is evidence of slowly or rapidly escalating behaviors of a disorganized type (e.g., psychotic behaviors).
4. Severe disorders of mood are noted (i.e., depression).

5. Fixed or persistent sets of behaviors which are dangerous to the self or others (i.e., mutilization of self or severe aggression towards others) are noted.

All of these symptom clusters can produce serious interference with the person's ability to learn or to interact appropriately within the mainstream of community life. Within the extensive list of psychiatric syndromes, it is important to analyze what target behaviors are specifically interfering with the person's ability to effectively learn and live in normalizing environments. This analysis involves: 1) specific identification of the interfering behaviors; 2) measuring the frequency, intensity, and location; 3) arriving at an objective professional assessment as to whether or not the behaviors are major roadblocks to ongoing learning, work, or appropriate involvement of the person in the normal social-recreational routines of life.

Accordingly, it is clear that this treatment process involves a combined working relationship between behavioral analysis-oriented programmatic staff and mental health professionals. Otherwise, balanced treatment-management programs are rarely achieved. In actual life situations, a teacher, parent, or workshop trainer is confronted with a person who usually presents one of the aforementioned five symptoms. The client is referred to a cooperating mental health specialist. The interfering behaviors are described; frequency and extent are measured and objectively resolved. If the behaviors are deemed to be of low frequency and noted to be rather easily redirected by a program of personnel intervention tactics, no further specialized professional attention is needed. If these and similar first level extrinsic alteration tactics are unsuccessful, however, the specific balanced analysis techniques should be utilized and closely assessed for efficacy. It is usually noted that when this second level modification tactic has not been successful, a psychoactive agent is warranted. At this point, a decision is reached based primarily on what psychotropic medication would best allow programmatic staff to most effectively, developmentally, and behaviorally work with the person. The treatment question becomes, what medication, dosage, and administration schedule would most readily and effectively enable programmatic staff to assist the person in becoming tractable so that he or she can begin to acquire appropriate and normalizing behaviors? For example, a very disturbed adolescent may be hitting others 30 times per day, running away 2 times per day, and biting his wrists 10 times per day. This symptom cluster obviously presents many barriers to ongoing attempts to keep the youngster in teaching and training programs. If necessary, the dosage of the medication should reduce these behaviors sufficiently so that programmatic staff can work more directly on the acquisition of appropriate skills and behaviors. Thus, in the example above the selected psychoactive agent should ideally serve to reduce the number of inappropriate and disruptive behaviors to a tolerance level wherein the ongoing teaching-training programs can again become effective.

Accordingly, the initiation of an active medication requires close monitoring by the mental health professional. Adjustments relative to the type of medications, dosage, and schedule of administration should be made. All concerned persons should understand the basic process involved in balancing the use of these agents with intensive ongoing developmental programming. This typically can be described as:

1. *Initiation Phase* There is a gradual "hooking on" of the medication in terms of the medication reducing the inappropriate behaviors to the point where the programming "takes hold." This needs to be closely and sensitively monitored so as to avoid sedative effects.
2. *Accumulation Phase* As the effect of the medication joins forces with the intensive developmental programming, both the acquisition of appropriate behaviors and skills begin to accelerate, and the inappropriate behaviors begin to decelerate, diving downward often in direct proportion to the accelerating appropriate learning.
3. *Reduction Phase* Once the accumulation phase begins to stabilize, it is time to focus on the reduction and/or elimination of the medication. Concomitantly, intensive developmental programming must continue and extend into extrinsic interpersonal transactions that permit behavioral improvement to stabilize.

The primary purpose of the medication should be to help the person arrive at a threshold state of readiness for learning, and thus make the person maximally accessible to the ongoing teaching and training process. Because there is minimum and maximum therapeutic effect for most psychoactive agents, it is the professional team, along with the parents, that must decide when to increase and decrease each agent.

MODERN GUIDELINES FOR UTILIZING PSYCHOACTIVE AGENTS

It is the consensus among mental health professionals that while these psychoactive medications have spurred major changes in the treatment and management of mental illness, especially in hospitalized or institutionalized patients, these agents are extremely potent and may be subject to potential abuse. The potential abuse may revolve around the medical risks to patients because of the side effects previously noted (e.g., tardive dyskinesia). Indiscriminantly high dosage utilization exceeding standards of use advocated by the Food and Drug Administration and prolonged use of the drug without periodic monitoring as to its effectiveness are major concerns.

The efficacy of some multidrug administration practices (e.g., polypharmacy, the practice of administering more than one psychoactive drug simultaneously) has been seriously questioned, especially because some of these practices have not been validated by research findings.

Because the possible benefits and/or risks of these psychoactive agents may significantly affect the patient's life, they, the actual consumers and/or contractor for this service, should be permitted to make their own decision as to whether to undergo such treatment. Although a number of complex issues are noted herein (e.g., competency, children's rights, etc.), it is becoming increasingly clear that the consumer's choice should be included in allied issues such as aversive behavioral modification, electroconvulsive treatment, and psychosurgery.

Because the actual or delayed potentially toxic effects of many of the major psychoactive agents in pregnant women or children is not clearly understood, special caution has been voiced as to their use with such persons. Similar concerns have been raised as to the potential hazards of these agents with elderly citizens.

EVOLVING MEDICOLEGAL PARAMETER

Beyond the above noted concerns there has been a veritable legal and regulatory revolution in the attitude toward the use of psychopharmacologic agents on retarded citizens. Legal cases stemming from the benchmark case of *Wyatt v. Stickney* (1972) have distinctly shaped the modern guidelines in this area. It is advisable to be aware of the impact of these legal changes and how they are viewed by national regulatory groups. For example, Section C of the *Wyatt v. Stickney* case stated:

> Residents shall have the right to be free from unnecessary or excessive medication. The resident's record shall state the effects of psychoactive medications on the resident. When doses of such are changed or other psychoactive medications are prescribed, a notation shall be made in the resident's record covering the effect of the new medication or new dosages and the behavior changes, if any, which occur.

Furthermore, Section D of this federal court order notes:

Medication shall not be used as punishment, for the convenience of staff, as a substitute for habilitation program, or in quantities that interfere with the resident's habilitation program.

It is clear that this legal case will have a major impact on the prescribing and utilization patterns of psychoactive agents in mentally ill-mentally retarded persons. To date, it has become the precedent for many far-reaching legal decisions in New York, Minnesota, Pennsylvania, Texas, and Nebraska. Beyond the initial focus on institutionalized retarded persons, these legal and regulatory changes are beginning to have a similar impact on the psychopharmacologic usage patterns in community-based populations of retarded citizens.

It is clear that a new approach to the clinical utilization of psychoactive agents is being mandated. Furthermore, the recently published standards concerning these agents and overall programming efforts for the mentally retarded by the Accreditation Council for Mental Retardation/Developmental Disabilities are slowly becoming the professional yardstick of accepted procedures for clinical utilization. The following guidelines summarize the published standards.

1. There should be a thorough review of possible alternative treatment interventions which can quell disturbing sets of behaviors. Similar to the posture noted in this volume by Watson (Chapter 6), it is often noted that the initiation of enriched program components and/or changes in the interpersonal milieu often effects major changes in retarded persons' behaviors without having to utilize more technical treatment interventions. There is a need to assess closely whether recent crisis features (e.g., reversible interpersonal and/or environmental changes) are operative, and initiate changes if necessary. After waiting a reasonable period of time, reassess whether the behavioral problems are still present. If they are present or have not been appreciably altered by initial treatment efforts, then the specific behaviors should be specifically described via an objective method for obtaining a baseline. This initial baseline should describe *what* behaviors (e.g., auditory hallucinations, hyperactivity, assaultive behavior toward others, etc.), their *frequency,* and the specific manner in which they disrupt the mentally ill-mentally retarded person's *developmental progress.* This guideline permits the use of an objective baseline for deciding whether to utilize psychoactive agents or to continue, stop, or increase/decrease their dosage.

2.   A treatment plan must be formulated which can be shared with the retarded person (if competent, or with his parents/guardian) and with the key members of his or her treatment team. The treatment plan focuses on obtaining consent for the use of a psychoactive agent and outlining the projected result of these agents in the overall programming efforts on behalf of the afflicted individual.

3.   The use of these agents must always be within an overall treatment approach (see McGee and Pearson, Chapter 11, this volume), clear provisions must be made for monitoring the efficacy, nonefficacy, side effects, and other actions of the psychoactive agents on a given individual. It is herein recommended that a 30-day limit be placed on all prescription orders, and the patient should be evaluated at least weekly by the prescribing physician. Separate monitoring by other members of the treatment team should always be welcomed; "excessive" data is a luxury that is very necessary and useful.

4.   The prescribing physician should be requested to review and record the *current* effect of the prescribed medication on the baseline behaviors recorded in guideline 1. If clearcut and/or expected changes have occurred (or have not occurred), changes in the dosage prescribed should be made at this time or in extreme cases, at sometime within a 6-month period of monthly monitoring efforts. It should be noted that a helpful pharmacologic assessment tactic here is the use of "drug holidays." Specifically, these drug holidays are planned reductions (or careful withdrawal) of the prescribed medications at regular intervals. This tactic helps to assess the effects of the medication on the original baseline behaviors and lessen the incidence of tardive dyskinesia.

5.   A conservative set of principles has clinically evolved to: a) avoid the utilization of more than one major psychoactive agent at one time; b) avoid combining major and minor psychoactive agents at one time; c) avoid the use of *any* psychoactive agent beyond the levels approved by the Food and Drug Administration; and d) practice special caution in utilizing this agent in pregnant women or to individuals under 12 years of age.

6.   Knowledge on the part of all treatment staff (not just the prescribing physician) as to adverse effects of the psychoactive agents should be provided. An ongoing in-service training program is an excellent vehicle for transmitting up-to-date information on this topic.

7. Lastly, a guideline that is gaining much popularity nationwide is the formation of a special psychoactive drug review committee. Care should be taken to have this committee composed of individuals who are not employed by the facility, program, or institution. Rather than an adversarial role for this committee, its focus must at all times be on providing constructive input and external monitoring so as to ensure that high quality professional care is being administered at all times.

Utilization of the above seven guidelines will, in the author's opinion, fully permit the rise of state-of-the-art utilization of psychopharmacologic agents as helpful adjuncts to the modern care and treatment of mentally ill-mentally retarded citizens.

SUMMARY

Psychopharmacologic agents are beneficial as selective adjuncts in the treatment of the symptoms of mental illness as they occur in both the mentally retarded and the nonmentally retarded populations. In order to provide the benefits of modern psychoactive agents to the care of mentally ill-mentally retarded individuals in the least restrictive environment, there must always be the professional posture of utilizing these agents with both caution and ongoing individualized care within a framework of periodic monitoring of the patient. A balanced treatment program, utilizing combined psychoactive agents and behavior analysis-based programs, seems most concordant with modern progress of help for dual diagnosis individuals.

REFERENCES

Campbell, M. 1972. Lithium and chlorpromazine: A controlled cross-over study of hyperactive severely disturbed young children. J. Autism Child Schizophr. 21:234–236.
DiMascio, A. 1969. Psychotropic drugs and induced hostility. Psychosomatics 10(3):37–38.
Dostal T., and Zvolsky, P. 1979. Antiaggressive effects of lithium salts in severe mentally retarded adolescents. Int. Pharmacopsychiatry 5:203–207.
Freeman, R. D. 1970a. Problems and care of the mentally retarded. In: N. R. Bernstein (ed.), Diminshed People, pp. 277–304. Little, Brown & Company, Boston.
Freeman, R. D. 1970b. Psychopharmacology and the retarded child. In: F. J. Menolascino (ed.), Psychiatric Approaches to Mental Retardation. pp. 294–367. Basic Books, New York.

Goetzl, U., Grunberg, F., and Berkowitz, B. 1977. Lithium carbonate in the management of hyperactive aggressive behavior of the mentally retarded. Compr. Psychiatry 16(6):591–606.

Greenblatt, D. S., and Shader, R. I. 1974. Benzodiazepines in Clinical Practice. Raven Press, New York.

Lipman, R. S. 1970. The use of psychopharmacological agents in residential facilities for the retarded. In: F. J. Menolascino, (ed.), Psychiatric Approaches to Mental Retardation. pp. 387–398. Basic Books, New York.

Lipman, R. S., DiMascio, A., Reating, N., and Kirson, T. 1978. Psychotropic drugs and mentally retarded children. In: R. S. Lipman (ed.), Psychopharmacology: A Generation of Progress, pp. 1437–1499. Raven Press, New York.

Mason, B. D., and Menolascino, F. J. 1976. The right to treatment for mentally retarded citizens: An evolving legal and scientific interface. Creighton Law Rev. 10:124–166.

Paulson, G. W., Rizvi, C. A., and Crance, G. E. 1975. Tardive dyskinesia as a possible sequel of long-term therapy with phenothiazine. Clin. Pediatr. 10:953–955.

Rivinus, T. M. 1980. Psychopharmacology and the mentally retarded patient. In: L. S. Szymanski and P. E. Tanguay (eds.), Emotional Disorders of Mentally Retarded Persons. University Park Press, Baltimore.

Sprague, R. L. 1977. Overview of psychopharmacology for the retarded in the U.S. In: P. Mittler (ed.), Research to Practice in Mental Retardation, Vol. 3. University Park Press, Baltimore.

Sprague, R. L., and Werry, J. S. 1971. Methodology of psychopharmacological studies with retarded. In: N. R. Ellis (ed.), International Rev. Res. Ment. Retard. 5:147–217.

Tu, J.B. 1979. A survey of psychotropic medications in mental retardation facilities. J. Clin. Psychiatry 40:125–130.

Werry, J. S., and Sprague, R. L. 1972. Methylphenidate and haloperidol in children. Arch. Gen. Psychiatry 32:790–795.

Wyatt v. Stickney. 1972. 344 F. Suppl. 387.

Chapter 8

Social Work Challenges

Meeting the Mental Health Needs of Mentally Retarded Young Adults

Michael J. Monfils

Mentally retarded adolescents and young adults face a variety of challenges as they adjust to their changing life circumstances. The retarded late adolescent must adapt in a relatively short time to parental and societal demands that he or she live independently and engage in productive work activities. These tasks accentuate the need of the individual to develop new skills in self-direction and social interaction. These skills, however, are not easily acquired due to the many developmental changes that occur throughout the course of adolescence. During this developmental period retarded individuals may also experience an intensification of normal adolescent conflict within the family, exacerbated by the retarded individual's delay in maturation. For example, the adolescent characteristically begins to challenge parents by rebelling against their authority and values. Parents of retarded adolescents at times feel frustrated by a loss of control over their son's or daughter's inconsistent behavior and may disagree regarding appropriate ways of providing for his or her growth toward adulthood. Their planning for the eventual separation of the young person from the home can be anxiety provoking for the entire family. Such conflicts in families with mentally retarded members can periodically bring families into contact with social workers and other professionals who are called upon to intervene at times of crises. It is crucial that treatment intervention focus on enhancing the normal development of the retarded young adult by facilitating his or her passage to a new level of maturity and independence.

In the past the mental health needs of mentally retarded young adults were dealt with primarily in institutional settings. Mental health professionals are now realizing, however, that retarded individuals are able to utilize a broad variety of generic community services, such as mental health clinics and centers, schools, and vocational training centers. The various professions are thus being challenged to provide the full spectrum of services that the retarded will need in order to adjust satisfactorily to community living.

Within the range of mental health services that are needed by retarded adolescents and young adults there remains an important niche for the community-based inpatient service. The author's perspective is that of a social worker on an inpatient unit offering short-term psychiatric treatment for retarded adolescents and adults. This chapter describes, through the use of actual case examples, how various treatment modalities may be utilized to meet the needs of retarded young adults and their families in an inpatient setting. Various strategies for working in conjunction with other community agencies and resources, such as through consultation and education, in the joint treatment and management of these adolescents and young adults are also explored.

ATTITUDES AND VALUES OF PROFESSIONALS

Mental health professionals who truly desire to be of service to retarded young persons and their families might well begin this endeavor by looking inward rather than outward. As Mackinnon and Frederick (1970) have pointed out, professionals need to examine closely their own attitudes, feelings, and prejudices about working with the retarded. It is of the utmost importance to accept retarded citizens as they are, and to develop positive attitudes about mental retardation, attitudes that stress the individual's potential for continued learning and growth. The professional needs to cultivate a commitment and a type of therapeutic enthusiasm for this unique and interesting area of human service.

In developing relationships with mentally retarded young adults, professionals may also benefit from a review of their own styles of relating and communicating. Rather than expecting or demanding change from a client, the mental health worker may wish to look at his or her own patterns of interaction and the ways in which those patterns affect the client. Because retarded adolescents, for example, often relate very directly on a verbal level without any facades, the helping individual will need to develop a relationship quickly based on mutual respect and trust.

Professionals from various disciplines should engage in careful scrutiny of their own value systems, and may wish to review the ways in which their values are communicated to mentally retarded individuals. For instance, social workers have historically stressed the importance of respect for the dignity, worth, and uniqueness of the individual; however, many social workers have also participated in practices that have actually contributed to the dehumanization of the retarded (Horejsi, 1979). It is therefore important for practitioners to develop a strong commitment to basic human rights and to ensure that the rights of their clients are respected.

One of the basic rights that retarded persons have at times been denied is that of self-determination, which includes such aspects as the ability to choose one's place of residence and type of employment or training. Mentally retarded persons are now beginning to assert themselves and are informing practitioners that they do not wish to be overprotected, but rather are willing to accept responsibility for making their own decisions and for speaking on their own behalf (MR 78, 1979).

Mental health professionals must ask themselves whether they are encouraging opportunities for self-assertion and expression on the part of retarded individuals. Such expression can also be seen as handicapped persons participate in cultural and artistic endeavors such as drama, dance, music, and painting. The role of the helper becomes one of allowing clients to learn from their own mistakes and to develop their unique creative abilities.

CASE HISTORIES

The Adolescent in the Primary Family

Tom is a mildly retarded 16-year-old adolescent living with his family. He was admitted subsequent to a recent increase in verbal and physical outbursts, primarily in the home setting. Several days prior to admission he was involved in an argument with his mother during which he struck and kicked her several times. His behavior was described by his parents as becoming increasingly argumentative, demanding, aggressive, and difficult to manage over the past 6 months.

This is the first psychiatric hospitalization for Tom, who enjoys good physical health and is a large, strong adolescent weighing

190 pounds. He has a history of a seizure disorder, which is under control with appropriate medication. His parents first realized that he was retarded when he was about 2 years of age, when his speech and ability to walk were delayed. He was able to enter the public school system at age 6, however, and is currently attending a special education program.

Tom's father is employed in a responsible professional position, which often requires long work hours, 5 to 6 days a week. He displays a great deal of anxiety regarding Tom's situation and the need to hospitalize him. Tom's mother, who has a part-time job, has borne the primary responsibility of caring for him. She indicated feelings of being overwhelmed and simply exhausted by the daily burden of disciplining Tom, as indicated by her statement, "At times I feel like I just don't care and want to give up."

In addition to Tom there are three other children in the home. An older brother, who is a college student, and Tom seem to enjoy a close relationship. Two sisters, one older and one younger than Tom, are high school and junior high school students, respectively. All three of the other children seem to be well adjusted, and there is no history of psychiatric care for any other family members.

Treatment Comments   A starting point in assessing the strengths and weaknesses in this family is the compilation of a thorough history of the patient and family. Satir (1967) has commented upon the importance of utilizing a history taking process in working with families. Such a process enables the professional to evaluate the family unit in terms of role relationships, decision making processes, and familial values regarding the presence of a retarded member. The careful taking of such a history allows the professional to discover patterns of interaction and methods of problem solving that are unique to each family. It also permits the helper to formulate an assessment of the identified patient's family support system and to begin to determine what type of therapeutic intervention would be most appropriate.

While recording a detailed developmental history of the patient and family, the human service professional begins to build and solidify a therapeutic relationship with the family. This relationship, which is characterized by concern, acceptance, empathy, and genuineness on the part of the helper, is a key factor in working with the family. Perlman (1979) has articulated the importance of developing a therapeutic relationship in working with individuals and families. Without the establishment and maintenance of this working alliance, efforts at change within the family will be incomplete. It is the promotion of rapport and communication within the relationship that lays the groundwork for further intervention with the family. The history of this particular family reveals a family constellation that has been functioning adequately up until the past several months. Halpern and Berard (1974) have noted the importance of including the stable family in the treatment process whenever possible. A brief inpatient hospitalization now serves as a means of crisis intervention, a period of respite for the family, and allows everyone to review the patterns of interaction taking place within the family. The treatment team functions as a support system for the family, with the goal of preventing a premature out-of-home placement for Tom.

Adolescence is generally viewed as a period of time during which the individual explores the boundaries or limitations of personal freedom. As Josselyn (1975) has observed, the adolescent actually values his or her parents highly while at the same time protesting the behavioral limits that are imposed by them. This developmental characteristic is apparent in the case of Tom, who is testing the boundaries of acceptable behavior within the family.

Because this family seems to be an essentially healthy unit with the recent onset of a crisis, a brief therapy approach was indicated. Kaffman (1973) has demonstrated a high degree of improvement in families with the use of a short-term family therapy approach. Additional research, as reviewed by Gurman and Kniskern (1978), also attests to the effectiveness of brief, time-limited therapies in working with families. Brief therapy attempts to stabilize the entire family unit and restore healthy coping mechanisms in individual family members.

Wolberg (1977) has developed a methodology for short-term therapy that can be readily adapted for use with families with a retarded adolescent. Once a supportive relationship has been established with the family, the therapeutic process proceeds to an examination of the major conflicts within the family. The role of the therapist is to assist family members in understanding and clarifying areas of conflict. The family is then able to examine alternative courses of action and to experiment with new behaviors and ways of interacting. The therapist challenges family members to change, verbally reinforces constructive behaviors, and assists the family in integrating new knowledge and in planning for the future.

In working with Tom's parents throughout the course of his 5-week hospitalization, efforts were made to assist them in realizing that his behavior represented a normal adolescent attempt to manipulate and explore the boundaries of his environment. His parents were encouraged to adopt a firm, consistent approach, one in which expected behaviors would be clearly established and enforced. Tom's father was able to explore ways in which he could adjust his own schedule and priorities in such a manner that he would be able to invest productive time and energy in his son.

Throughout one's work with the retarded adolescent who is living at home, it is important to evaluate the amount of realistic stress that parents are experiencing (Menolascino, 1977). As in the case of Tom, the day-to-day responsibility of caring for a retarded child in the home can at times be overwhelming. Parents can often be greatly aided by means of a referral to such resources as a parent group or respite care service. Toward the conclusion of Tom's hospitalization contact was made with the local youth chapter of the Association for Retarded Citizens, which made arrangements to include him in regularly scheduled recreational groups and programs. This arrangement would involve him in meaningful social and educational activities, while at the same time providing his parents with periodic relief from the responsibilities of caring for him.

Society often places a negative value upon mentally retarded persons (Mandelbaum and Wheeler, 1960) because they are viewed by some individuals as being deviant and different. The inpatient setting is thus an ideal time to assist family members in examining their own attitudes and values regarding the presence of a retarded member in the family (Menolascino, 1977). Efforts must be made to stress the retarded adolescent's potential for learning, growth, and development, and thereby to enable families to value their children positively. A realistic yet hopeful assessment of the adolescent's developmental potential is imperative.

Tom responded well to the structure and limitations that were placed upon him in the inpatient milieu, and a brief therapy approach to the needs of the family proved effective in engaging them in the treatment process. A low dose of neuroleptic medication was also used and was beneficial in Tom's overall management.

Three months after discharge a follow-up contact with the family indicates that Tom continues to adjust satisfactorily in his home and school settings, with no serious incidents of verbal or physical aggression.

The Late Adolescent without a Family Support System

Glen is an 18-year-old youth who falls within the borderline range of intellectual functioning and was referred for inpatient evaluation and treatment due to recent aggressive and antisocial behaviors. He is facing an assault and battery charge because of a recent attack on a female staff member at his group home, and also has a history of petty thefts at his home and place of employment. Glen has been a resident in community-based foster and group homes for the past 4 years, and also is employed at a workshop, but recently has been refusing to attend the workshop program.

This young man was anoxic at birth, and his early developmental milestones including speech and walking were delayed. He subsequently demonstrated hyperactivity and learning difficulties in school. Glen's situation is further complicated by the fact that he is lacking a supportive family system. His parents were divorced when he was 2 years of age, and his father's current whereabouts are unknown. His mother has remarried and lives nearby, but has chosen to remain detached from him. She has seven other children in the family, and states that she is too busy to visit Glen or participate in his treatment program. Furthermore, she does not feel that there is any way that she can really be of help to him.

Although Glen is 18 years of age and is in good physical health, he is small in stature, measuring 5 feet 4 inches tall and weighing about 100 pounds. He frequently engages in immature, attention seeking behaviors, and has not developed appropriate interpersonal relationship skills. He largely denies responsibility for his impulsive actions, and becomes very sullen and argumentative when confronted about his behaviors. At times he can become quite verbally abusive toward other individuals. Psychologic testing reveals that he is highly confused, suspicious, and agitated, and that he possesses very low self-esteem.

Treatment Comments   Individuals such as Glen present substantial challenges for mental health professionals. Whereas Tom (in the first example) is exploring the limits of acceptable behavior primarily in the family context, Glen is testing out acceptable societal limitations and may be heading toward some type of disposition in the criminal justice system. The inpatient treatment team in this instance functions as a backup system for Glen's community-based program, and will consult regularly with the staff members of the community program throughout his treatment.

Lidz (1976) has postulated that the major tasks of late adolescence revolve around the search for an ego identity and the development of the capacity for intimacy with others. In the case of Glen, his negative self-image was an important barrier to achieving a constructive realization or sense of his own identity. Scanlon (1978) believes that the consistent use of supportive, educative relationships is essential in helping persons with low self-esteem to develop a positive self-concept. Therapeutic relationships were utilized with Glen in the contexts of both individual and group psychotherapy, and a well structured behavioral approach was also designed.

Therapists such as Lott (1970) and Schild (1971) have outlined the rationale and methodology of individual psychotherapeutic approaches with the retarded. The therapist will often need to adopt a flexible approach in working with retarded young persons in individual therapy, without relying on any one particular technique or philosophy. A behavioral counseling orientation (Stamm, 1974) is one of several approaches that may be utilized. It should be noted, however, that there is a need for additional research demonstrating the effectiveness of particular counseling approaches with mentally retarded persons. Browning and Keesey (1974), for example, in their review of seven studies on counseling with the retarded, found only one study which had an adequate research design according to their criteria. Nevertheless, one derives the impression from reviewing the literature that human service professionals do find individual psychotherapy to be an important and useful treatment method with the retarded.

In individual therapeutic sessions with Glen the author assisted him in conducting a self-appraisal, wherein he was able to realize that he did possess some personal strengths and positive attributes. He was also given an opportunity to ventilate his feelings of estrangement from his mother and family, and to resolve feelings of anger and resentment toward his family situation. In addition, difficulties in meeting behavioral expectations and in relating appropriately to other patients and the staff were reviewed, and alternative courses of behavior were explored.

Group therapy approaches with mentally retarded persons have been used by a variety of professionals in diverse settings, and are not really a recent development. As early as the 1940s, Cotzin (1948) described a group therapy approach that was used with retarded adolescent boys. Other authors such as Vail (1955) and Astrachan (1955) reported on both successful and unsuccessful experiences in developing groups for mentally retarded young adults.

More recently, Slivkin and Bernstein (1970) have commented on the benefits of a group approach with an institutionalized adolescent population as a preparation for community placement. Lee (1977) reported on a study that demonstrated that group counseling with moderately retarded adults can prove effective in enhancing their social adjustment skills. In their review of the literature on group therapy with retarded individuals, Vance, McGee, and Finkle (1977) concluded that group counseling can assist these persons to understand and accept themselves, to improve social relationships, and to cope with the problems of everyday living.

Group work with retarded citizens can also encompass the teaching of appropriate social and behavioral skills. Perry and Cerreto (1977), for example, have described the development of a social skills training program that was conducted in a group setting with retarded young adults. Granat (1978) suggests that group assertiveness training can be useful in the habilitation and vocational placement of mentally retarded persons. The use of role playing and modeling in teaching appropriate social skills to mildly and moderately retarded adults has been outlined by Bates (1980). Promising approaches such as these need to be further refined and researched by group practitioners.

The group approach enabled Glen, who participated in therapy sessions with peers four to five times per week, to learn appropriate ways of handling conflicts with others. An additional goal was to teach him how to develop and maintain meaningful relationships with other persons. Once Glen was able to establish trust with the group members, he readily verbalized his feelings and concerns and was able to accept more responsibility for his behaviors.

The role of the group leader in working with individuals such as Glen is to provide an open, accepting atmosphere in which verbalization of feelings is encouraged. The leader will often need to function in a teaching capacity, providing structure and limits with respect to appropriate behaviors within the group. An active style of leadership is usually indicated in which the leader not only offers support, but also fosters insight and behavioral change in group members.

In addition to utilizing individual and group psychotherapeutic approaches with this young man, a program designed to shape and modify his antisocial behaviors was also essential. Birnbrauer (1976) has reviewed the benefits of using behavioral techniques, such as modeling and reinforcement principles, with the retarded. Behavior contracting, a technique that was used successfully by Douds, Engelsgjerd, and Collingwood (1977) in a study with juvenile offenders, was utilized with positive results with Glen. This approach involved a written agreement between Glen and the treatment team regarding responsibilities that he was expected to perform and privileges that he would receive if he carried out his responsibilities properly. The contract, when consistently used to firmly structure the limits of acceptable behavior, proved to be an effective means of modifying inappropriate behaviors.

Throughout the course of Glen's 8-week hospitalization, active consultation and education were carried out with the staff members of his community-based programs. This type of outreach, combined with thorough discharge planning, paved the way for the smooth transition of this youth back into the community. Low doses of antidepressant medication, which had been initiated when Glen first entered treatment, were gradually decreased until he was able to be discharged medication-free.

Follow-up contact with Glen's community counselor 2 months after discharge indicates that his staff members have continued the firm structured and reinforcement procedures that were begun in the facility, as well as supportive individual therapy. Glen is adjusting satisfactorily to a new group residence and has returned to his workshop program, with no outstanding behavioral difficulties or outbursts.

The Young Adult Emancipating from the Family

Brenda is a 23-year-old mildly retarded woman who is a current patient at the facility. She was admitted by her parents for treatment of depression and anxiety, and has been a patient at two other hospitals on three occasions within the past year, subsequent to suicide attempts.

This young woman, who attended special education classes up to approximately an eighth grade level, is in good physical health and has been residing with her parents. Her father, who is retired and in his late 60s, has a history of acute myocardial infarction. He is a concerned parent with good intentions, but has in the past suggested that perhaps an institutional placement might best meet Brenda's needs. Her mother, who is in her mid-60s, seems to be under a great deal of stress and relates feelings of being overwhelmed by Brenda's problems.

Brenda has been somewhat sheltered by her parents from normal social outlets and experiences. Approximately 8 months ago, just prior to her first suicide gesture, she moved with her parents to a retirement community. She has few friends and has never dated. With the exception of having participated in a day activity program for the past two summers, she has not been enrolled in educational or vocational programs that would allow her to develop independent living skills, career interests, and recreational pursuits. Her parents have been overprotective of her and express feelings of guilt and anxiety regarding their daughter's social and sexual development. Brenda's response to her constricted environmental circumstances has included manipulative and passive-aggressive behaviors such as the suicide gestures, as well as depression, repressed anger, and vulnerability to stress.

Brenda is the youngest of four children. Two brothers live out of state and maintain minimal contact with her. A third brother lives nearby and is very supportive and desiring to help. Approximately 6 weeks after admission to our program, Brenda left for a vacation with her family, during which her father became seriously ill and required hospitalization. Her behavior regressed, as she once again became sullen and depressed and was readmitted to the inpatient service. The entire family now faces crises revolving around her father's deteriorating health and the need to acquire appropriate residential and vocational services for her.

Treatment Comments This example illustrates graphically some of the difficulties that may be encountered by retarded young adults as they make the transition from home and family to community living and the world of work. Although this transition is often difficult, continued residence with the family can also result in unhealthy adaptations on the part of various family members. Goodman (1978), in his study of parents who had mentally retarded adult offspring still living at home, found that some of these parents developed maladaptive responses, such as unresolved concerns related to separation and avoidance in making plans for the future. It is unfortunate that a crisis situation often must serve as the catalyst for change in families with retarded young adults. The community-based inpatient service in this case becomes a bridge or platform between the family and other programs, such as group residences and vocational placements.

The young adult years are characterized by the adaptation of the individual to a number of crucial issues. These issues, according to Neugarten (1975), include the person's perspective of time, his or her structuring of the major themes of work and love, and changes in self-concept and identity. An additional important issue for the retarded young adult is separation from the nuclear family and the adjustment to semiindependent or independent living. Parents and other family members also may require opportunities to resolve their feelings about the separation of the retarded member from the home.

Fortunately, mental health professionals have a variety of techniques that may be utilized with individuals such as Brenda. Individual and group psychotherapy have been used in the hospital milieu as a means of allowing her to express and understand her feelings about her situation. Psychotherapy has also enabled her to discuss her family and realistic plans for her future with respect to out-of-home placement and vocational interests. Crisis-oriented brief therapy has been used as a support system for Brenda's parents as a means of assisting them in resolving their own guilt and disappointment over their daughter's situation.

At the present time plans are proceeding to refer Brenda to community-based residential and vocational programs. Her concerned brother, who is her legal guardian, has been in contact with the appropriate agency (Eastern Nebraska Community Office of Retardation), and that agency is in the process of evaluating Brenda for placement into its programs. The treatment team in this instance serves as an intermediary between the family and the agency, and will provide whatever information and assistance are necessary for the agency to reach a decision about serving her.

The importance of effective communication and cooperation between various professionals and agencies, as illustrated in this example, cannot be overemphasized. Social workers are often in an excellent position to mediate between systems and agencies on behalf of their clients. Horejsi (1979) has referred to this type of intervention between social systems as "boundary work." Boundary work in this instance can be seen as including such tasks as information and referral, case coordination, and discharge planning.

Because Brenda has had minimal exposure to a vocational setting, it is also imperative to assess her readiness for training or employment. Accordingly, arrangements have been made for a thorough evaluation by rehabilitation professionals at a nearby facility. The results of this evaluation will make it possible to place her into a vocational setting commensurate with her level of skills.

Mention has been made of this young woman's deficits in the areas of social experiences, ability to develop friendships, and independent living skills. One should not overlook the important contribution that can be made by individuals from disciplines like occupational and recreational therapy in ameliorating deficiencies such as these. Group experiences involving the development of communication skills, creative artistic expression, and leisure time pursuits are also important in the personal development of this young adult.

This example presents a portrait of a young mentally retarded woman who offers a variety of challenges to helping professionals. The inpatient service, working in conjunction with community-based mental health and mental retardation professionals, serves as a platform for Brenda's entry into new residential and vocational services. Continued support for her family members will enable them to deal with separation issues and other personal mental health needs.

IMPLICATIONS FOR PRACTICE

As social workers and other professionals strive to meet the mental health needs of retarded young adults, they will find that they actually have a variety of treatment methods and techniques at their disposal. Approaches that may be utilized range from individual and group psychotherapy to brief crisis-oriented family therapy to the application of behavior modification principles. The approaches that have been employed in an inpatient setting in the above examples can be readily adapted for use in other settings as well. The tasks that practitioners will face in the future include the swift application of new research findings to clinical practice settings so that professionals will be able to choose more easily the treatment method that best fits the circumstances of the particular client.

The variety of situations and problems that are presented by retarded adolescents and young adults points to the importance of flexibility on the part of mental health workers. A large number of helping roles, such as advocate, enabler, therapist, systems negotiator, and case coordinator, are available, and practitioners will need to be flexible in shifting from one role to another as circumstances demand.

The use of consultation and education will also enable human service professionals to reach out directly and indirectly to young retarded citizens and their families. Mental health-mental retardation consultation, as Shapiro (1972) has pointed out, can frequently be used at all levels of prevention. Education regarding modern concepts in mental retardation, such as normalization and the developmental model, will also continue to be essential in the provision of comprehensive mental retardation services to our communities.

In the future, professions such as medicine, psychology, and social work will be challenged to engage in continued research regarding mental retardation and in prevention efforts on all levels. If mental health professionals are serious about their intentions to offer effective services to young adult retarded citizens, they must also be committed to immediate intervention into the early childhood experiences and environmental factors that interfere with normal development (Menolascino and Eaton, 1980). As appropriate new programs and services are created for retarded children and adolescents, these individuals will be well prepared for assuming adult responsibilities and leading meaningful, productive lives.

CONCLUSION

Mentally retarded adolescents and young adults have mental health needs that are similar to those of other persons. Issues that assume importance include separation from family members, adjustment to new residential and vocational environments, and the ongoing need for friendships and meaningful interpersonal relationships. These young people thus present many exciting challenges for mental health professionals in both inpatient and community settings.

Professional helpers are encouraged to develop positive attitudes, values, and commitments toward working with retarded youths. Knowledge and appropriate use of a variety of treatment methods is seen as essential to effective intervention with these clients and their families. With the assistance of research efforts and prevention strategies, much can be done to meet the mental health needs of these individuals.

REFERENCES

Astrachan, M. 1955. Group psychotherapy with mental retarded female adolescents and adults. Am. J. Mental Def. 60:152–156.

Bates, P. 1980. The effectiveness of interpersonal skills training on the social skill acquisition of moderately and mildly retarded adults. J. Appl. Behavior Anal. 13:237–248.

Birnbrauer, J. S. 1976. Mental retardation. In: H. Leitenberg, (ed.), Handbook of Behavior Modification and Behavior Therapy. Prentice-Hall, Englewood Cliffs, N.J.

Browning, P., and Keesey, M. 1974. Outcome studies on counseling with the retarded: A methodological critique. In: P. Browning, (ed.), Mental Retardation Rehabilitation and Counseling. Charles C Thomas, Springfield, IL.

Cotzin, M. 1948. Group psychotherapy with mental defective problem boys. Am. J. Ment. Def. 53:268–283.

Douds, A. F., Engelsgjerd, M., and Collingwood, R. R. 1977. Behavior contracting with youthful offenders and their parents. Child Welfare 56:409–417.

Goodman, D. M. 1978. Parenting an adult mentally retarded offspring. Smith Coll. Stud. Social Work 48:209–234.

Granat, J. P. 1978. Assertiveness training and the mentally retarded. Rehabil. Counsel. Bull. 22:100–107.

Gurman, A. S., and Kniskern, D. P. 1978. Research on marital and family therapy: Progress, perspective, and prospect. In: S. L. Garfield and A. E. Bergin, (eds.), Handbook of Psychotherapy and Behavior Change: An Empirical Analysis. John Wiley & Sons, New York.

Halpern, A. S., and Berard, W. R. 1974. Counseling the mentally retarded: A review for practice. In: P. Browning, (ed.), Mental Retardation Rehabilitation and Counseling. Charles C Thomas, Springfield, IL.

Horejsi, C. R. 1979. Developmental disabilities: Opportunities for social workers. Social Work 24:40–43.

Josselyn, I. M. 1975. The adolescent today. In: W. C. Sze, (ed.), Human Life Cycle. Jason Aronson, New York.

Kaffman, M. 1973. Short-term family therapy. In: H. H. Barten and S. S. Barten, (eds.), Children and Their Parents in Brief Therapy. Behavioral Publications, New York.

Lee, D. Y. 1977. Evaluation of a group counseling program designed to enhance social adjustment of mentally retarded adults. J. Counsel. Psychol. 24:318-323.

Lidz, T. 1976. The Person. Basic Books, New York.

Lott, G. 1970. Psychotherapy of the mentally retarded: Value and cautions. In: F. J. Menolascino, (ed.), Psychiatric Approaches to Mental Retardation. Basic Books, New York.

Mackinnon, M. C., and Frederick, B. S. 1970. A shift of emphasis for psychiatric social work in mental retardation. In: F. J. Menolascino, (ed.), Psychiatric Approaches to Mental Retardation. Basic Books, New York.

Mandelbaum, A., and Wheeler, M. E. 1960. The meaning of a defective child to parents. Social Casework, 41:360-366.

Menolascino, F. J. 1977. Challenges in Mental Retardation: Progressive Ideology and Services. Human Sciences Press, New York.

Menolascino, F. J., and Eaton, L. F. 1980. Future trends in mental retardation. Child Psychiatry Human Dev. 10:156-168.

MR 78. 1979. Mental Retardation: The Leading Edge, Service Programs That Work. A Staff Report of the President's Committee on Mental Retardation. U.S Government Printing Office, Washington, DC.

Neugarten, B. L. 1975. Adult Personality: Toward a psychology of the life cycle. In: W. C. Sze, (ed.), Human Life Cycle. Jason Aronson, New York.

Perlman, H. H. 1979. Relationship, The Heart of Helping People. The University of Chicago Press, Chicago.

Perry, M. A., and Cerreto, M. C. 1977. Structured learning training of social skills for the retarded. Ment. Retard. 15:31-34.

Satir, V. 1967. Conjoint Family Therapy. Science and Behavior Books, Palo Alto, CA.

Scanlon, P. L. 1978. Social work with the mentally retarded client. Social Casework, 59:161-166.

Schild, S. 1971. Counseling services. In: R. Koch and J. C. Dobson, (eds.), The Mentally Retarded Child and His Family. Brunner/Mazel, New York.

Shapiro, I. M. 1972. Mental health-mental retardation consultation. In: E. Katz (ed.), Mental Health Services for the Mentally Retarded. Charles C Thomas, Springfield, IL.

Slivkin, S. E., and Bernstein, N. R. 1970. Group approaches to treating retarded adolescents. In: F. J. Menolascino (ed.), Psychiatric Approaches to Mental Retardation. New York, Basic Books.

Stamm, J. 1974. Behavioral counseling with the mentally retarded. In: P. Browning (ed.), Mental Retardation Rehabilitation and Counseling. Charles C Thomas, Springfield, IL.

Vail, D. J. 1955. An unsuccessful experiment in group therapy. Am. J. Ment. Def. 60:144-151.

Vance, H., McGee, H., and Finkle, L. 1977. Group counseling with mentally retarded persons. Pers. Guid. J. 56:148-152.

Wolberg, L. R. 1977. The Technique of Psychotherapy, Part Two. Grune & Stratton, New York.

PART III
TRAINING CHALLENGES

Chapter 9

The Role of Community Schools in Providing Mental Health Services for Retarded Individuals

Sidney W. Bijou

The role of schools in providing mental health services for retarded individuals should be no different than it is for any other group of individuals. It is the task of schools to provide retarded individuals with effective training in academic skills and knowledge, social behavior, and motivation in order to enhance their community adjustment and personal satisfaction. It is also the duty of schools to deal with classroom behavior problems and disorders in accordance with the best available knowledge and practices. There is no humanitarian justification for discriminating between habilitation and rehabilitation programs for retarded children versus any other category of individuals.

The brief historical sketch presented here of school mental health services for retarded individuals and prospects for the future is viewed from the vantage point of applied behavior analysis (Bijou and Baer, 1978; Bijou and Dunitz-Johnson, 1981), an approach that overlaps at many critical points with the more popular term *behavior modification* (Kazdin, 1978).

FROM THE TURN OF THE CENTURY TO THE END OF WORLD WAR II

At about the turn of the century, community schools in the United States began to cater to the mental health needs of retarded individuals (Reynolds, 1976). Considered barely tolerable by the school system, these children were enrolled in a limited number of day classes and "special classes" or "opportunity rooms," which quickly acquired derogatory connotations. They were provided with manual training curricula fashioned after the programs in use in residential training schools and hospitals that had been established in many states during the previous two decades. They were retained in school until they were "too old" to benefit from further formal education. Level of retardation was established by intelligence tests, and the teaching techniques employed varied as extensively as the personalities of the teachers. The prevailing attitude was that retarded individuals were incapable of learning academic skills and knowledge because they were "born that way."

FROM 1945 TO 1975

Shortly after World War II, many states launched large-scale special class and special school programs for handicapped children, most of them designed for the retarded. Admission to these classes was based on scores made on intelligence tests, which were frequently supplemented by personality tests, particularly when children were referred because of problem behavior. Accompanying the test results in the school psychologists' reports were diagnostic summaries and recommendations, most of which were couched in general and obscure terms. The manual-oriented curricula and teaching techniques employed in the new wave of special classes varied widely and changed with the vicissitudes of educational fads and fashions. Concurrently, colleges and universities—some with federal subsidies—initiated training programs for special teachers.

In the mid-1960s, about 15 years after the special class boom, a number of survey studies concluded that retarded children in special classes achieve no better academically than retarded children in regular classes (e.g., Johnson, 1962). Proponents of special classes argued that the findings were faulty, that gains other than academic were not taken into account, and so on. Opponents of segregated classes, on the other hand, claimed that teaching methods and classroom management techniques in special classes were essentially unguided and unanchored to any theory of teaching or learning; consequently, they were subject to the whims of educators. From the behavioral perspective, arguments about the relative merits of special class versus regular class placement are counterproductive; the basic issue is not type of classroom placement, but the competence of the teacher. Depending on the adequacy of his or her training, a teacher may be effective or ineffective in either a special class or an integrated class, despite the inherent differences in the two teaching situations.

Also in the mid-1960s, reports began to appear demonstrating that behavior analysis principles (Skinner, 1953) could be applied effectively to the education of young retarded children and to the treatment of behavior problems. A seminal study conducted at the Rainier School in Buckley, Washington (Birnbrauer, Bijou, Wolf, and Kidder, 1965), described a curriculum in reading, writing, and arithmetic, the behavioral teaching method and monitoring procedure, and the techniques for treating problem behavior. Other investigations with the same theoretical orientation expanded on the management of problem behaviors in one-to-one situations (Harris, Wolf, and Baer, 1964; Sloane, Johnston, and Bijou, 1967) and in group settings (Becker, Madden, Arnold, and Thomas, 1967). Further development in other parts of the country are outlined by Schiefelbusch (1979).

The salient features of the behavioral approach to delivering mental health and educational services to retarded children follow.

The Teaching Format

The applied behavior analysis teaching format consists of five basic components: 1) individual behavioral assessment; 2) individualized programmed planning; 3) teaching techniques based on operant learning principles; 4) program monitoring; and 5) active participation by parents and aides.

The objective of individual behavioral assessment is to inventory by criterion-referenced tests the competence of a child in *real-life* activities such as self-care, social behavior (including communication), gross and fine motor skills, and preacademic and academic behavior (e.g., Bluma, Shearer, Frohman, and Hilliard, 1976). Findings from such tests (Martuza, 1977) are expressed as degree of mastery of the tasks in the various categories. Levels of achievement are not converted into mental age scores and IQs as in psychometric or norm-referenced testing, and a child is not classified on the basis of intelligence or personality dimension.

The second feature of the behavioral approach—individualized programmed planning—utilizes the information from the behavioral assessment *to plan an initial instructional program,* one that is appropriate to a child's developmental competencies and the educational objectives established for him or her.

Contrary to popular belief, an individualized program does not mean that all instruction must be carried out on a one-to-one basis. It means that the teacher must always be sensitive to each child's learning history and response capacities, and must arrange teaching procedures so that teaching may be carried out either in a one-to-one situation with a teacher, parent, aide, or peer as tutor, or in small groups, or in independent assignments, with or without instructional devices.

The third characteristic of this approach—teaching techniques based on operant learning principles—pervades all the components of the instructional process, to wit, getting the child's attention, providing instructions for performing the task, prompting, reinforcing correct responses, and arranging conditions to generalize the learning acquired (Bijou, 1981a). A well-trained teacher knows how to modify the procedure in each of these phases to help a child make progress and enjoy the fruits of achievement regardless of the source of his or her difficulty in learning.

The hallmark of behavioral teaching on an individual or group basis is the fourth characteristic—monitoring progress in the instructional programs (Lund, Schnaps, and Bijou, in press). Keeping records of the child's responses and the teacher's mode of consequating the responses is probably the most productive way of evaluating progress. Interpretation of the records is unequivocal and straightforward: high rates of correct responding suggest continuation of the program; low rates of correct responding suggest reevaluation and modification of the teaching procedure. A self-correcting system such as this, which can be likened to a servomechanism on a ship or plane, leaves little room for "blaming the victim" for lack of progress.

The fifth and final feature of the application of behavior analysis to educational settings is based on the assumption that well-motivated, fairly intelligent persons—parents and aides—can be trained by the teacher to be capable teaching assistants. Understandably, the teacher must be properly trained to instruct paraprofessionals so that they can participate in the actual teaching process.

Treatment of Classroom Behavior Problems

Classroom behavior problems are generally viewed as problems of childhood pathology requiring assessment, diagnosis, classification, and treatment based on some variation of psychoanalytic, biophysical, or client-centered models (e.g., Kauffman, 1977). In a behavioral approach behavior problems are conceptualized as behaviors that interfere with classroom learning and are a consequence of a child's history and the conditions that prevail in the classroom (Bijou, 1981b). Mild problem behaviors are treated as classroom management problems. That is to say, in carrying out classroom routines, the teacher uses behavioral techniques designed to weaken mild forms of interfering behaviors, such as wandering attention, inappropriate contact with classmates, etc., by using mild forms of disapproval. At the same time he or she attempts to strengthen through positive reinforcement those behaviors that support learning: paying attention, complying with instructions, and enjoying the acquisition of new knowledge and skills.

Moderate and severe forms of classroom problem behavior, namely, persistent noncompliance, tantruming, running away, aggression, self-stimulatory behavior, and destruction of property, are treated by tailor-made programs requiring an observer and, on occasion, an aide. Programs for these kinds of problems involve: 1) specifying the problem in objective, countable terms; 2) obtaining a baseline of its frequency of occurrence; 3) planning a program designed to weaken the problem behavior and strengthen the behavior that supports classroom learning; and 4) recording the occurrence of the problem under the treatment condition. If the data show the treatment program to be effective, it is continued until it is no longer needed. On the other hand, if the data show that the program is not achieving the desired results, it is modified and the record keeping procedure is resumed. If, after several revisions of the program, the problem continues to be so severe that it cannot be ameliorated by this strategy, the teacher seeks assistance from an agency in the school or community.

FROM 1975 TO PRESENT

Since 1975 four developments have markedly extended the application of behavioral principles to the education and treatment of retarded individuals: 1) the establishment of behavioral models for the preschool education of handicapped children; 2) the results of the national Follow Through research project on the elementary education of disadvantaged children; 3) the general recognition that applied behavior analysis is a method of choice for the education and training of severely and profoundly retarded individuals; and 4) the enactment of PL 94-142, the Education for All Handicapped Children Act of 1975.

Behavior models and training centers were established for young handicapped children at the University of Illinois (Bijou, 1972a, 1972b); for young deviant children at the University of Kansas (Baer, Rowbury, Baer, et al., 1976); for moderately and severely handicapped children in Monmouth, Oregon (Fredericks, Baldwin,

Grove, et al., 1977); for Down's syndrome babies and children at the University of Washington (Hayden and Haring, 1976); and for young handicapped children at the University of Arizona (Bijou, 1977). In addition, a successful behavioral model for training parents to train their young handicapped children in the home was developed at Portage, Wisconsin (Shearer and Shearer, 1976).

The objective of the national Follow Through project, administered by the U.S. Office of Education with funds from the Office of Economic Opportunity, was to evaluate the relative merits of the major teaching models for the elementary education of economically disadvantaged children. Follow Through was so named because it was viewed as a program that would follow through on educational efforts initiated in the Head Start program for preschool socially disadvantaged children. The eight models that could be evaluated on substantial data included: Direct Instruction (University of Oregon), behavior analysis (University of Kansas), parent education, the Southwest Laboratory approach, cognitive curriculum, the Bank Street School approach, open education, and TEEM (The University of Arizona). Although the findings have been interpreted variously (e.g., ABT Associates, 1976, 1977; House, Glass, McLean and Walker, 1977), it has become increasingly clear that the Direct Instructional Model and the behavior analysis model, both based on applied behavior analysis, were the most effective approaches in educating disadvantaged children from kindergarten through the third grade (Bereiter and Kurland, 1978; Becker and Carnine, 1980, 1981).

During the latter part of the 1970s, special educators in general acknowledged that behavioral techniques were the most promising approach for the education and training of severely and profoundly retarded individuals. The majority of textbooks geared to this population were behaviorally oriented, and much of the research in this area was beginning to be focused on problems of individualized instruction (e.g., Guess, Horner, Utley, et al., 1978), using single-subject designs (e.g., Hersen and Barlow, 1976).

PL 94-142 was enacted as a backlash of federal legislation in the sense that members of the U.S. Congress, partially because of pressure from concerned parents and parent organizations, expressed their dissatisfaction with the progress of children placed in special classes through the testing-classification procedure mentioned earlier. Among its various stipulations, the law expressly requires that classroom instruction be individualized, that parents be involved in the individual educational program, that the rights of children be protected in all special educational programs (the concept of the least restrictive alternative for education and treatment), that records evaluating the progress of children be kept, and that parents be informed periodically of their children's progress.

The implementation of PL 94–142 has created problems, two of which are fairly serious. The first results from a gap between the requirements of the law and the competence of the teachers. Teachers were unprepared to comply with the law; they had not received the necessary training, neither from their colleges and universities nor from their in-service school programs. As a result, there has been an unfortunate widespread solution to the problem: principals and superintendents, wanting to comply with the law so that their schools and school districts can qualify for the federal funds involved, have asked their teachers to adhere to the stipulated guidelines, and the teachers have discharged their duties as well as they can. In essence, they have continued to teach in the usual way, yet describe their procedures in language that fulfills the stipulations of the law.

A second problem stemming from PL 94–142 is the imposition of additional work on an already crowded schedule. Teachers and administrative officers are required to spend more time on program planning, committee meetings, parent conferences, recordkeeping, and report writing. And the pity of it is that all this extra expenditure of effort has not been compensated for by evidence that the children are making better progress.

The problems generated by this well-intentioned law can be resolved gradually by systematic and comprehensive in-service training programs. There is little doubt that such an undertaking would not only enhance instruction for retarded and other handicapped children, but would encourage the development of other serviceable procedures over and beyond the original intent of the law.

PROMISES FOR THE FUTURE

Clearly, educational and mental health services for retarded children have improved over the past 20 years, and the application of behavioral principles has contributed to these changes. What, from the behavioral point of view, are some of the promising directions for continued improvement? Several are worthy of note.

One promising direction for improved services for the retarded is the acceleration of teacher training in applied behavioral analysis through in-service programs, demonstrations, and outreach projects designed to deal with the details of arranging teaching conditions so as to enhance learning and reduce problem behavior. When teachers gain facility with behavioral techniques, they will take pride in seeing their children progress on a day-to-day basis. Future training of teachers, however, must include more of the available knowledge about behavioral teaching than is currently disseminated. Mastery of a wider range of behavioral principles and techniques will enable teachers not only to improve their ability to teach academic skills and knowledge, but also to teach concomitantly, in a planned way, such desirable attributes as concentration on the task at hand and working independently and productively.

A second direction involves instructing paraprofessionals to use behavioral techniques for teaching and training. Many psychologists agree that they can serve the public best by sharing their techniques and procedures with those who are on the front lines in child rearing, education, vocational trainging, and counseling. Now that some of the principles and concepts for effective instruction are beginning to be understood, we can turn our efforts toward making them more explicit so that any person interested and capable of working in some area of education, training, and treatment will be able to comprehend and use them. There is no need or justification to restrict training in behavioral techniques to professionals.

Another promising direction is the application of the behavioral approach to the education and training of *all* children with developmental problems. The instructional techniques used with severely and profoundly retarded individuals are equally appropriate for mildly and moderately retarded individuals, for children with learning problems in reading, writing, and arithmetic, and for those having physical handicaps or behavior problems and disorders. That this approach is effective for all developmentally delayed children is strongly suggested by the results of the Follow Through study.

A fourth promising direction concerns the prevention of mild and moderate retardation, particularly when the condition is associated with handicapping sociocultural conditions. Findings from behaviorally oriented research on early intervention and on preschool and primary education can be brought together in a single, unified program to prevent retardation at the upper ranges, which constitute the largest segment of the retarded population (Bijou, 1983).

A fifth promising direction for improving educational and mental health services to the retarded pertains to increased efforts to safeguard the rights of retarded individuals as they participate in educational and training programs. Ethical and human rights committees and peer review committees have been established in some residential institutions, community schools districts, and group homes to review aversive practices in habilitation and rehabilitation programs that not only provide retarded individuals with much needed advocates, but also lead to upgrading the practices of teachers and child care workers. Although all too often we see that the recommendations of review committees are not implemented, this is usually the result of inadequate staff training and not mere indifference. The closing of this gap can be effected through in-service training that would provide up-to-date information on legal and ethical guidelines and training in well-established behavioral techniques for changing behavior. It is the additional responsibility of committees appointed to safeguard the rights of retarded individuals to alert administrators to the need for improved staff training.

REFERENCES

ABT Associates. 1976. Education as Experimentation: A Planned Variation Model. Vol. III. ABT Associates, Cambridge, MA.

ABT Associates. 1977. Education as Experimentation: A Planned Variation Model. Vol. IV. ABT Associates, Cambridge, MA.

Baer, D. M., Rowbury, T., Baer, A. M., et al. 1976. A program test of behavior technology: Can it recover deviant children for normal public schooling? In: T. D. Tjossem (ed.), Intervention Strategies for High Risk Infants and Young Children. pp. 213-234. University Park Press, Baltimore.

Becker, W. C., and Carnine, D. W. 1980. Direct instruction: An effective approach to educational intervention with the disadvantaged and low performers. In: B. B. Lahey and A. E. Kazdin (eds.), Advances in Clinical Child Psychology, Vol. 3. Plenum Publishing Corp., New York.

Becker, W. C., and Carnine, D. W. 1981. Direct Instruction—A behavioral theory-based model for the comprehensive educational intervention with the disadvantaged. In: S. W. Bijou and R. Ruiz (eds.), Behavior Modification: Contributions to Education. pp. 145-210. Lawrence Erlbaum Associates, Hillsdale, NJ.

Becker, W. C., Madsen, C. H., Jr., et al. 1967. The contingent use of teacher's attention and praise in reducing classroom behavior problems. J. Spec. Ed. 1:287-307.

Bereiter, C., and Kurland, M. 1978. Were some Follow Through models more effective than others? Paper presented at the American Educational Research Association, Toronto.

Bijou, S. W. 1972a. The technology of teaching young handicapped children. In: S. W. Bijou and E. Ribes-Inesta (eds.), Behavior Modification: Issues and Extensions. Academic Press, New York.

Bijou, S. W. 1972b. These kids have problems and our job is to do something about them. In: J. B. Jordon and L. S. Robbins (eds.), Let's Try Doing Something Else Kind of Thing. Council of Exceptional Children, Arlington, VA.

Bijou, S. W. 1977. Practical implications of an interaction model of child development. Except. Child. 44:6-14.

Bijou, S. W. 1981a. Behavioral teaching of young handicapped children: Problems of application and implementation. In: S. W. Bijou and R. Ruiz (eds.), Behavior Modification: Contributions to Education: pp. 97–110. Lawrence Erlbaum Associates, Hillsdale, NJ.

Bijou, S. W. 1981b. Management of individual behavior problems and disorders in the classroom. Paper presented at the 11th International Symposium on Behavior Modification, Lima, Peru.

Bijou, S. W. 1983. The prevention of mild and moderate retarded development. In: F. J. Menolascino, R. J. Neman, and J. A. Stark (eds.), Curative Aspects of Mental Retardation. Paul Brookes Pub. Co., Baltimore.

Bijou, S. W., and Baer, D. M. 1978. Behavioral Analysis of Child Development, Rev. Ed. Prentice-Hall, Englewood Cliffs, NJ.

Bijou, S. W., and Dunitz-Johnson, E. 1981. Interbehavior analysis of developmental retardation. Psychol. Rec. 31:305–329.

Birnbrauer, J. S., Bijou, S. W., Wolf, M. M., and Kidder, J. D. 1965. Programmed instruction in the classroom. In: L. P. Ullmann and L. Krasner (eds.), Case Studies in Behavior Modification. pp. 358–363. Holt, Rinehart & Winston, New York.

Bluma, S. M., Shearer, M. S., Frohman, A. H., and Hilliard, J. M. 1976. Portage Guide to Early Education: Checklist. Cooperative Educational Service Agency 12, Portage, WI.

Fredericks, H. D., Baldwin, D. N., Grove, D. N., et al. 1977. A Data Based Classroom for the Moderately and Severely Handicapped. 2nd Ed. Instructional Development Corp., Monmouth, OR.

Guess, D., Horner, R. D., Utley, B., et al. 1978. A functional curriculum sequencing model for teaching the severely handicapped. Mimeographed manuscript, Department of Special Education, University of Kansas, Lawrence.

Hayden, A. H., and Haring, N. G. 1976. Early intervention for high risk young children: Programs for Down's syndrome children. In: T. D. Tjossem (ed.), Intervention Strategies for High Risk Infants and Young Children. University Park Press, Baltimore.

Harris, F. R., Wolf, M. M., and Baer, D. M. 1964. Effects of adult reinforcement on child behavior. Young Child. 20:8–17.

Hersen, M., and Barlow, D. H. 1976. Single Case Experimental Designs: Strategies for Studying Behavior Change. Pergamon Press, New York.

House, E. R., Glass, G. V., McLean, L. D. and Walker, D. E. 1977. No simple answer: Critique of the "Follow Through" evaluation. Mimeographed report, University of Illinois, Urbana.

Johnson, G. O. 1962. Special education for the mentally handicapped—A paradox. Except. Child. 29:62–69.

Kauffman, J. M. 1977. Characteristics of Children's Behavior Disorders. Charles E. Merrill, Columbus, OH.

Kazdin, A. E. 1978. History of Behavior Modification: Experimental Foundations of Contemporary Research. University Park Press, Baltimore.

Lund, K. A., Schnapps, L., and Bijou, S. W. Let's take another look at record keeping in a special class. Teach. Except. Child. In press.

Martuza, V. R. 1977. Applying Norm-referenced and Criterion-referenced Measurement in Education. Allyn & Bacon, Inc., Boston.

Reynolds, M. C. 1976. Trends in Education: Changing Roles of Special Education Personnel. The University Council for Educational Administration, Columbus, OH.

Schiefelbusch, R. L. 1979. Advances in school and classroom learning. In: L. A. Hamerlynck (ed.), Behavioral Systems for the Developmentally Disabled: I. School and Family Environments, pp. 3–22. Brunner/Mazel, New York.

Shearer, D. E., and Shearer, M. S. 1976. The Portage Project: A model for early childhood intervention. In: T. D. Tjossem (ed.), Intervention Strategies for High Risk Infants and Young Children. University Park Press, Baltimore.

Skinner, B. F. 1953. Science and Human Behavior. Macmillan, New York.

Sloane, H. N., Johnston, M. K., and Bijou, S. W. 1967. Successive modification of aggressive behavior and aggressive fantasy play by management of contingencies. J. Child Psychol. Psychiatry 8:217–226.

Chapter **10**

Roles of the Community Mental Health Center in Providing Services for Mentally Ill-Mentally Retarded Citizens

Donald A. Swanson and Frank J. Menolascino

The last 30 years have witnessed a dramatic increase in the recognition of the wide range of services needed to meet the needs of mentally retarded citizens and spurred the establishment of many specialized programs and agencies designated to serve these needs. Educational, recreational, vocational, and residential programs have been established to provide services to an increasing number of mentally retarded persons. Despite these dramatic advances, there continues to be a pressing need for mental health services for mentally retarded citizens. The mental health services that are available tend to be few in number and poorly coordinated. Similarly, the President's Committee on Mental Health (PCMH) and the President's Committee on Mental Retardation (PCMR), in their respective 1978 reports, have identified significant gaps in the availability of appropriate mental health services for mentally retarded individuals and their families. For example, the PCMH report noted:

> Information gathered from many state coordinators indicates that the mental health field still responds to the myth that mentally retarded persons cannot and do not profit from psychotherapeutic intervention. Others report that mental health staff are unfamiliar with mental retardation and relate their unwillingness to treat to lack of knowledge and training. In many cases, their unwillingness to treat mentally retarded persons is attributed to their lack of knowledge and training. Mental

health delivery systems for mentally retarded persons are described as unresponsive, woefully inadequate, and often nonexisting. There appears to be a tendency for the mentally retarded client to be bounced back and forth between mental health and mental retardation professionals, with neither agency offering an adequate service delivery plan to meet the client's needs. Often the individual is shuffled among mental health, mental retardation, and correctional institutions. Some states report that limited services are available for mentally retarded persons in local clinics and the frequent referrals to State hospitals. There are, however, some treatment programs scattered across the country that are providing generic mental health services to mentally retarded persons and their families in the community, based on individual developmental needs (p. 7).

In its recommendations for resolving the above noted crisis of few available services for retarded citizens who are mentally ill, the PCMH further stated:

Community Mental Health Centers should have the responsibility for the provision of specific mental health services for mentally retarded persons and their families. The current Community Mental Health Center's program structure should be carefully reevaluated to identify specific priorities and the range of services that will strengthen the delivery of appropriate community-based mental health care for mentally retarded persons and their families. Those Centers which cannot meet this condition should be responsible for reimbursing or contracting for specific services to meet the needs of these individuals. There are highly successful prototypes that can be used as models for effective care (p. 10).

Thus the challenge of providing special training for mental health personnel goes beyond the community mental health center (CMHC) model and must address the provision of specific training for all mental health personnel wherever they practice (Cohen, 1978). An overview of basic and advanced training challenges for all mental health personnel is presented in Chapter 11 of this volume.

The potential roles of the CMHCs in meeting the mental health needs of the mentally retarded is the purpose of this chapter.

THE COMMUNITY MENTAL HEALTH CENTER

The CMHC national legislation of 1963 embodied some of the most progressive ideologies and models of care existent in mental health activity at that time (Kennedy, 1963). Borrowing heavily from public health models of service delivery (i.e., levels of prevention, catchment area designations for geographic-population coverage, mandated basic services and their mode of availability, etc.), it was predicated that *all* mentally ill citizens could be served within a short distance from their home. At that time, concurrent trends in mental retardation had witnessed the establishment (by local parent groups on behalf of their children and adults) of opportunity centers for education and training, sheltered workshops, and a global push for the modern programs of service that had earlier been envisioned by the President's Panel on Mental Retardation (1963). Working closely together in their initial thrusts of public information, legislative bills, and the establishment of a nationwide system of service delivery, panel members created great optimism that retarded citizens would equally benefit from the anticipated fruits of the proposed CMHC national network and the concurrently emerging programs of services for the mentally retarded.

Within a decade, the initial promises of the CMHC for the mental health service needs of the retarded were noted to be seriously wanting. Increasingly, there were noted disquieting voices that mental health professionals tended to ignore the retarded citizen because more exciting challenges were viewed elsewhere, or because of perplexity and lack of understanding of the varied personality phenomena noted in mentally retarded citizens. These perceptions resulted in divergent pathways for both the CMHC thrust and the increasingly more active national parent advocacy efforts on behalf of the mentally retarded. Having taught a graduate course in community psychiatry during the early 1970s, one author vividly recalls the increasing autonomy of the CMHC from the mental retardation programs in the United States and the reasons brought forward for supporting this widening gap between the initial promise of generic services for all mentally ill citizens and the increasing selectivity of CMHC caseloads. Gone was the CMHC thrust of serving *all* mentally ill citizens; the magnitude of the apparent mental health needs tended to overwhelm the individual centers and they retracted their visions so as to keep within their descending 8-year budgetary guidelines.

Simultaneously, the mental retardation field embraced the ideology of normalization (Wolfensberger, 1972) and reconceptualized the basis for mental health problems in retarded citizens and their parents (Olshansky, 1970), and there was a growing awareness that in the minds of many professionals, the word *mental* was the only major link between the fields of mental health and mental retardation. This latter trend has reached its logical conclusion in those states in which organized associations for the retarded have successfully supported legislative efforts to clearly separate their state's mental health and mental retardation systems of services. Rather than bridging the gap between these two service systems, the latter trend of separation of services (which has been energetically pursued to the present) has tended to exclude the retarded from the generic mental health services (including their local CMHC programs), the use of which is central to the concept of normalization. Unfortunately, this separation of service systems has not resulted in enhanced mental health services for the retarded citizen within autonomous mental retardation programs. As a distinguished colleague said, "It seems that the *new* retardation systems have redefined the *medical model*, replete with older approaches—and the emotionally disturbed retarded citizen still waits to be served."

Before directly addressing the possible role(s) of CMHCs in serving mentally ill-mentally retarded citizens, the current status of these centers needs review. It should be recalled that President Kennedy's benchmark legislation in 1963 envisioned the hope to blanket our country, via the catchment area concept of a CMHC for every 75,000 to 200,000 population base, with 2,000 CMHCs by 1985. It was viewed as the ultimate answer to (indeed, even the demise of) the traditional state mental hospital. The initial years were auspicious regarding the many construction grants and allied staffing grants awarded, and when the CMHC programs hit their high tide in 1977, there were 850 CMHC programs in operation. Yet a dramatic shrinkage of the number of CMHC programs in the United States has occurred—747 centers in 1978 and only 648 operative at the close of 1979. This trend has also had very negative impact on the numbers of mentally ill-mentally retarded citizens served in these CMHCs. A recent analysis of the National Institute on Mental Health data concerning this service component of the CMHC to retarded citizens confirms this trend. In 1979 (the last year for which national statistics are available), the number of mentally ill-mentally retarded citizens seen in the CMHCs was 2.8% of the total individuals served. As to a percentage of known need based on incidence-prevalence of the symptoms of mental illness in the mentally retarded, this figure should be closer to 15%, not 2.8%.

These recent trends in shrinkages of the number of operating CMHC programs in our country and the persistently low number of retarded citizens with mental illness who were/are actually served therein, calls for a reevaluation of the current and future roles of CMHCs. Training needs and allied modern models of service delivery also became a central concern in discerning what should be the current and future roles of the CMHC in serving mentally retarded citizens who are also mentally ill.

SPECIFIC POTENTIAL ROLES OF CMHCs

First, it should be clearly noted that at least 50% of the population do not have a CMHC as a local resource. Those who do have this service should—as clearly recommended by the PCMH (1978)—demand that the CMHC have a direct responsibility for the provision of specific mental health services for mentally retarded persons (with allied mental illnesses) and their families. Full utilization of the basic CMHC components of emergency services, inpatient, outpatient, transitional, and consultation and education can greatly strengthen the appropriate delivery of mental health services to community-based retarded persons and their families. Models for utilizing portions of this CMHC approach are noted by Cohen (PCMH, 1978), Menolascino (1977), and Provitt (1977). True, there are major training (and retraining) issues involved in the full utilization of current CMHC personnel for the task of promoting generic mental health services for their local retarded citizens; however, it is difficult to argue with one of the key underpinnings of the normalization concept: fully utilizing local generic services. Tarjan and Keeran (1974) have cogently discussed this need for redirecting the current and future CMHC efforts toward serving the retarded.

As previously noted, there persists in many states a vocal demand for clear if not total separation of mental health and mental retardation services; yet, separation of these two major systems of human service requires that people in need must decide in advance which of the two systems to approach in their search for help. The frequent overlap and blurring of diagnostic differentiation between mental illness and mental retardation—especially early in life— present serious problems. For example, in the severe disorders of children such as the childhood psychoses or infantile autism, parents must select the correct service system. If they have a 4-year-old child who is withdrawn, has minimal language, and displays primitive stereotyped motor behaviors, the challenge becomes, should they seek services from a mental health system or a mental retardation system for their child? Frequently, such children are referred from one system to the other, and this diagnostic merry-go-round perpetuates the specious arguments concerning mental versus physical developmental problems. Furthermore, if retarded adults have emotional problems in addition to and/or as a result of their intellectual limitations, where should they go for services? Do their local mental retardation system counselors try to help them as best they can? Should they be referred to a private mental health practitioner? Who will correlate the "old" (retardation) problems with the needs of the "new" (mental illness) symptoms? All too often, what actually occurs is a continuation of the merry-go-round with the afflicted individuals being passed between the two service systems. Frequently, neither of these systems provides the needed services (of appropriate quality and quantity) to meet the persisting cry for help.

The current intent of federal laws and state service systems is for mentally retarded persons who need mental health services to receive them in their local CMHC. For example, Section 504 of the Vocational Rehabilitation Act underscores the mandate to provide handicapped individuals with such services. Exclusion from such generic services, because of allied handicaps is specifically viewed and could jeopardize an agency's federal funding base. In other words, family counseling to help parents in the daily behavioral management of their retarded son must be provided by a CMHC *if* that center also provides such counseling to families of nonretarded children or youth who are having similar behavioral management problems. Likewise, a mentally retarded adult who is distinctly anxious cannot be denied CMHC services because of perceived clinical difficulties (i.e., a more complicated clinical picture because of the presence of the allied handicap of mental retardation) in providing needed mental health services. There *is*, however, a wide gap between federal and state legal mandates for services, and these may *not* directly translate into a guarantee that the actual provision of service will occur.

Services that can be readily provided by CMHC personnel include individual and group psychotherapy, play therapy, consultation to nursing homes, marriage counseling, drug therapy consultation, transitional and day hospital programs, self-help and social skills training, providing consultation (direct and indirect) to group homes and developmental or special education programs, inservice training programs, specific behavioral intervention consultation (e.g., behavioral modification), etc. Services to children and families include family counseling, specific help as to crisis management, the provision of respite services, and parental education as to child management techniques. True, these traditional mental health services need a necessary attitudinal set and specific changes in professional techniques when utilized on behalf of the mentally retarded. Selan (1978) notes:

> Few non-retarded persons take the time to listen and respond to the feelings which retarded persons express, and few adults form lasting dependable relationships with retarded persons. The social worker, psychiatrist, or psychologist who does so will discover that retarded persons respond quickly to individual attention, form almost im-

mediate rapport, and will achieve concrete goals in a comparatively short time. The methods of traditional psychotherapy, however, have to be adapted to the concrete level on which many retarded persons operate (p. 48).

Similarly, Rubin (1981) and Monfils (1981) have outlined the technique changes necessary to successfully utilize the major current individual and group therapy approaches.

CMHC personnel can provide group psychotherapy sessions at the group homes where the retarded individual resides, and thus avoid the persisting stigma of attendance at a mental health facility. In this regard, the writers have elaborated a series of visual overheads that are utilized to initiate or focus such group therapy transactions. The mobility of both the professional and the equipment (i.e., an overhead projector) permits itinerant mental health services to be truly mobile while utilizing modern concepts and audiovisual aids. Similarly, such group techniques can also be utilized in a preventive fashion by providing orientation group sessions for retarded individuals who have just returned from an institution to their new group home. Lastly, beyond the mental health focus of these services, they are also excellent professional vehicles for teaching adult career education topics. Because these activities help to focus the retarded citizen's interest in self-learning activities, while structuring their "after 5 o'clock" activities, they can be a potent alternative to the unstructured aimlessness of the evening hours for these adult retarded citizens, whether they are mentally ill or not.

CMHC caregivers need to obtain proficiency in the specialized techniques, general care principles, and specific interpersonal and intrapersonal needs of mentally retarded. In conjunction with awareness-sensitivity courses for helping CMHC personnel mitigate the prevalent professional myths about the retarded, the above are direly needed as orientation and inservice training ingredients. These training exposures, special techniques, and necessary attitude changes fit in nicely with the basic training background that the majority of mental health professionals already possess.

EXTENSION OF THE ROLES OF THE CMHC

The Mental Retardation Specialist

An early modification of the CMHC, which was intended to directly impact on the needs of the mentally retarded, was the mental retardation specialist position. Herein, a number of CMHC personnel are specifically designated to provide mental health services for retarded citizens and their families. Often, the specialist has had specific training in mental retardation and extended experience in mental retardation programs in institutions or community-based programs. Levie, Roberts, and Menolascino (1979) discuss the specific functions of a mental retardation specialist within a CMHC setting. A more recent innovation is the utilization of parents of the mentally retarded, who have received special training in mental health, in this role. Truly, this type of approach *does* bridge the gap quite nicely.

Program Innovations

An excellent brief survey of progressive programs for the retarded citizens who have associated mental illness, is provided in the 1978 PCMR Report (PCMR, 1978). Two of these programs will be reviewed as examples of recent program innovations beyond the CMHC concept. The description of these progressive programs is drawn largely from the PCMR Report.

The Rock Creek Foundation for Mental Health (Bethesda, Maryland) is a nonprofit organization founded in 1973. The foundation has combined the humane enthusiasm and professionalism of its staff with a range of treatment modalities to serve 33 young adults who are both mentally retarded and emotionally disturbed. The foundation's approach to its clients, like many mental retardation programs, stresses normalization through work experiences, but its most striking feature is its determined utilization of a wide variety of psychotherapeutic approaches seldom employed with mentally retarded clients.

The psychiatrist-director of the Rock Creek program has explained his profession's traditional unwillingness to use psychotherapy with retarded individuals as follows:

> Most psychiatrists are bright individuals and they like to work with other bright persons who can become more like their psychotherapists. For this reason, those having high achievement levels—like medical students—are preferred patients. But when a mentally retarded person comes for psychotherapy, he is quickly "referred away." Such referrals are polite diversions, so the psychiatrist doesn't have to say what he really feels, "Get out of my office . . . I don't want to talk to you . . . I don't want to recognize that you have feelings too." Of course, a retarded person will never develop like a medical student can, but that handicapped person can be helped to find an emotional stability and a career within his range that is every bit as satisfying. Unfortunately, most psychiatrists fail to see value in such an opportunity (p. 62, PCMR, 1978).

A public health administrator who is familiar with Rock Creek's clientele provides an excellent insight into the plight of emotionally disturbed-mentally retarded individuals:

> Many of these people have needed psychiatric intervention almost all of their lives, but such needs were ignored. As young children, their aberrant behaviors were ascribed to mental retardation syndromes. During adolescence—when most attended special education classes—their bizarre actions were tolerated just as long as such acts were not sexual or violent. For example, one young lady literally believed she was Cinderella, but none of her special education teachers did anything about it. The real shock came after these disturbed persons leave the special education classes. Then, they are rejected by one adult program after another. When this happens the families are forced to keep their disturbed children in the home with no programs or to send them to an institution. That's a bitter set of alternatives for parents to face after at least 20 years of hard work and sacrifice (p. 63, PCMR, 1978).

This recognition of society's failure to provide for the mental health needs of retarded individuals led the director and administrator to establish the Rock Creek Foundation in 1973. Since its inception, the foundation has not failed to accept the fact that their clients are apt to be those deemed most difficult by other treatment agencies: the mildly and moderately retarded with severe emotional and behavioral disturbances.

The young retarded adults who are treated at the foundation engage in a 40-hour week of day activities that include behavior therapies from the field of developmental disabilities, and the expressive therapies more usually employed in psychiatric settings. What is most striking about the foundation's treatment milieu is the pervasive attitude of humaneness that has broken down some of the barriers between staff and clients. There are no one-way vision mirrors (to permit staff to observe clients secretly) because this device would undermine the staff-client equality they are fostering. Similarly, there are no separate lounges for staff and clients, nor do they patronize separate bathrooms or activity areas. Rather, a spirit of togetherness binds staff and clients in all their daily activities, including lunching and shopping together during free times. The foundation provides no mealtime programs; instead, the clients are encouraged to go to restaurants or bring their own lunches, with the belief that such activities are more normalizing and further the client's experience in the community.

Rock Creek does not transport its clients; they are trained to utilize public transportation in the greater Washington, DC., area. Despite the difficulties and potential problems this may involve, the foundation considers such experiences and the neighborhood terrain as the milieu in which their clients must gain skills in order to achieve developmental growth. One aid to the foundation has been the neighborhood's interest in the clients; local businessmen have come to know Rock Creek staff and clients on a personal basis. In fact, one local fast-food facility even trains its counter employees in recognizing the skills and limitations of the clients who come there frequently for lunch.

The Rock Creek Foundation employs many treatment modalities for specific emotional disturbances in mentally retarded individuals. Examples of these treatment modalities include: 1) individual therapy; 2) group therapy; 3) family therapy; 4) community meetings; 5) structured activity groups; 6) task-oriented groups; and 7) a vocational program ladder. The last treatment modality noted, vocational rehabilitation, is a very important ingredient of a modified CMHC model. Because mental illness can be extremely expensive in terms of client's time and energy, there is often a need to rejuvenate the client's sense of purpose. Thus, beginning clients at Rock Creek are paid the minimum wage to complete successfully daily chores like maintaining the coffee urn, vacuuming the floor, or emptying the wastebasket. From this first successful taste of work, the clients (most of whom have not held a job before) progress through a demanding step-by-step process of adapting to work that in the client's view gives him or her a feeling of dignity and achievement. One part of this adaptation is participation in small career exploration groups that travel to industrial settings to observe people at work to inquire about working conditions and find out how to qualify for a job in such a setting. The success of Rock Creek's vocational program has much to do with the effect to which it is graduated on a continuum, progressive, and fully supported by staff. Both vocational counselors and therapy staff members perform a detailed number of follow-along functions, supporting the client and reinforcing his or her progress even after full-time employment is achieved.

In summary, it should be noted that the Rock Creek program utilizes many of the therapeutic approaches, professional staffing patterns, and multidisciplinary approaches that have been the hallmark of the CMHC movement. Variants of this excellent program are thus possible to establish within CMHC contexts across our country. It is for this very reason that the Rock Creek program is viewed (and functions) as a program of national significance (as to readily transferrable treatment-programmatic modalities to other geographic-population areas) at this time.

The *Regional Intervention Program* (Nashville, Tennessee) focuses on a younger age group of mentally ill-mentally retarded citizens, and utilizes a very advanced parent-as-therapist approach.

Mental health professionals often forget the situational difficulties and emotional isolation of the parent with a behaviorally disordered child. It is tempting to "explain" such a child's tantrums, screaming, and destructive behavior by blaming the parents: the parents are "permissive," "too indulgent," "they don't discipline the child." In the clinical management of mentally ill-mentally retarded children, however, these generalizations typically do not apply. In contrast, more typically, one notes parents who are neither incompetent or permissive. Indeed, these parents have usually raised two or three well adjusted children. Their usually successful past child-rearing tactics tend only to exacerbate their dual-diagnosis child's problem. Furthermore, the very atypical nature of these behavioral disturbances makes the parents feel that it is their "cross to bear," because few neighbors have similar experiences to share with them. Indeed, the neighbors tend not to understand the nature of these problems. These factors often coalesce to perplex these parents to the point at which they feel very lonely as they increasingly isolate themselves.

It was to meet the special needs of such parents that the Regional Intervention Program (RIP) was established. This treatment program has no shortage of persons who can help families who have preschoolers with combined symptoms of mental retardation and mental illness. There is no waiting list because help begins immediately after a parent contracts the program. The therapists are not only well trained, they are also parents of children with the same problems. In the entire program, there are only six master's level professionals and they serve as resource persons.

In the RIP treatment approach, each specific treatment target is individualized; however, the treatment sequence utilized tends to follow a general pattern and the following vignette drawn from the PCMR Report (p. 65–66) illustrates the treatment pattern utilized via the experiences of a young couple with their dual-diagnosis young child.

It began on Monday morning, a year and a half ago, when a thoroughly battle-weary Mary Sanders and Jamie met with their pediatrician. The physician spoke of a film presentation he had seen in which the RIP was described. He suggested that Mrs. Sanders call to see if Jamie could be helped by the program. She called immediately. Two days later, Mrs. Sanders attended an intake conference at

RIP which was conducted by a trained parent who skillfully handled 14 checklists, authorizations, and negotiations. Included in the issues discussed was a parent participation contract. After it was thoroughly explained, Mary Sanders signed an agreement that she would: 1) appear with Jamie for each session (every weekday morning for more than a year) and take primary responsibility for her son's treatment as recommended by her son's treatment team members; 2) pay no fees, with the understanding that continuance in the program depended upon her work in relation to Jamie and the program as a whole; and 3) receive support from parents and, in a short time, give support to new parents. She also agreed to pay back the program with 6 months' daily service after Jamie's treatment was completed. As the intake conference was concluded, Mrs. Sanders was assigned a parent case manager and a support parent, and was told that treatment would begin at RIP in 2 days.

On the first day at RIP, Mrs. Sanders and Jamie were asked to spend 20 minutes in the generalization training room, a simulated three-room apartment—living room, bedroom, and kitchen—where she and her son were instructed to play with a specific number of toys, on cue, while two parent observers and the case manager watched through a one-way mirror and systematically recorded what was happening. As soon as the session began, Jamie's behavior turned violent; toys hurtled through the air—some striking the mother. The session was stopped abruptly when Mrs. Sanders began to cry. Immediately, the observers and the mother went into a feedback session, in which Jamie's behavior was discussed and Mrs. Sanders given emotional support. Mrs. Sanders and Jamie were then scheduled for another generalization training session on the following Monday.

During the weekend, Mary and Phillip Sanders received a visit from their support parent who was placed on call to the Sanders at any time, day or night, during Jamie's treatment period. The Sanders spoke with their support by telephone no less than 15 times in the following months. Although the conversations primarily provided much needed emotional support, technical advice was given as well. For example, the support parent advised the Sanders on how to make their home childproof by storing breakable items and installing gates and barriers. The support parent also helped the family develop in-home programs having to do with Jamie's mealtime and nighttime behaviors. On the next Monday and on the days following the generalization training feedback sessions were continued. From these sessions, it was learned that everybody had been unintentionally reinforcing Jamie's violent acts by giving him extra attention when he committed them. With this knowledge, the mother and child began a long series of regular sessions called individual tutoring. Again, the case manager and parent observers first watched the sessions and joined Mrs. Sanders in feedback, helping her develop skills that could turn off bad behavior and turn on good behavior. Jamie also spent time in an intake classroom, where his developing health behavior was reinforced in a group setting.

After 1 year of hard work by the therapists and the entire Sanders family, Jamie began to progress dramatically. He had established more self-control, and his parents were able to remove the childproofing devices from his home. At RIP, Jamie was promoted to a language/community class for handicapped children and normal children who served as models. (Because the normal children who attend this class are the brothers and sisters of the handicapped child, the arrangement relieves parents from the added expense of daycare.)

This fall, Jamie is attending a public school. His entry into a special education class was assisted by well trained parents who serve as liaison workers. They set up meetings with public school faculty members at which they described Jamie's progress at RIP and his immediate program needs. In Jamie's first month at school, the liaison workers made three follow-up visits to the school on the child's behalf and remain available as advocates should such services be needed.

Because RIP is a dynamic program that changes as the needs of the handicapped child and his family change, the Sander's experience makes visible only the edge of a rich program that contains the following basic concepts which have been shaped through the years:

1. An efficient, three-tiered organization keeps RIP cohesive and flexible at the same time. On the first level, all on-line service delivery functions are carried out by parents. On the second level, the six professional resource persons serve as an advisory and resource force. The third level is a seven-member evaluation committee of parents and community professionals—chosen by the parents—who monitor all treatment activities and report monthly to the Tennessee Department of Mental Health and Mental Retardation.

2. The parent-child relationship is the heart of the program. Every program component is constantly adjusted so that optimum success can be realized in this single, crucial relationship. The pro-

gram's dynamism is due mostly to intense parent participation. One RIP professional explained why:

Professional agencies simply cannot shift as rapidly. Professionals spend time and energy, each developing his own professional role which "locks" the agency into a more constant, unchanging service pattern. The only thing that is constant at RIP is that parents will always deliver the on-line therapies.

3. RIP is governed by a management-by-objectives system which keeps RIP remarkably accountable. For example, behavioral targets are time-bound and numerically delineated as measures that incorporate predetermined sequential activities; they are individually formulated for each family-child relationship. These behavioral targets are evaluated every 6 months. Utilizing a unique point system, an account of the behavioral targets reached (and not reached) is passed onto the evaluation committee, which in turn produces the overall progress reports.

4. RIP is flexibly data-based because careful measurement of input-process-output variables are utilized in all program operations. Although some data-based programs perfect a single, rigid system, RIP has developed 25 different types of change-producing systems. Such flexibility permits highly individualized programs tailored to the specific needs of each family.

5. There are no fees. While the state pays the operating costs, the parent pay back plan (a minimum of 9 hours per week for 6 months) has kept the RIP remarkably cost-efficient. Over the years, only 15% of the enrolled families failed to pay back their contracted obligations, and many of these parents were officially released from the obligation because of family tragedies or hardship. A complex system of detailed tasks is performed by parents. They serve as intake workers, support parents, case managers, and liaison workers. They are also teachers, clerical workers, and some are trained as video camera operators who periodically videotape parent-child interactions. Finally, RIP training is seen as rehearsal training. Success in the training setting is put into perspective. The real test of RIP's success takes place in such settings at the home, the grocery store, the restaurant, and the public school.

Since 1969, more than 420 families have received help from RIP. This program clearly demonstrates that when the service to be delivered is clearly delineated, and when all tasks in delivering the service are broken down into many different jobs (with exact procedures, targets and time limits), and when every task is kept under the scrutiny of evaluators, then a cadre of parents with a special need to become involved can develop into highly motivated and efficient therapists.

Utilization of parents of currently mentally ill-mentally retarded children as future trainers of other parents who pass down the same roads with their mentally ill-retarded son or daughter is a forceful reminder of one of the initial goals of the CMHC thrust: to train the community and its parental-indigenous resources to eventually provide their own services. The RIP program has major benefits far beyond its rapid transferability to other diverse demographic-socioeconomic areas of the United States. The cost-service benefit considerations of this program are definitely a plus. More importantly, its outstanding utilization of the large manpower pool of trained volunteers addresses a major concern. Specifically, it is becoming abundantly clear that excellent human services of sufficient quantity may be beyond economic resources. The RIP program clearly shows how a large manpower pool, when added to an excellent treatment-training model, can obviate the need for large financial outlays. Lastly, it should be noted that the RIP prototype can be engrafted onto a CMHC operation with relative ease. Thus it can extend the base of the CMHC and better enable it to serve *all* of the needy citizens in its catchment area.

Outreach and Consultation-Education Services

Often the CMHC can provide its most specific set of services to the retarded citizen who is also mentally ill by having readily available outreach and consultation services. The outreach services can be helpful in activities ranging from very early diagnosis to follow-up and follow-along services. These types of activities also provide for full attention to the continuity of services, which is a vital component of modern service delivery programs.

Similarly, consultation and education provide excellent entry points for both direct contact (i.e., client contact) and indirect contact (i.e., non-client contact as in providing expertise to a special education teacher, a program administrator, etc.). This model of service stretches the availability of mental health manpower to provide an excellent cost-service benefit ratio. The potential for cross-fertilization of viewpoints, techniques, and ideologies is also an outstanding aspect of these consultative services.

Because other contributors to this volume explore the outreach and consultation-education challenges that are available in the CMHC at some length, they will not be further elaborated.

Private Practitioners

Intertwined with the above components is the rapidly evolving cadre of mental health personnel who work part-time at a CMHC (or other mental health programs) and are available for delivering services in a private practice model or for providing in-service training skills. This particular aspect of the manpower pool of the CMHC is rapidly developing because it permits a wider variety of vocational opportunities for mental health personnel. Furthermore, its flexibility permits wider utilization of the CMHC personnel, and the diversity of challenges and opportunities that are present in these private practice arrangements can be a strong antidote to staff burnout. Private practice consultants are increasingly becoming available to serve mentally ill-mentally retarded citizens where they actually reside. Watson (Chapter 6, this volume) reflects on the availability of such services to institutionally based retarded citizens. Furthermore, the recent excellent film by Foxx (1980) entitled, "Harry: Behavioral Treatment of Self-Abuse," vividly portrays the effective use of advanced behavioral analysis techniques—provided on a consultative basis—with an extremely disturbed mentally retarded individual. The portability of both the techniques and the service providers who deliver these services out in the field is a unique feature of these consultation arrangements.

Another private practice consultation trend that is rapidly being disseminated is the role and services of the clinical pharmacologists. Their value in initiating (and monitoring) drug disbursement systems is an increasingly noted consultative role in community-based mental retardation service systems. Furthermore, the clinical pharmacologist is a valuable colleague in outlining drug reduction (or redirection) programs wherein the role and need for psychoactive or anticonvulsant drugs are continually questioned as a valid part of an ongoing individualized treatment plan.

For the mentally ill-mentally retarded citizen, these rapidly evolving models of care bring the private practice model of care directly to them—replete with a new base of one-on-one individuality, high professional competence, confidentiality, and reasonable costs—all within the mainstream mode of obtaining human services.

Mental Health Services within Transitional Living Facilities

A variation of the basic-extended services provided by a CMHC, which has been very useful in providing direct services to the retarded, is the use of a network of transitional living facilities. Specifically, a growing national trend is the establishment of the two-to-four geographically dispersed group homes in conjunction with the day hospital segment of a CMHC operation. The group homes seem to function most optimally when operated as small, homelike facilities (e.g., four to six individuals per group home), and the population characteristics permit a wide variety of homogeneous (or heterogeneous) matching of factors such as sex, age groupings, and types or levels of disorders. The provision of group homes also facilitates participation in generic community services. They provide a major cost saving so as to avoiding unnecessary inpatient hospitalization or the need to use other specialized (and expensive) community-based services. Lastly, the group home facilities are excellent training sites for professional trainees in social work, medicine, clinical psychology, special education, nursing, and vocational rehabilitation.

CONCLUSION

Some key current and future roles of CMHCs in the provision of mental health services for mentally ill-mentally retarded citizens have been reviewed. The CMHC has an excellent potential for becoming the key component of locally available clinical mental health resources for retarded citizens. To effect minimal social-vocational dislocation, major emphasis has been directed toward close-to-home and family treatment of *all* mentally ill citizens. This aspect of modern mental health services delivery has brought with it the professional-moral responsibility, within a demographic area, for the establishment and promotion of mental health programs in prevention, early case finding, and treatment for *all* citizens. These goals are realized through aid in program planning, the actual provision of a spectrum of modern mental health services, direct and indirect consultation, and mental health education. Although the CMHC model is currently in a state of flux, the Mental Health Systems Act holds great promise in shoring up its conceptual, service delivery, and financial bases. It *does* have the potential for delivering mental health services as a generic human service for mentally retarded citizens who experience mental illness. Within this model of generic service delivery, it can enlarge the services provided by local educational, vocational, and retardation systems of service. Rather than stress the current problems and apparent competition between different systems of human service, an attempt has been made to present the CMHC as an excellent community resource for working with and across other generic service systems for the betterment of all retarded citizens whose lives become complicated by mental illness.

REFERENCES

Cohen, A. M. 1978. Options to meet the mental health needs of mentally retarded persons. Working paper prepared for President's Commission on Mental Health, Washington, DC.

Foxx, R. M. 1980. Harry: Behavioral Treatment of Self Abuse. Research Press, Champaign, IL.

Kennedy, J. F. 1963. Mental illness and mental retardation. (Message from the President of the United States presented to the House of Representatives, 88th Congress, Document No. 58). U.S. Government Printing Office, Washington, DC.

Levie, C., Roberts, B., and Menolascino, F. 1979. Providing psychiatric services for clients of community-based mental retardation programs. Hosp. Commun. Psychiatry 30(6).

Menolascino, F. 1977. Challenges in Mental Retardation: Progressive Ideology and Services. Human Sciences Press, New York.

Monfils, M. 1981. Tailoring group psychotherapy approaches to retarded citizens with mental illness. Presented at the Annual Meeting of the American Psychiatric Association, May, New Orleans.

National Action to Combat Mental Retardation. 1962. The President's Panel on Mental Retardation. U.S. Government Printing Office, Washington, DC.

Olshansky, S. 1970. Chronic sorrow: A response to having a mentally defective child. In: L. N. Robert (ed.), Counseling Parents of the Mentally Retarded. Charles C Thomas, Springfield, IL.

President's Commission on Mental Health. 1978. Report of the Liaison Task Panel on Mental Retardation. U.S. Government Printing Office, Washington, DC.

President Committee on Mental Retardation. 1978. Mental Retardation: The Leading Edge. Service Programs That Work. U.S. Department of Health, Education and Welfare, Washington, DC.

President's Panel on Mental Retardation. 1963. A Proposed Program for National Action to Combat Mental Retardation. U.S. Goverment Printing Office, Washington, DC.

Provitt, E. 1977. Community mental health centers: Use of resources for mental health service/treatment needs of the mentally retarded. Working paper prepared for the President's Commission on Mental Health, Washington, DC.

Rubin, R. 1981. Individual psychotherapy approaches with mentally ill-mentally retarded individuals. Presented at the Annual Meeting of the American Psychiatric Association, May, New Orleans.

Selan, B. H. 1978. Psychotherapy with the developmentally disabled. Health and Social Work, 1 (1):73–85.

Tarjan, G., and Keeran, C., Jr. 1974. An overview of mental retardation. Psychiatr. Ann. 4(2).

Wolfensberger, W. 1972. The Principle of Normalization in Human Services. National Institute on Mental Retardation, Toronto.

Chapter 11

Personnel Preparation to Meet the Mental Health Needs of the Mentally Retarded and Their Families

Role of the University-Affiliated Programs

John J. McGee and Paul H. Pearson

This chapter examines one aspect of the complex problem of meeting the mental health needs of mentally retarded citizens and their families: the preparation of personnel through the national network of university-affiliated programs (UAPs) as well as other universities and community colleges. In order to adequately examine this area of personnel preparation:

1. The nature and extent of the mental health needs of mentally retarded persons and their families from the perspective of personnel preparation are analyzed. In doing so, it is pointed out that this population tends to be the last served and the least served. The types of mental health services and trained personnel required for this population are outlined.
2. The role of UAPs is defined and the ways in which UAPs and other postsecondary education centers might more closely focus on these particular personnel preparation needs are demonstrated. Because the UAPs comprise a national network of interdisciplinary training activities in the area of developmental disabilities, they must play an important role in the preparation of personnel to meet the mental health needs of mentally retarded persons and their families.

3. A manpower developmental model is outlined that could be adopted on a national and local level in order to train parents, paraprofessionals, and professionals to meet these needs.
4. The linkages that must exist between programs and personnel preparation and between mental health and mental retardation systems are outlined.

THE MENTAL HEALTH NEEDS OF
MENTALLY RETARDED PERSONS AND THEIR FAMILIES

It is clear that the mental health problems of the mentally retarded and their families have been neglected. Those involved in the provision of direct care or the administration of community-based services for the mentally retarded acknowledge the emotionally disturbed client as their biggest challenge and the hardest one for whom to obtain adequate services. That there is an increased prevalence of behavioral and emotional disturbance in individuals with mental retardation is beyond question. Rutter and his colleagues (1970a, 1970b, 1976) have provided the most conclusive proof through a brilliantly conceived series of epidemiologic studies over the past 15 years. They have found that prevalence of mental retardation or brain damage increased the vulnerability to psychologic disorder by a factor of 2 to 3 times that found in the normal population. Where there is both this increased vulnerability as well as psychosocial pathology in the family, the risk of psychiatric disorder is further increased.

There is, however, considerable question and confusion as well as many myths and misconceptions concerning the nature of emotional disturbance among the mentally retarded. A comprehensive review of the literature on this topic clearly noted the persistence of soft data herein (Parsons and May, 1979).

The lack of precise information cannot be used to excuse the present sad state of affairs in meeting the mental health needs of mentally retarded persons and their families. As pointed out in the report of the Liaison Task Panel on Mental Retardation to the President's Commission on Mental Health (1978): "Traditionally these people have fallen through the cracks. They have, unfortunately, been neglected by both mental health and mental retardation systems."

A survey (McGee, 1979) revealed that families, when confronted with a mentally retarded child with behavioral needs, were typically the last and the least served by either the mental retardation or the mental health service systems. In the survey the large majority of parents and professionals agreed that the most difficult population to deal with were mentally retarded persons with behavioral and communication deficits. It was felt that this group receives the fewest services and is often dumped into other programs with both inadequate staffing and services. When asked what would be required to meet the needs of this population adequately, parents and professionals alike responded as follows: 1) the preparation of service providers; 2) parent training; 3) respite services; and 4) long-term and short-term community-based residential services.

The President's Commission on Mental Health (1978) forcefully stated that the mental health needs of the families of mentally retarded persons have long been ignored, or worse, mishandled:

> Paradoxically, the parents of mentally retarded individuals have a long history of being mishandled by professionals, including mental health professionals. They have, for example, sometimes been miscast as emotionally disturbed people in desperate need of psychiatric care. Their sorrow for their children has been inappropriately interpreted at times as psychopathology. Their militant demands for improved services have been dismissed as manifestations of displaced hostility....

Traditionally, the service delivery system for the treatment and therapy of children with special needs seems to have been founded on the following two incomplete assumptions: 1) the habilitation of the child alone is sufficient, and 2) what is good for the child is good enough for the family.

The mental health needs of the entire family unit cannot be ignored. These assumptions, of course, disallow for the unique nature of all other family members and their particular human needs. Professionals too often fail to consider the range of normal feelings that the daily care of a child with special needs may evoke on the part of the parents and the impact these feelings have on the capacity of the family to deal with the normal and special needs of the child (e.g., pain, anger, guilt, sadness, frustration, and helplessness, as well as hope, joy, perseverance, sharing, and feelings that may be intermixed to varying degrees). The Joint Commission on the Mental Health of Children (1970) insightfully stated:

> Any commitment to children is a commitment to the family union... we must not lose sight of the fact that any service, or lack of service, which affects one member of the family affects all members, brothers and sisters as well as parents.

Tymchuk (1979) stated that when a parent begins to suspect difficulty with the development of his or her child and seeks help, there are four typical responses:

1. There may be no help or information available. This may evolve into negative feelings toward self and/or child.

2. There may be help available to the parent(s); however, nothing will be done to help the child (e.g., instruction on feeding or toilet training). How often are parents still told "Just take your child home and love him or her." Thus, the original confusion and frustration of the parents may return.

3. There may be help available for the child, but not the parents (i.e., the feelings of the parents are ignored).

4. Occasionally, there may be help available both for the family and the child.

Families need a variety of mental health supports on an ongoing basis. The large majority of the time, competent professionals, given some minimal preparation, should be able to prevent mental illness in the family due to the presence of a mentally retarded family member (Freeman and Pearson, 1978). The preventive measures are fourfold: 1) to provide accurate information on what the problems are, what caused them, and how to deal with them; 2) to deal with parental feelings, emotions, and attitudes; 3) to offer information regarding child health and development in general and future steps for the child in particular; and 4) to provide help with parenting skills.

Thus, it seems that this population is a last frontier in the development of family-centered and community-based services. The major corollary, of course, to this service gap is the lack of well trained personnel to meet the needs of these families and their children. Additionally, it becomes clear that the question of manpower development for this complex population must also be considered in the context of the development of comprehensive solutions.

THE ROLE OF THE UNIVERSITY-AFFILIATED PROGRAMS

The need to train an array of personnel to meet the mental health needs of mentally retarded persons and their families is, as mentioned earlier, one of the major corollaries of serving the mentally retarded emotionally disturbed and their families. Here, the UAPs have a unique role in the preparation of personnel to meet the needs of mentally retarded citizens and their families. The UAPs have had a historical responsibility for this personnel preparation.

The university-affiliated facilities, as they were originally called, had their origin in legislation (PL 88-164) signed into law by President Kennedy in1963. They had their conceptual origins in recommendations made by the 1962 President's Panel Report, *National Action to Combat Mental Retardation.* This panel enunciated the need of individuals with mental retardation for a continuum of care.

The report traced out *two* fundamental consequences of the continuum of care concept for the education of professionals, paraprofessionals, parents, and volunteers: 1) the need for systematic training in how to relate theory to practice; and 2) the need for professional training conducted in service settings that are models of practice and management. The panel further emphasized the principle of professional education which holds that the student acquires his or her professional skills best in settings which exemplify the most advanced practices of that profession. Together these two points provide the basic concept of the UAP program.

The panel also recommended periodic reassessment of these concepts. Thus, in 1976, a special task force reported its findings and recommendations in a document titled, *The Role of Higher Education in Mental Retardation and Other Disabilities.* The task force assessment of the progress made by the University Affiliated Programs stated:

> Experience with the UAF program to date has validated each of the original program concepts stated by the 1962 President's Panel on Mental Retardation...[They also stated] more attention should be given to assuring that the program proportionately benefited all developmental disabilities... [and that] the purposeful specialization of selected UAFs constitutes a valuable national resource. The next major evolutionary step of the UAF program is development of a national network which will allow specialized knowledge to be purposefully developed and made systematically available on a nationwide basis.

On the matter of training, the task force had the following recommendations:

> Interdisciplinary training is a basic element in the effort to prepare leaders and certain other personnel who will work effectively with the complex problems associated with mental retardation and other types of developmental disabilities.

Of particular relevance to this problem was a recommendation that besides practitioners with a strong disciplinary identity who work within an interdisciplinary context, trained personnel are needed who can work *across* the traditional systems of health, education, and social services. The task force also recommended that UAPs should maintain closer contact with trends in community and institutional programs and the resultant manpower demands that are being generated and that they should establish linkages with appropriate programs outside their parent universities, including affiliations with community or junior colleges, so as to give special attention to the number of students in these schools who will be given opportunity to gain skills in developmental disabilities.

In general, the UAPs have a primary mandate to provide inter-disciplinary training to professional and direct care personnel as well as to parents and volunteers and to provide this training in service settings that are models of practice and management. UAPs provide direct services to individuals with mental retardation and their families, as well as diagnostic and assessment services. Lastly, UAPs establish linkages with other educational and service agencies through cooperative agreements and the provision of consultation and technical assistance.

Although only 19 construction grants were awarded under PL 88-164, there are now over 40 programs that identify themselves as UAPs in 35 states (see Figure 11.1).

Several years ago, these programs established a national organization, the American Association of University-Affiliated Programs for the Developmentally Disabled, for the purpose of increasing the flow of information between the different programs, to provide a central repository for data on the activities of the UAPs, and to develop standards and criteria to evaluate such programs. This last goal is difficult because no two UAPs are alike, each reflecting the particular combination of interested talent available in that area. This diversity and individual specialization can be one of the strengths of the UAPs, provided a true network is maintained that will allow specialization knowledge to be purposefully developed and made available on a nationwide basis.

UAPs AND THE MENTAL HEALTH
NEEDS OF THE MENTALLY RETARDED

Ideally, Figure 11.2 depicts the UAP model for the preparation of manpower to meet the mental health needs of mentally retarded persons. It seems, however, that the UAPs have not systematically focused on this unique population. Historically, the UAPs have performed well using the above model for other complex areas of developmental disabilities, for example, the severely retarded, the multiply handicapped, the medically fragile, etc. Mentally retarded persons with severe mental health needs still tend to be the recipients of inadequately trained personnel and inappropriate programs. At best, the typical UAP has historically prepared manpower to meet the mental health needs of mildly mentally retarded persons. Even today the preparation of manpower for severely behaviorally involved mentally retarded persons is rare.

Figure 11.1. Distribution of UAPs.[1]

PROBLEMS CITED BY UAPs

In responding to this survey study, 22 of the UAPs listed the following major problems related to the preparation of personnel to meet the mental health needs of mentally retarded persons and their families: 1) the dichotomy between mental retardation and mental health is not a "clean" one; 2) mental health programs are reluctant to deal with anyone labelled mentally retarded, and mental retardation pro-

[1]University of Alabama at Birmingham; University of California, Irvine and Los Angeles; University of Southern California, Los Angeles; University of Colorado Medical Center, Denver; Georgetown University Medical Center, Washington, DC; University of Miami, Florida; Athens and Atlanta, GA; Chicago; Indiana University, Bloomington; Indiana University Medical Center, Indianapolis; University of Iowa, Iowa City; Kansas City, Lawrence, and Parsons, KS; University of Kentucky, Lexington; Louisiana State University Medical Center; New Orleans; Johns Hopkins University, Baltimore; Children's Hospital Medical Center, Boston; Walter F. Fernald State School, Waltham, MA; University of Michigan, Ann Arbor; St. Paul-Ramsey Hospital, St. Paul, MN; Jackson, MS; St. Louis, MO; University of Nebraska Medical Center, Omaha; Kean College of New Jersey, Union; Yeshiva University, Bronx; New York Medical College, Valhalla; The Roosevelt Hospital, New York; University of Rochester Medical Center, Rochester; University of North Carolina, Chapel Hill; Ohio University, Athens; University of Cincinnati; Ohio State University, Columbus; University of Oregon, Eugene; University of Oregon Health Sciences Center; Temple University, Philadelphia; Rhode Island Hospital, Providence; Winthrop College, Rock Hill; University of South Carolina, Columbia; University of Tennessee, Memphis; University of Texas Health Sciences Center at Dallas; Utah State University, Logan; University of Washington, Seattle; University of Wisconsin, Madison; West Virginia University, Morgantown.

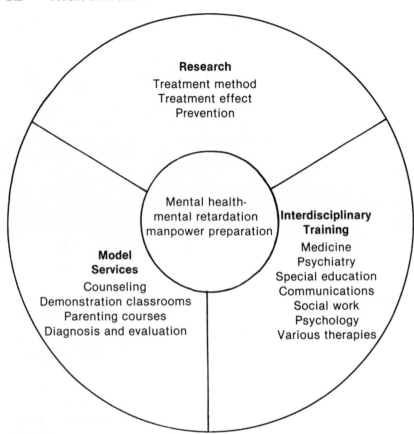

Figure 11.2. UAP model.

grams often are not competent to deal with these needs as they become more severe; 3) both community-based programs and institutions for the mentally retarded are too often unwilling to service mentally retarded persons with severe behavioral problems; 4) 24-hour supervision and support is often necessary for such clients; this service component is often thought of as being unrealistic; 5) severely aggressive mentally retarded persons and persons with autisticlike behaviors require well prepared, interdisciplinary based manpower, yet they generally receive the least prepared personnel; 6) community mental health centers generally have few personnel trained to work with mentally retarded persons; 7) psychiatrists are often not interested in mentally retarded persons; 8) diagnosis may be available, however, treatment is often scarce; and 9) many of the mental health problems seen in retarded persons and their families are preventable given early intervention, but few programs seem prepared to provide these services.

PERSONNEL PREPARATION MODEL

In this review of current personnel preparation trends, it is clear that there are few UAPs that have a comprehensive or adequate focus on this problem. Almost all of the UAPs deal with the preparation of personnel for this population *along* with the general, ongoing interdisciplinary training of professionals; however, there rarely seems to be any special or exemplary commitment to this population. It seems that only recently have the UAPs been confronting this major frontier of training need.

Of all of the needs of mentally retarded persons, the dual diagnosis of mental illness and mental retardation requires a truly interdisciplinary approach. The UAPs are in a unique position to help with personnel preparation. The President's Commission on Mental Health (1978) recommended several personnel preparation guidelines that should be underscored: 1) mental health professionals should be trained to provide adequate services to retarded people who are mentally ill; 2) mental health professionals should be familiar with the principle of normalization and the developmental model; 3) mental health professionals should be trained in the diagnosis and the treatment of mental illness in mentally retarded persons; 4) human service workers who are in frequent contact with retarded persons should be offered training and supportive services in basic mental health skills; and 5) ongoing communication linkages should be established between those working in the field of mental health and mental retardation.

An entire array of paraprofessionals and professionals must be educated through the UAP and other postsecondary education systems if the mental health needs of mentally retarded citizens are to be met in the family and in community settings. Figure 11.3 shows the range of personnel whose manpower needs must be closely examined and in all the major service delivery areas of today's new community alternatives in which personnel must be trained: educational, vocational, residential, and support services.

Keeping in mind that more than 80% of the personnel who come in contact with mentally retarded persons in service programs are paraprofessionals (NIMR, 1972), much work must be done to develop basic mental health skills (e.g., general behavioral-developmental skills) in this level of personnel. Also, the tremendous role that parents and families play in the development of sound mental health must not be forgotten. Both continuing education, parenting skills, and ongoing in-home support services play an important role in this endeavor. Of course, as mental health needs become more complex, mentally retarded persons, as any other citizen, should

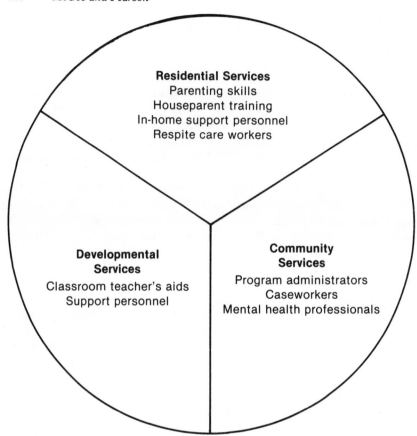

Figure 11.3. Range of personnel.

have the right to have his or her needs met through the appropriate mental health professionals. It is in this area that UAPs have the long-range challenge of developing broader linkages—across the nation—between developmental disabilities and the mental health professions. An obvious challenge for creative interdisciplinary education challenges is present in such personnel preparation.

An overview of a personnel preparation model that focuses on the mental health needs of mentally retarded persons is presented in Figure 11.4.

The model presented in Figure 11.4 focuses on the entire range of needs of mentally retarded persons and the personnel required to meet these needs, from routine to most complex. As the needs become more complex, the level of specialization becomes greater, but the number of professionals involved becomes smaller. A large percentage of mental health needs can be prevented or, when present,

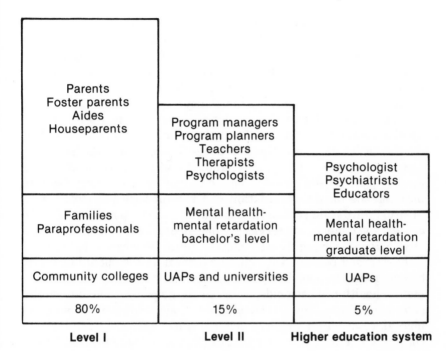

Figure 11.4. Level of skills by personnel needs.

cared for by well prepared parents and paraprofessionals. As the needs become more complex, the prerequisite for sensitive and well trained community mental health professionals becomes more clear-cut.

THE RELATIONSHIP OF PERSONNEL AND SERVICES

As noted earlier, the resolution of the mental health needs of mentally retarded persons and their families is complex and will only occur over time. It will require the development of community-based alternatives and the preparation of personnel to support the mentally retarded-emotionally disturbed in these alternatives. In the past, individuals who were *both* mentally ill and mentally retarded were most likely institutionalized or forgotten. These nonoptions required little more than custodial care workers and, thus, little personnel preparation. Today, however, the situation is substantially different. Both constitutional rights and modern, community-based service alternatives demonstrate that even the most severely involved mentally retarded persons can have their multiple and highly specialized needs met in their home communities and their families.

As the various services and appropriately trained personnel that have been recommended throughout this chapter evolve over the next 5 to 10 years, there will be increasing focus on the issue of the locus of responsibility for the delivery of mental health services to mentally retarded citizens. Figure 11.5 depicts a preliminary model for finalizing this locus of responsibility.

The large majority of mentally retarded persons (Level 1) have routine mental health needs. This group should be able to have their mental health needs met through the general mental retardation service system, given adequately trained and sensitive staff. Acute mental health needs (Level 2) should be met by an ongoing interface between the mental retardation and mental health systems, with mental retardation professionals assuming the responsibility for the *acquisition* of adequate services, while mental health personnel actually *deliver* their highly specialized clinical services. Finally, mentally retarded persons with chronic mental illness should be under the care and responsibility of appropriately trained and sensitive mental health professionals. Thus, the large percentage of mentally retarded persons (Level 1) should have their needs met through the mental retardation delivery system with appropriate interfaces (Levels 2 and 3) with the mental health system being utilized for the remainder of these special service needs.

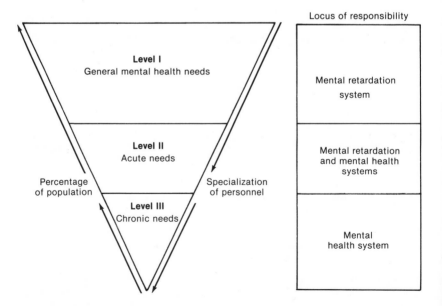

Figure 11.5. Population needs.

SPECIFIC LEARNING FOCI

Although a detailed description of the learning content that personnel serving the mentally retarded-emotionally disturbed should be
competent in is not the intent of this chapter, it is useful to summarize some of the principal content goals that relate to the preparation
of personnel to service this population: 1) the developmental model;
2) the principle of normalization; 3) the types and range of mental illnesses found in the mentally retarded; 4) descriptive diagnoses;
5) the theory of applied behavioral analysis; 6) managing persons
with aggressive and self-abusive behaviors; 7) the role of psychoactive medications; 8) types of residential, educational, vocational, and
social-recreational models for the mentally retarded-emotionally
disturbed; 9) teaching and training techniques for this population; 10) parent training mechanisms as a preventive-supportive
strategy; 11) the coordination of mental retardation-mental health
services; 12) counseling techniques for families of the mentally
retarded-emotionally disturbed; 13) counseling techniques for the
mentally retarded-emotionally distrubed; 14) sexuality and the mentally retarded; and 15) types of allied medical challenges (e.g., seizure
control). These broad goals can be applied to the various types of
paraprofessionals and professionals involved with this population.

More specifically, Roeher (1979) has suggested a curriculum
guide that can be adapted to the personnel preparation needs for
those serving this population. Tables 11.1 and 11.2 are adaptations
of Roeher's curriculum guide for Levels 1 and 2 personnel preparation for the Levels I and II skill that was reviewed in Figure 11.4.

CONCLUSION

The days when the needs of mentally retarded citizens are being
cared for primarily through institutionalization are over. Today's retarded citizens—of all levels of severity—should be living with their
families or in their communities. This brings with it the need for adequately prepared personnel in all communities across the United
States (i.e., parents, paraprofessionals, and professionals).

The general disregard of the mentally retarded person with severe behavioral needs has resulted in frustration after frustration for
families and for the retarded persons. The manpower model described will require new ideologies to be adopted by some. It will also
require an interface between the UAPs and allied entities such as
community colleges. Significantly, it will require strong linkages between the mental retardation-development disability systems and
the mental health system.

Table 11.1. Suggested topics for Level 1 curriculum guide

Unit	Main focus/potential topics
1. Human service ideologies	Normalization and integration Personal dignity, individualization Self-determination, developmental orientation
2. Orientation to human services	Orientation to mental retardation and mental health Definition, causes, and prevalence of mental retardation and mental illness
3. Human growth and development	Biologic concepts Physical growth and development and relevant theories Affective domain, sexuality
4. Learning during the developmental period	Piaget, social learning factors that enhance/limit learning Cultural deprivation Emotional at-risk factors by levels of retardation
5. Observational techniques and report writing	Observation—formal and informal Assessment tools (achievement, social, behavioral) Recording and reporting—oral and written Confidentiality
6. Human relations	Helping relationships Communicating with others (parents, professionals, volunteers, clients, laymen)
7. Individualized planning as basis for program development	Individualized educational planning Behavioral objectives Short- and long-term goals Sequential planning and task analysis Including consumers in process Motivating
8. Recreation and leisure time activities	Activation Participation Using community resources Fitness Client interests and service match
9. Teaching-learning strategies and techniques	Importance of environment Enthusiasm Increasing attention Shaping/prompting Successive approximation

	Informal reinforcement
	Specific techniques
	Positioning/handling
	Peer and role modeling
	Representational, symbolic, and abstract learning
	Overlearning and repetition
10. Behavior management and problem solving	Conflict resolution
	Encouraging appropriate social behaviors
	Hyperactivity
	Stereotypic behaviors
	Aggressive behaviors
	Self-injurious behaviors
	Noncompliance
	Disruptiveness
	General discipline
11. Basic health and medical information	Nutrition and diet
	Exercise
	Basic hygiene
	Dental care
	Self-concept development
	Use of medications (general)
	First aid
	Prosthesis/orthotics
	Screening for physical problems
	Seizure regulations and management
	Bowel and bladder problems
	Medications, administration and effects of

The large percentage of mental health needs of mentally retarded children and adults can be met through: 1) a comprehensive array of family centered and community-based developmental services such as the early availability of parent counseling and family support services designed to bring the locus of service delivery directly to the family whenever possible; 2) a variety of community-based residential alternatives, short- and long-term, ranging from a variety of ongoing respite care services to long-term residential alternatives in the community; 3) socially integrative leisure time activities; and 4) different degrees of specialized mental health professional services to provide the secondary (i.e., consultant) or primary (direct care) back-up services for the above components.

All of these require, as mentioned earlier, an entirely new type of personnel, both paraprofessional and professional. UAPs are beginning to confront this challenge. Again, UAPs must develop a new

Table 11.2.   Suggested topics for Level 2 curriculum guide

Unit	Main focus/potential topics
1. Ideologic issues, advanced	Normalization and its implications Biomedical issues and concerns Service comprehensiveness Problems with integration Least restrictive doctrine Service coordination between mental retardation and mental health services
2. Advanced issues in mental retardation and mental health	Definitions Epidemiology International issues Causes Prevention
3. Specialization area	Educational models Residential models Vocational models Supportive community services
4. Legal and human rights	Handicapism Systemic prejudice Least restrictive doctrine Right to treatment and services Guardianship Protective services Citizen advocacy Recent laws and court decisions Use of punishment
5. Social psychology	Theroretical emphasis Group dynamics Social status Roles Deviancy Labeling Social systems Societal management of deviancy
6. Learning and development, focus upon adults	Emphasis upon expanding familiarity with learning theories and basic psychologic foundation Relearning and retraining Adapting theories to adult needs Independent living skills
7. Behavior modification	Introduction to formal use of behavior modification Reinforcers Observable behavior Charting and recording

		Baseline Precision teaching
8.	Family of the retarded person	Role of parents in service delivery Parent, professional, and client relationships Parent growth/development Decision making Basic information and needs of families with handicapped member Voluntary associations
9.	Current trends in mental retardation services	History of mental retardation Current priorities and emphasis Service coordination
10.	Prevention of mental retardation	Community awareness New techniques and technologies Basic information
11.	Effective communication	Conducting meetings Use of audiovisual equipment Public education Persuasion and speaking techniques
12.	Strategies for self-renewal and continuing growth	Professional development Using journals, etc. Short- and long-term training Personal renewal strategies

type of manpower for those mentally retarded persons and families with chronic or acute mental health needs. Their mental health needs can be alleviated through: 1) training programs for mental health and mental retardation professionals in the diagnosis and treatment of mental illness in mentally retarded persons; 2) initiation of ongoing in-service training programs that embody modern concepts of the dual diagnosis of mental illness-mental retardation for generic human service personnel who come into contact with mentally retarded persons and their families; and 3) the development of specialized mental health services available through community mental retardation programs (e.g., behavioral modifications programs) and community mental health centers or private mental health practitioners (e.g., individual psychotherapy or inpatient psychiatric care).

Thus, the preparation of personnel to meet the mental health needs of mentally retarded persons and their families will require a national commitment of the UAPs toward a realistic interface with the mental health delivery system and the community-based mental retardation service system alternatives. Consumer organizations such as the National Association for Retarded Citizens can play an important role, nationally and locally, through their active advocacy for the support of the training models recommended here.

REFERENCES

American Association of University-Affiliated Programs. 1976. The role of higher education in mental retardation and other disabilities. American Association of University-Affiliated Programs, Washington DC.

Freeman, R. D., and Pearson, P. H. 1978. Counseling with parents. In: J. Appley (ed.), Care of the Handicapped Child. Clinics in Developmental Medicine, No. 67. J. B. Lippincott Co., Philadelphia.

Joint Commission on Mental Health for Children. 1970. Crisis in Child Mental Health's Challenge for the 1970's. Harper & Row, New York.

McGee, J. J. 1979. The needs of autistic children and their families. Unpublished paper, Meyer Children's Rehabilitation Institute, Omaha, NB.

National Institute on Mental Retardation. 1972. A National Mental Retardation Manpower Model. National Institute of Mental Retardation, Toronto.

Parsons, J. and May, J. 1979. The nature and incidence of emotional disturbance among mentally retarded individuals. Doctoral research paper (unpublished), Florida State University, Tallahassee.

President's Commission on Mental Health. 1978. Report of the Liaison Task Panel on Mental Retardation, Vol. IV. U.S. Government Printing Office, Washington, DC.

President's Panel on Mental Retardation. 1962. A Proposed Program for National Action to Combat Mental Retardation. U.S. Government Printing Office, Washington, DC.

Roeher, A. 1979. University affiliated facilities: A primary resource in improving services for developmentally disabled persons. American Association of University-Affiliated Programs, Washington, DC.

Rutter, M., Graham, P., and Yule, W. 1970. A Neuropsychiatric Study in Childhood. Spastics International Medical Publications, London.

Rutter, M., Tizard, J., Yule, W., Graham, P., and Whitmore, K. 1976. Research report: Isle of Wight studies, 1964–1974. Psychol. Med. 6:313–332.

Rutter, M., Tizard, J., and Whitmore, K. (eds.). 1970. Education, Health and Behavior. Longmans, Green & Co., Ltd., London.

Tymchuk, A. J. 1979. Parent and family therapy intervention with parents of the mentally retarded. Unpublished paper, University of California, Los Angeles.

PART IV
CONCLUSION

Chapter 12

Conclusion

Frank J. Menolascino and Brian M. McCann

The contributors to this book clearly illustrate that the dual diagnosis of mental illness and mental retardation poses both major diagnostic difficulties and intriguing treatment challenges. For example, the differential diagnosis issues involved in separating the social-adaptive behavioral indices of a moderately retarded individual from his or her concurrent problems in interpersonal transactions are professionally quite knotty at times. Yet resolution of these dual diagnostic difficulties can clarify the selection of treatment considerations such as *what* technique, appropriate for *which* person, with *their* specific problems in living can most effectively restabilize their mental health status. These considerations are recurrent themes in mental health and mental retardation activities, and the continuing clarification of what exactly exists in these complex retarded citizens is bringing forth a new era of professional involvement. Specifically, one increasingly notes in the professional literature (in both mental health and mental retardation) an increasing focus on descriptive diagnosis (i.e., what *is* clinically present versus the past over-focus on possible causative mechanisms or indirect dynamic formulations). For example, the objective measurement and recording of bizarre behaviors on an objective descriptive scale has increasingly replaced the hypothesized presence of problems in reality testing. Also, clinicians seem more comfortable in viewing and describing multiple symptom phenomena and acting directly on same via multiple treatment interventions, rather than following the traditional training principle of seeking the major cause for the symptom configuration and the rather myopic treatment postures that flow from same. Admittedly, the challenge of viewing a handicapped person, who may well display six to eight major presenting symptoms, tends to bewilder the clinician. It is increasingly clear that the evolving posture of descriptive diagnostic clarification, as a prelude to specific treatment intervention, will continue to erase the aura of bewilderment that clouded the vision of health professionals toward the dual-diagnosis person in the past. Concomitantly, the rapid growth of the multidisciplinary team concept (in both mental health and mental retardation) has brought a rapidly increasing number of professionals with a wide range of professional talents and skills to help clarify these complex clinical challenges.

In the past, many professional myths colored the expected behavioral symptoms in retarded citizens and led to stilted diagnostic approaches that tended to eschew treatment interventions or prognostic expectations. A recurrent theme in this book is the focus on what actually constitutes the behavioral repertoire of the retarded, as separate from the products of professional stereotypes as to same. For example, in the past many professionals had been trained to believe (or had fixed personal views before ever starting advanced training) that "slow" persons displayed qualitative or quantitative differences in their expression of the signs and symptoms of mental illness (in contrast to normal persons), and it became understandably very difficult for them to note the similarities among *all* mental health patients. A clear instance of this excessive focus on extraneous factors that indirectly imply behavioral characteristics is the professional roadblock, which has commonly been noted in the stereotype that Down's syndrome persons are the "Prince Charmings" of the mentally retarded: overly friendly, very affable, given to mimicry, and devoid of personality conflicts. This particular behavioral stereotype has unfortunately lead generations of professionals *not* to view (and try to understand) the behavioral picture that is directly before them, but rather the traditional interpretation of expected behaviors.

A particularly strong antidote to the past and ongoing overreliance on behavioral stereotypes in the retarded has been the behavioral analysis approach and its direct treatment aspect: behavior modification. This particular treatment approach has ushered in a *past* professional posture wherein a premium was placed on clear descriptions of current behavior, rather than almost obsessive professional focus on underlying psychodynamics and its treatment corollary: one can only treat what *is* present whether in the mentally ill-mentally retarded or the mentally ill nonretarded. Herein a wide variety of modified treatment approaches specially tailored to the needs of the retarded (as clearly noted by Rubin, Watson, and Monfils in this book) can be utilized. True, the psychoanalyst would scoff at such a simplistic view of human behavior, but he or she would concede that behavioral improvement *is* what most conflicted or mentally ill persons are requesting, and the psychoanalytical goal of reeducation of the personality is increasingly viewed professionally as a rare luxury both in its attainment and the interest of patients in same. In other words, most people want to obtain prompt relief for their headaches (read: disturbing feelings) and are not overly interested in knowing the symbolic basis for same. This professional posture of utilizing a wide variety of direct treatment approaches to specifically described behaviors has been a hallmark of developmentally oriented treatment-management approaches in the field of mental retardation over the last two decades. It is now, and will increasingly in the future, be more actively extended to the instances of mental illness that so frequently complicate the path of so many retarded citizens through life.

It is interesting to note that the three subgroups of the mentally retarded who currently present the most complex sets of clinical challenges also have behavioral or personality problems as one of their core problems. Indeed, as one views these three subgroups— the severely retarded-multiply handicapped, the mentally ill-mentally retarded, and the retarded person with criminal proclivities (i.e., the "defective delinquent")—the role and nature of their primitive, abnormal, and atypical behavioral problems (Menolascino, 1972) are quite striking. Although the primitive behaviors of the severely retarded-multiply handicapped directly emanate from their very restricted utilization of delayed special sensory and language abilities as to interpersonal tactics for dealing with the external world, it is instructive to note that these limitations have direct repercussions on their families, their caregivers, and general society. These complex severely handicapped individuals tend to wear out their parents, both physically and emotionally. They also represent a huge dosage of reality to overzealous treatment personnel who literally cannot seem to wait for or tolerate, the typically very slow developmental timetables noted in these retarded citizens. This group has forcibly demanded a careful rethinking of *where* they should be served (Within their family? A community-based facility? Institutional placement?) and *how* they are served (Full day programs? Individually tailored partial day programs? Extra attention in the daily treatment programs to ongoing social-recreational parameters, rather than on developmental-work parameters?). Far from being resolved (Ellis et al., 1981; Menolascino and McGee, 1981) this location-allocation issue of society's resources remains as a challenge to all professionals in both the mental retardation and mental health fields.

Many of the contributors to this book have noted both the complexity and the reality-based challenges that mentally ill-mentally retarded persons present to the professional interviewer. For example, it is increasingly being noted that deinstitutionalized retarded citizens tend to be ill-equipped to understand or adjust to the complexities of their new homes in the community (Bruininks, Meyers, Sigford, and Lakin, 1981). Whether based on factors such as internment in large public institutions wherein passivity and conformity were the behavioral adjustments expected in the large congregate care models, or their limited internal equipment for managing more demanding sets of expectancies, the affected individual's resultant response has too often been the same: bewilderment, poor psychosocial adjustment, and, at times, major and prolonged emotional turmoil. This challenge has become an acute one as the population of public institutions for the retarded has decreased from 185,000 to 125,000 over the last decade. Specifically, how and where shall the recently deinstitutionalized be served so as to avoid the above noted personal adjustment problems? In addition to those in this book who addressed this issue, the authors suggest some future challenges. Although local mental health treatment resources such as the Community Mental Health Center, private mental health practitioners, and similar current mental health treatment facility-personnel come readily to mind, we would suggest that a more energetic outreach posture will be needed. Remembering the demonstrated difficulty in motivating nonretarded mentally ill citizens to attend (and continue at) these community resource settings, the dual-diagnosis individual is in need of a far more direct linkage. Specifically, we foresee an increase in mobile mental health services wherein the service is provided in the group home, or the group therapy is provided at the sheltered place of employment. Simultaneously, we will note an enhanced focus on training mental retardation personnel in mental health treatment techniques so that they can utilize their new treatment skills as an ongoing part of their daily work in education, training, and residential facilities. Thus, the direct (i.e., service) and indirect (i.e., training) components of modern mental health consultation practice can and should be accomplished concurrently.

Similar professional challenges surround the allied issue of attempting to provide modern services for the chronically delinquent adolescent retarded or the adult retarded person who displays chronic maladaptive, aggressive, or abnormal sexual proclivities. Indeed, the demonstrated difficulties in providing effective treatment are more marked in this population because the field of corrections (where the bulk of these individuals may belong, rather than inappropriate referral to the mental retardation service systems) has a far less firm base of professional involvement or ongoing parental support then do the developmental-educational-mental health systems of care. For example, the latter systems of care tend to more actively support and advocate for the previously discussed two subgroups of complex retarded persons. Although the number of "defecting delinquents" is numerically not great, they do tend to tie up excessive amounts of staff time, and their behavioral volatility is an ever present disruptive influence to general programs of service. It is a truism that the adolescent delinquent *can* and should be treated via the current models of care in adolescent psychiatry; this truism awaits fuller implementation as increasing numbers of mental health personnel become actively involved. Yet the adult retarded person, who consistently has legal entanglements secondary to his or her poor impulse control, does not tend to respond to mental health treatment approaches. Herein the authors believe the future trend will be to involve the mentally retarded more directly in correctional systems of care, with the provision of mental health inputs and mental retardation service on an ongoing consultation basis.

The presentations herein on training the current and future cadres of professionals to serve dual-diagnosis persons focused on correcting the essential lack of such training in the past and the unidimensional nature that characterizes most of the more recent training activities in both mental retardation and mental health. Modern training programs must focus on basic concepts and sets of experiences which the varied members of an interdisciplinary team will need so as to be truly professionally proficient, up-to-date as to modern diagnostic and treatment approaches in the field, and cognizant of the national trends that impact directly or indirectly upon the retarded. Exposure to these basic concepts and sets of experiences in the field of mental retardation will permit the current and future mental health trainee to more readily understand and appreciate clinical transactions with retarded citizens and their parents. Understanding of the unique needs of retarded citizens—whether or not they are also mentally ill—prepares the mental health trainee to enlarge his or her range of expertise so as to encompass the utilization of treatment-management techniques that are consistently helpful (i.e., specially tailored individual and group psychotherapy techniques) to this dual-diagnosis population. Beyond this systematic exposure to the basic and applied training components, an allied benefit for the mental health trainee will be a clearer understanding of current health issues: a closer study of the similarities and dissimilarities of societal postures toward the chronically handicapped and the key biologic and psychosocial research issues in the field of mental retardation are examples. Complementarity of experiences from each field of expertise will produce a far more knowledgeable and compassionate mental health treater for whatever population the individual focuses on in his or her future professional careers.

As noted earlier, retarded citizens with mental illness have tended to fall into the gap which has increasingly separated mental retardation from mental health services. In the past, these citizens' needs have been almost totally unmet as both service systems have floundered in their interest and/or ability to address these challenges directly. Those who have been closely identified with the fields of mental retardation and mental health have striven for years to clarify the distinction between mental retardation and mental illness. They have often been frustrated by the general public's confusion of the two conditions, and have also been concerned by the past tendency of some professionals to apply mental health approaches inappropriately to mental retardation. Fortunately, these erroneous interpretations and professional postures are increasingly being viewed as largely representing historical professional postures. The developmental model has been generally adopted as the most appropriate basis for mental retardation services, and no longer does any professional group claim dominance over the field of mental retardation, which is now recognized, as it should be, as requiring an interdisciplinary approach. However, although it is now clearly recognized that mental retardation is not a form of mental illness, this awareness is obviously not a guarantee against mental illness actually occurring in mentally retarded citizens. Thus, retarded citizens may develop emotional problems and/or mental illnesses just as can nonretarded individuals. This increased clarification of diagnostic issues has now been translated into actual treatment models that *are* effective for the mentally retarded and show what *can* be done for these dual-diagnosis individuals.

Index